Authenticity in the Language Classroom and Beyond: Adult Learners

Edited by Sarah Rilling and Maria Dantas-Whitney

Maria Dantas-Whitney, Sarah Rilling, and Lilia Savova, Series Editors

TESOL Classroom Practice Series

 Teachers of English to Speakers of Other Languages, Inc.

Typeset in Typeset in ITC Galliard and Vag Rounded
by Capitol Communication Systems, Inc., Crofton, Maryland USA
Printed by United Graphics, Inc., Mattoon, Illinois USA
Indexed by Pueblo Indexing and Publishing Services, Pueblo West, Colorado

Teachers of English to Speakers of Other Languages, Inc.
700 South Washington Street, Suite 200
Alexandria, Virginia 22314 USA
Tel 703-836-0774 • Fax 703-836-6447 • E-mail tesol@tesol.org •
http://www.tesol.org/

Publishing Manager: Carol Edwards
Copy Editor: Laurie Arnston
Additional Reader: Kelly Graham
Cover Design: Capitol Communication Systems, Inc.

ISBN 9781931185608
Library of Congress Control No. 2009929406

Table of Contents

Series Editors' Preface vii

Chapter 1
Authenticity, Creativity, and Localization in Language Learning 1
Sarah Rilling and Maria Dantas-Whitney

Authentic Design: Tasks, Materials, and Curricula

Chapter 2
Where Can I Get My Shoe Fixed? Authentic Tasks for Students
in EFL Settings 11
Jan Edwards Dormer

Chapter 3
Sharing Our Culture With Visitors: English for Tour Guides 19
Janet M. D. Higgins

Chapter 4
Oh, the Places You'll Go: Creating a Class City Guide 29
Laura Ramm

Chapter 5
Magazine as Project-Based Learning 37
Hoang Thi Ngoc Diem

Chapter 6
Language Training à la Carte 47
Peggy Allen Heidish

Authentic Language: Skills, Content, and Culture

Chapter 7
Using Authentic Texts to Facilitate Culturally Relevant Extensive
Reading Programs in Tajikistan 63
  Lori Fredricks

Chapter 8
The English of Math—It's Not Just Numbers! 71
  Kathy Ewing and Bill Huguelet

Chapter 9
Readers' Theater: Turbo-Charged Language Acquisition 85
  *Gary Carkin, Sarah Dodson-Knight, Alexis Gerard Finger,
  Silvia Rodriguez Spence, Nigel A. Caplan, and Judy Trupin*

Chapter 10
Inexpensive, Effective ESP Material Development for the
EFL Classroom 99
  Marvin D. Hoffland and Oswald Jochum

Authentic Connections: Community Partnerships

Chapter 11
Exploring the Global Landscape Through Language and
Service Learning 109
  Beth Kozbial Ernst and Megan Allen

Chapter 12
Creating a Technical Career ESL Program Through
Community Partnerships 117
  Gilda Rubio-Festa and Rebeca Fernández

Chapter 13
Climate Change and Other Hot Topics on Campus:
Project-Based Learning 129
  Marianne Stipe and Lora Yasen

Chapter 14
This Class Is a Disaster: Public Information, Natural Disasters,
and the ESL Classroom in the United States 143
  Christopher Miles and Bill Powell

Contents

Authentic Purpose, Authentic Medium: Technology in Language Learning

Chapter 15
The Times They Are A-Changin': Strategies for Exploiting Authentic
Materials in the Language Classroom 155
Alex Gilmore

Chapter 16
Lights, Camera, Action: Scripts for Language Learning 169
Gregory Strong

Chapter 17
Authentic Video as Passport to Cultural Participation
and Understanding 181
Christopher Stillwell

Chapter 18
Sharing the Food and Fun Through Restaurant Review Blogs:
An Integrated-Skills Project Approach 191
Timothy R. Healy

Chapter 19
Using Wikis for Collaborative Writing and Intercultural Learning 199
Geoffrey P.J. Lawrence, Terry Compton, Clayton Young, and Hazel Owen

Chapter 20
Developing Specialized Discourse Resources for International
Teaching Assistants Using a Multimedia Wiki 213
Barbara Gourlay, David Kanig, Joan Lusk, and Stewart Mader

Chapter 21
I Tube . . . Do YouTube? Virtual Portfolios for Reflective Learning
and Peer Review 223
Kathleen Snyder-Parampil and Joel Hensley

Chapter 22
Medical Doctors Using Authentic Webcast Lectures to
Learn Lexical Phrases 231
Susan Olmstead-Wang

References 239

Index 253

Series Editors' Preface

The TESOL Classroom Practice Series showcases state-of-the-art curricula, materials, tasks, and activities reflecting emerging trends in language education and in the roles of teachers, learners, and the English language itself. The series seeks to build localized theories of language learning and teaching based on students' and teachers' unique experiences in and out of the classroom.

This series captures the dynamics of 21st-century ESOL classrooms. It reflects major shifts in authority from teacher-centered practices to collaborative learner- and learning-centered environments. The series acknowledges the growing numbers of English speakers globally, celebrates locally relevant curricula and materials, and emphasizes the importance of multilingual and multicultural competencies—a primary goal in teaching English as an international language. Furthermore, the series takes into account contemporary technological developments that provide new opportunities for information exchange and social and transactional communications.

Each volume in the series focuses on a particular communicative skill, learning environment, or instructional goal. Chapters within each volume represent practices in English for general, academic, vocational, and specific purposes. Readers will find examples of carefully researched and tested practices designed for different student populations (from young learners to adults, from beginning to advanced) in diverse settings (from pre-K–12 to college and postgraduate, from local to global, from formal to informal). A variety of methodological choices are also represented, including individual and collaborative tasks and curricular as well as extracurricular projects. Most important, these volumes invite readers into the conversation that considers and so constructs ESOL classroom practices as complex entities. We are indebted to the authors, their colleagues, and their students for being a part of this conversation.

Adult language learners in particular have specific learning goals that reflect their lives within a global society, and adults negotiate multiple and changing identities throughout their personal, academic, and professional lives. Chapters in *Authenticity in the Language Classroom and Beyond: Adult Learners* highlight how teachers have the ability to transform language instruction from a mechanical learning experience to a dynamic interaction to assist learners in reaching real-world goals. Rather than focus only on native-speaker norms of language production, English language instruction can provide adult learners with opportunities to create and act on their own texts, engage with meaningful audiences, and develop interactions that mirror their purpose for learning. The chapters in this volume demonstrate how language teaching practices engage learners in authentic experiences, using and producing texts to meet international and localized communication needs.

All the chapters in this volume demonstrate that authenticity is more than just the materials we use. Authenticity also means using language for real purposes. It means engaging students in collaborative learning, involving discussions, negotiations, and decision making. Authenticity is creating real uses for English, not just holding native-speaker language and culture as the sole model. With English increasingly being used as a lingua franca to connect second language speakers, authenticity takes on new meanings as we seek to develop learners who can face the challenge of communicating effectively in an increasingly globalized world.

Maria Dantas-Whitney, Western Oregon University
Sarah Rilling, Kent State University
Lilia Savova, Indiana University of Pennsylvania

CHAPTER 1

Authenticity, Creativity, and Localization in Language Learning

Sarah Rilling and Maria Dantas-Whitney

Communicative language teaching (CLT) has been advocated for several decades based on an understanding of language learners as both cognitive and social beings, each with different and changing needs, interests, and motivations. In recent years, authenticity has taken a central role in discussions of what it means to teach and learn language. In the early days of CLT, the focus of discussion was authentic texts, which were seen as autonomous objects produced by native speakers to be studied in language classes and emulated. More recent notions of authenticity are framed in broader terms to include learner cognition, engagement, collaboration, problem solving, critical analysis, and the development of language for specific and often localized communication purposes.

In the introduction to TESOL's *New Ways in Using Authentic Materials in the Language Classroom*, Larimer and Schleicher (1999) define authentic materials in the language classroom as "oral and writing texts that occur naturally in the target language environment and that have not been created or edited expressly for language learners" (p. v). The contributors to the *New Ways* volume demonstrate how teachers employ creativity in incorporating meaningful texts to reach realistic and real-world goals, rather than merely using texts as input or model. However, we still must ask: Whose texts and whose language standards should be used? Who sets the goals for language learning? What is the role of authentic cognitive and social processes, such as completing tasks or collaborating on projects? Can we empower students to gain a sense of ownership—both of input and output—in the language classroom? In other words, how can we avoid relegating authenticity to that "catchphrase currency whose value is taken for granted without further enquiry" (Widdowson, 1998, p. 705)?

In a useful history of authenticity, Lindholm (2008) writes that the concept emerged during the Enlightenment as a mechanism for humankind to come closer to the divine through authentic experience. It was not until the early 20th century that authenticity became commodified and the search for authenticity became a search for ownership of authentic materials. More recently, however, and especially in applied linguistics and language teaching, the concept of authenticity has subsumed experience and materialism, both defined locally.

Bringing experience to classroom instruction is not always an easy task, and unfortunately, as far too many of us know from personal experience, "school learning is often about disembodied minds learning outside any context of decisions and actions" (Gee, 2005, p. 39). In such classrooms, learning too often is rendered rote, disengaging, and inauthentic. Gee argues that learning is not meaningful unless we can connect language, activity, and purpose through talk, action, and text. Simulations have the potential for integrating talk, action, and text, but as Seargeant (2005) demonstrates, this does not always occur. Seargeant explored English language vacation theme parks for Japanese tourists in Japan, which offer "authentic" interactions with native speakers in a simulated foreign travel experience. Although this simulation engages language learners in tourist activities, the author questions how authentic these interactions really are and whether any real-world purpose is involved. Does the native speaker employee of the park—as the sole embodiment of English—really meet an authentic purpose, or are stereotypes only reinforced and English sold as a commodity but not incorporated into the world outside the park? Perhaps this can only be answered by the theme park guests themselves as they venture into the wider world where English may well serve as a better medium of communication than Japanese in international travel.

Although simulations have the potential to bring talk, action, and text together, other classroom techniques connect language, activity, and purpose, such as tasks with real-world applications (Guariento & Morley, 2001; Ur, 1998). Rather than focus on material authenticity, Widdowson (1998) argues that even teacher prepared or modified material can serve an authentic purpose: "Contrived language has to be such that learners will learn from it and develop the capacity for authentication that they can exploit when they encounter actually occurring language in the real world" (p. 715). The goal of using and creating language for real-world purposes within language instruction is to bring authenticity to the learning experience, not to the texts themselves. Pedagogical tasks have the potential to provide learners with a framework and tools for approaching real-world tasks as we "engage learners in the kinds of *cognitive processes* that arise in communication outside the classroom" (Ellis, 2003, p. 336). As Widdowson (2003) reminds us, classrooms are not context-neutral spaces: "The original communicative context that constituted [learners'] 'guide and support' is no longer in evidence, so it has to be reconstituted in some way" (p. 105). Rather than material authenticity, situational and interactional authenticity may play a greater role in language teaching (Ellis, 2003). When learners authenticate classroom experiences and texts, they are more likely to incorporate language and communication strategies to meet real-world purposes outside the classroom.

Through tasks, teachers can connect language, activity, and purpose by drawing learners' attention to successful strategies for processing instructional materials and interacting meaningfully with peers, teachers, and others to meet real-world goals, in both social and academic contexts. Strategy training helps learners develop autonomy in language learning and use as they apply what they are learning to their lives beyond the classroom. Authenticity within language teaching practice encompasses learners interacting with classmates, teachers, and others to negotiate meaningful solutions to tasks (potentially even extensive simulations) through problem solving by using available English language resources both in and outside the classroom. Teachers engage learners in integrating talk, text, and action to solve real problems and reach real-world goals. As we move from second- to third-millennium language teaching practices, we must address the "needs and interests of students; engaging them in authentic, real-life tasks; allowing them ownership of the curriculum" (Felix, 2005, p. 88). When teachers meet learners' needs and interests through their curricular choices, and when we engage learners in setting their own learning objectives to meet career and academic goals, our classrooms, whether real or virtual, become places where authentic purposes are achieved, as many of the chapters in this volume demonstrate.

The digital age brings new possibilities for engaging learners with authentic materials and experiences, interactions, and publication opportunities. Multimodal communications are increasing both inter- and intra-nationally (Warschauer, 2000), and technology has the potential to "expand students' literacy practices beyond linear text-based reading and writing" (Cummins, 2006, p. 53), perhaps engaging learners' multilingual abilities. As with any new technology, learning digital literacy first and foremost requires access, along with instruction and consistent practice. Without an authentic purpose, audience, and goal, the use of technology in the classroom is ineffective. Engagement with various technological literacy projects and tasks is a common theme of many of the chapters in this volume, demonstrating how 21st century language learners are authenticating multimodal spaces for themselves.

Around the globe, and even within English speaking countries, there is a shift in focus from Anglo- and Western-centric standards and norms of English to localized usage and literacy practices, including multilingual ones. English is an international language of communication, and as such, it has a range of norms and forms around the world based on localized and world varieties of English (Jenkins, 2006). Allowing learners to draw on local language use and literacy practices builds authenticity into instruction as learners validate English within their own social and professional networks and begin addressing their own goals for using English in real, meaningful, and individualized ways. When learners can connect real language use with actual life goals, they begin to build an identity in which English plays an integral and authentic role (Norton & Toohey, 2002).

As Widdowson (2003) reminds us: "Standard English is not simply a means of communication but the symbolic possession of a particular community, expressive of its identity, its conventions, and values" (p. 39). Language instruction can assist learners in understanding and meeting the needs of an imagined audience, for example, as they produce language with formal or informal forms; include multilingual use (Dray, 2003); select discipline-specific lexicon or structures to vary language for specific purposes (Hyland, 2000); or include graphic or multimedia elements. When learners can draw on individual and group resources through cooperation, collaboration, and negotiation, they develop expertise and language skills to meet real-world goals.

Language use, whether written or oral, engages us with social networks and communities. "The notion of authenticity can be understood not so much as an individualist obsession with the self but rather as a dialogical engagement with community" (Pennycook, 2007, p. 3), and "community" is a malleable concept, especially within international contexts.

Whether in foreign or second language learning, we are asking our learners to envision themselves as users of English. Currently, nonnative speakers outnumber native speakers of English (Jenkins, 2007), thus changing our metaphor of "target" language and culture as teachers reposition themselves within student-centered instruction. Learners build identities as target users of English and develop their own purposes and goals for language learning. Teachers can model goal setting, and collaborations between teachers and students can lead to meaningful instruction in moving learners toward individualized goals. Instruction draws on appropriate notions of target culture, not necessarily only Anglo-centric ones. As Seargeant (2005) demonstrates with the tourist theme parks in Japan, language teachers cannot provide all of the meaningful contexts that are necessary to practice all potential language forms. TESOL's position statement on nonnative English speaking (NNES) teachers demonstrates the value our profession places on language teachers, regardless of first language:

> The distinction between native and nonnative speakers of English presents an oversimplified, either/or classification system that does not actually describe the range of possibilities in a world where English has become a global language. . . . All English language educators should be proficient in English regardless of their native languages, but English language proficiency should be viewed as only one criterion in evaluating a teacher's professionalism. Teaching skills, teaching experience, and professional preparation should be given as much weight as language proficiency. (TESOL, 2006)

Adult language learners in particular have specific learning goals that reflect their life goals within a global society, and, as Miller (2007) points out, adults also negotiate multiple and changing identities throughout their personal, academic, and professional lives. Language teachers have the ability to transform language instruction from a mechanical learning experience to a dynamic interaction to assist learners in reaching real-world goals. Rather than focus only on native-speaker norms of language production, English language instruction can provide adult learners with opportunities to create and act on their own texts, engage with meaningful audiences, and develop interactions that mirror their purpose for learning. The chapters in this volume demonstrate how language teaching practices engage learners in authentic experiences, using and producing texts to meet international and localized communication needs.

This volume, *Authenticity in the Language Classroom and Beyond: Adult Learners*, is divided into four sections. The introductory section, "Authentic Design: Tasks, Materials, and Curricula," focuses on how various practitioners design their curricula to meet specific localized learner needs. Jan Edwards Dormer, in "Where Can I Get My Shoe Fixed? Authentic Tasks for Students in EFL Settings," focuses on a curriculum that employs a theme- and task-based approach to engage students in Indonesia and Brazil in language learning. A major component of each level of Dormer's curriculum includes a project serving local needs and involving students in authentic communications and negotiations. In "Sharing Our Culture With Visitors: English for Tour Guides," Janet M. D. Higgins demonstrates how learners apply the concept of the "guided walk" in developing language skills useful in the tourist industry, their area of academic study. Higgins' students practice describing guided walks using online, print, and local sources. Laura Ramm's adult education students in the United States ("Oh, the Places You'll Go: Creating a Class City Guide") develop local city guides useful for other second language speakers in the community. Practice leading to the development of guides includes a scavenger hunt, map and direction activities, and field experience. Hoang Thi Ngoc Diem's curriculum has students developing magazines collaboratively ("Magazine as Project-Based Learning"). She discusses the steps in project development and presents sample rubrics used in assessment. Peggy Allen Heidish presents the support curriculum for graduate students, including those who are international teaching assistants, at her university in the United States ("Language Training á la Carte"). Workshops and credit courses are offered ranging from assisting students with specific skills (e.g., writing to incorporate source texts, pronunciation) to strategies (e.g., reading strategies, job interviewing).

The second section of the book, "Authentic Language: Skills, Content, and Culture," presents four chapters exploring various approaches to language teaching for authenticity. Lori Fredricks describes a curriculum employing reading resources based on local culture, history, and literature ("Using Authentic Texts to Facilitate Culturally Relevant Extensive Reading Programs in Tajikistan"). She details the process of selecting readings and building extracurricular or community-based programs using reading resource rooms and reading clubs. In "The English of Math—It's Not Just Numbers!" Kathy Ewing and Bill Huguelet break the myth that the language of math is universal. They report that students face similar difficulties talking about and understanding math concepts in the vastly different contexts of universities in the United States and Oman, and they share activities that successfully engage students with the language of mathematics. Gary Carkin, Sarah Dodson-Knight, Alexis Gerard Finger, Silvia Rodriguez Spence, Nigel A. Caplin, and Judy Trupin present an active and imaginative way to get students to develop confidence and skill in speaking through drama practices ("Readers' Theater: Turbo-Charged Language Acquisition"). Using a Vygotskyan framework, the authors show how a range of text types, from poems and short stories to plays and textbook readings, can provide rehearsal and performance opportunities to learners in a variety of instructional contexts. Marvin D. Hoffland and Oswald Jochum, in "Inexpensive, Effective ESP Material Development for the EFL Classroom," present easily accessible authentic materials from local industry that teachers use in business and scientific English lessons at two institutions in Austria. Creativity in designing lesson materials to accompany real business documents and collaborations with community partners provide students with examples of how English is used to promote business and industry both internationally and locally, bringing English to life for these students.

The third section of the book, "Authentic Connections: Community Partnerships," focuses on practical teaching ideas to connect learners with their local communities to develop specific language skills and increase cultural understanding. In "Exploring the Global Landscape Through Language and Service Learning," Beth Kozbial Ernst and Megan Allen engage their second language learners with community service through local nonprofit agencies. This service provides students with opportunities to explore local resources and connect with community members. Gilda Rubio-Festa and Rebeca Fernández ("Creating a Technical Career ESL Program Through Community Partnerships") demonstrate how their career-oriented educational programs team with local employers to create practical training opportunities for the large influx of immigrants their community has experienced in recent years. Pathways are created to assist students in succeeding in technical career programs, and community connections assist students in working toward realistic career goals. Marianne Stipe and Lora Yasen's chapter ("Climate Change and Other Hot Topics on Campus: Project-Based Learning") describes student involvement in a regional conference on climate change and sustainability. Through a variety of contacts with a local high school and their affiliate university, students researched sustainability and prepared poster presentations for the conference, building community connections, knowledge, and language and presentation skills. Finally, Christopher Miles and Bill Powell present ideas for making resources on disaster preparation and survival accessible to second language speakers in communities devastated by natural disasters such as Hurricane Katrina ("This Class Is a Disaster: Public Information, Natural Disasters, and the ESL Classroom in the United States"). Through various community-based language activities, these authors heighten student awareness of disaster preparation and survival, and they suggest locally available resources that teachers in other areas might employ.

The fourth and final section of the book, "Authentic Purpose, Authentic Medium: Technology in Language Learning," focuses on various accessible media for language learning. The first three chapters highlight the use of video in the language classroom. Alex Gilmore connects film and television use in the classroom to the types of communicative competence students can develop ("The Times They Are A-Changin': Strategies for Exploiting Authentic Materials in the Language Classroom"). Gilmore explores various definitions of authenticity to show that film and television programs can be used productively for sociopragmatic learning. In "Lights, Camera, Action: Scripts for Language Learning," Gregory Strong describes multiple activities focused on film and television scripts. He provides an overview of the types of scripts available and presents practical ideas on how students can make their own scripts to engage in authentic language practice. Christopher Stillwell, in "Authentic Video as Passport to Cultural Participation and Understanding," presents a series of questions for teachers to ask when selecting video materials and tasks for learners. He suggests various activities to engage students in repeated viewings using subtitles and other textual supports, and he presents resources for using video in class.

The final five chapters in this section focus on computer media in language teaching. Timothy R. Healy's students went to local restaurants and wrote authentic reviews in a blog ("Sharing the Food and Fun Through Restaurant-Review Blogs: An Integrated-Skills Project Approach"). Stages in the writing process as well as electronic literacies are practiced as students write for an authentic purpose: sharing their ideas on local restaurants. In an interactive learning project between students in Canada and the United Arab Emirates, Geoffrey P. J. Lawrence, Terry Compton, Clayton Young, and Hazel Owen describe a wiki they used for collaborative writing projects focusing on research of a famous person ("Using Wikis for Collaborative Writing and Intercultural Learning"). The authors provide step-by-step suggestions for such online collaborations. In "Developing Specialized Discourse Resources for International Teaching Assistants Using a Multimedia Wiki," Barbara Gourlay, David Kanig, Joan Lusk, and Stewart Mader present materials and activities they have devised for graduate students (international teaching assistants) to improve their pronunciation of discipline-specific vocabulary. They describe a series of activities chemistry students can use in developing their comprehensibility. Kathleen Snyder-Parampil and Joel Hensley have their students create virtual portfolios on YouTube ("I Tube . . . Do YouTube? Virtual Portfolios for Reflective Learning and Peer Review"). They show how this Internet resource can be used as a private class forum where students can post video assignments online and critique and comment on each others' work. Finally, Susan Olmstead-Wang uses Webcasts of medical professionals at conferences to assist faculty at her university in Taiwan to develop professional presentation skills ("Medical Doctors Using Authentic

Webcast Lectures to Learn Lexical Phrases"). By focusing on lexical phrases that mark discourse structures, these medical professionals can improve their professional conference presentation skills.

All the chapters in this volume demonstrate that authenticity is more than just the materials we use. Authenticity also means using language for real purposes. It means engaging students in collaborative learning, involving discussions, negotiations, and decision-making. Authenticity is creating real uses for English, not just holding native-speaker language and culture as the sole model. With English increasingly being used as a *lingua franca* to connect second language speakers, authenticity takes on new meanings as we seek to develop learners who can face the challenge of communicating effectively in an increasingly globalized world.

———

Sarah Rilling, associate professor of English at Kent State University in the United States, teaches applied linguistics courses such as ESP, world Englishes, L2 writing, and task research and design. She is co-editor (with Elizabeth Hanson-Smith) of Learning Languages through Technology *(TESOL, 2006). Her teaching, research, and language learning have taken place in the United States, Germany, and Japan.*

Maria Dantas-Whitney is an associate professor of ESOL/bilingual education at Western Oregon University in the United States. She is past president of Oregon TESOL and ORATE (Oregon Association of Teacher Educators). She is co-editor (with Nick Dimmitt) of Intensive English Programs in Postsecondary Settings *(TESOL, 2002) and is currently a Fulbright scholar in Oaxaca, Mexico.*

Authentic Design: Tasks, Materials, and Curricula

CHAPTER 2

Where Can I Get My Shoe Fixed? Authentic Tasks for Students in EFL Settings

Jan Edwards Dormer

A colleague excitedly showed me the colorful document in her hands. "Look!" she exclaimed, "This is the final copy of the booklet that my English class created. It's called *A Foreigner's Guide to Malang,* and the university wants to actually publish it for distribution!" For her English class in an Indonesian university, the booklet was the culmination of activities done throughout the semester through our task-based syllabus. The theme for the semester had been community. Students had explored their own city as they dealt with issues such as health care, transportation, and marketing—in English. But their exploration was always guided by a specific purpose: to answer the question, What does a foreigner need to know in order to live here?

The pursuit of this information resulted in teams of students working on different community-oriented projects, both in and out of class. The student teams interviewed foreign visitors and residents. They collected and created maps. They compared notes on prices and services. And finally, the teams compiled the pictures, maps, comparisons, charts, transportation routes, and much more in the final booklet, of which the teacher and students—and also the university's English department—were justifiably so proud. Students had been able to use English in a country where English is a foreign language, for a real and useful purpose. It was authentic.

CONTEXT

Finding authentic tasks for English classes in English as a foreign language (EFL) settings is not easy. Having taught English in Brazil and Indonesia for the past

13 years, I have often grappled with the question of how to increase intrinsic motivation by giving students a real reason for using English. English is not used widely in either country for interpersonal or transactional communication, although it is a required subject in junior high and high school, as well as in many elementary schools. Most university programs also include English. But all of this formal study of English has not resulted in the ability to use English for real communicative purposes for the majority of students. A few students actively explore English language Web sites, watch foreign movies, or listen to music with English lyrics. And some students make a beeline for any foreigner they see on the street, immediately engaging in conversation. But the majority of my adult students have been a bit less enamored with English. When they watch movies, they read the Portuguese or Indonesian subtitles. When they encounter a foreigner, they really hope that the person can speak the local language. They are enrolled in English classes either because of a cultural perception that "every educated person needs to know English" or because their jobs or studies require it.

For these students, fostering a communicative goal for language learning is tough. Communication with classmates in English can seem stilted and artificial. Role plays in English language textbooks on going to the bank or going shopping are even more artificial. For some students, these types of activities result in a classroom orientation to language learning, creating a mental categorization of language as knowledge rather than as vehicle for real communication. Such students fossilize at pre-intermediate levels, never gaining quite enough proficiency, fluency, or courage to engage in conversation or business with foreigners or write an e-mail in English. Without authentic purposes for learning, it can be difficult for students to move to the intermediate level where they can begin to reap the benefits of their years of classroom learning.

CURRICULUM, TASKS, MATERIALS

A Thematic, Task-Based Curriculum

Our school in Brazil had recently switched from a textbook series to an in-house curriculum. The new program consisted of five levels (see Table 1), the first of which was an introduction to English, focusing on the acquisition of vocabulary and phrases. Levels 2–5 each centered on a broad theme, with a task orientation to the classroom activities undertaken at each level. Each level generally comprised a semester of study, with 4–6 classroom hours per week. Students were placed at appropriate levels based on an initial placement test.

Discovering an Authentic Task

Our curriculum engaged students in many real-world tasks, and I thus found myself continually searching for ways to make classroom activities more authentic. I set up a store with cereal boxes and other packaged food from the United States

Table 1. Theme and Content for Each Level

Level	Theme	Content
1	Introduction to English	letters, numbers, colors, food, body, clothing, school, personal information
2	Home and Family	introductions, descriptions, jobs, home life, family, house, schedules and habits
3	Community	the neighborhood, stores, services, directions, professions
4	The World	culture, customs, holidays, geography, countries
5	Personal Development	relationships, traditions, beliefs, worldview, problems and solutions, change, the future

where play American money was exchanged and students could practice such skills as reading ingredient lists and verbalizing amounts of money. These were, indeed, authentic activities. For Grellet (1981), authenticity means "none of the original text is changed and also . . . its presentation and layout are retained" (p. 8). Certainly, the original presentation and layout of text on my cereal boxes was retained! But despite this use of authentic materials, it was still in the classroom. We still were not getting past the classroom orientation of language learning that I wanted so much for my students to see beyond.

One day, quite by accident, a new approach dropped into my lap. I was having a casual conversation with some students before class, asking them where I could get a shoe fixed. As I listened to their conversation, they haltingly pieced together sentences using directions, sequence words, comparatives, and much more. I asked them questions about quality, price, location, and time. They answered and asked me additional questions: What kind of shoe was it? Did I need it done quickly? Would I like someone to go with me? The questions and answers continued on into the beginning of class, and it occurred to me that it was the richest class we had had in a long time! Students were motivated to talk. They enjoyed telling me about places and services in their city. And what really made it authentic was that I truly needed the information they were giving me.

According to Brown's (2001) definition, my students were engaged in a "real-world" task. Telling me where to get my shoe fixed engaged the learners in a "practical task that language users engage in 'out there' in the real world" (p. 244). True, the conversation was happening in a classroom. But it just as easily could have happened on the street. It was not a part of a course book but instead was an attempt to exchange real information out of a real need for that information. The authenticity in this exchange did not stem from an authentic text; rather, it was an *authentic task* developed from an authentic need to communicate. According to Mishan (2005), authenticity "is a factor of the learner's involvement with the task" (p. 70). My learners were involved in communicating with me for a real purpose.

"Information for Foreigners" as Authentic Tasks

After the shoe-fixing dialogue, I got excited. What if we could build such authentic tasks into every level of our task-based syllabus? Could this be the spark that would ignite the desire to learn English for real communication for some of our students? I surveyed the themes we had chosen for each level (see Table 1). My mind raced as I envisioned the possibilities for authentic tasks that would provide foreigners with needed information at each level. In Level 2, students could show foreigners how people live in their country. There would be opportunities to promote understanding of differences in family relationships, jobs, food, housing, daily schedules, and home life. The theme of community in Level 3 would provide countless opportunities for students to tell about various places in their cities or towns. Level 4 could acquaint foreigners with local celebrations and holidays, as well as help them understand how to be culturally sensitive in action, speech, and dress. And finally in Level 5, students could show others who they are as people: their traditions, worldviews, problems, and dreams for the future. Creating such documents could be motivating, self-affirming, and, most importantly, authentic.

Identifying Specific Tasks

We designed the tasks to provide information for foreigners in the form of a product at each level called a class project. These class projects take a variety of forms, including booklets, DVDs, Web sites, presentations, and posters. The class project develops naturally over the course of the semester as various portions of it relate to specific units in the overall course syllabus. After deciding on the class project, specific portions of the project are identified within each unit, as unit tasks. For the most part, these tasks are already in our syllabus in some form and require minimal adaptation to make them fit the goals of the class project. Table 2 shows the themes and class projects as well as a few sample unit tasks for each level.

Unit tasks are prepared as group work, with different groups taking on different tasks. We chose this approach not only to save time but also because it increases the authenticity of the task, especially since students could choose tasks that drew on their own areas of expertise. Because one group completes each task, each group's product is essential to the overall project. Students always know that their contributions will be used, increasing their motivation to do a good job.

Sometimes within group work, tasks were further broken down into individual or pair tasks, as shown in Figure 1. This task-based hierarchy provides a natural way to progress from large class, to small group, to individual or pair work, while still working together toward a common goal.

Table 2. Theme and Tasks by Level (Indonesian Context)

Level	Theme	Class Project	Sample Unit Tasks
2	Home and Family	Create a booklet about how people live in Indonesia.	• Write about and illustrate different types of Indonesian homes. • Write about and illustrate typical Indonesian food. • Create guidelines for foreigners when visiting Indonesian homes.
3	Community	Create a guide to your city for foreigners.	• Make a map that shows important places in the city. • Make charts comparing and contrasting favorite restaurants, hair salons, and stores. • Give pictures and explanations of different kinds of jobs in Indonesia.
4	The World	Create a cultural guide for foreigners.	• Tell about the many languages and cultures of Indonesia through pictures and text. • Create guidelines for foreigners on cultural norms. • Provide pictures, descriptions, and histories of celebrations and holidays.
5	Personal Development	Create a video documentary about the people in the class: their life realities, beliefs, and dreams for the future.	• Videotape each class member, telling who they are, the realities of their lives, and their goals and dreams. • Create video segments on current issues in Indonesia, including class members' involvements in development and change.

REFLECTIONS

Difficulties Encountered

"It's not a real class."

For students from traditional educational backgrounds, going around the city making maps may not seem like a suitable activity for an English class. And, there is indeed reason for caution. We found that sometimes it is all too easy to get caught up in the project and not engage in real language learning during the activities.

Teacher and student awareness can ensure that language learning does remain at the forefront. Questions teachers may want to ask as they evaluate learning effectiveness include the following:

1. **The development of oral language:** Are the students using English as they complete their tasks? If not, is there a time subsequent to the task or

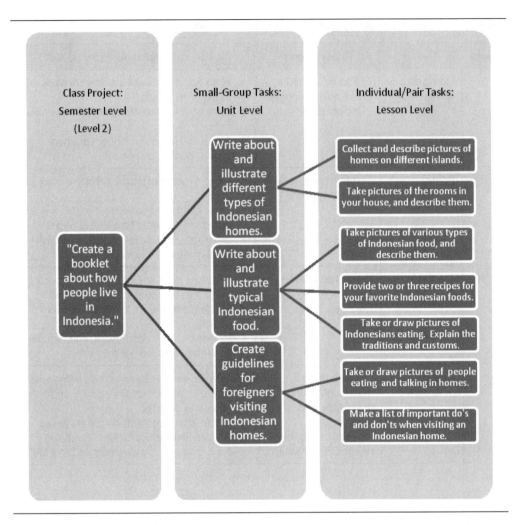

Figure 1. Sample Tasks for Level 2 (Indonesian Context)

information-gathering activity during which students report back to the class using English?

2. **The development of reading and writing:** Does the project require sufficient writing? Do students need to include more or higher level textual explanations and headings along with pictures or graphics? Can additional reading sources be found on the Internet or in local flyers or videos designed for tourists? Such sources of information may not only provide data needed to complete the project but may also provide models of specific language use.

3. **The acquisition of vocabulary and structure:** Are students keeping records of new vocabulary and structures that they are noticing and learning in the course of completing the tasks?

Language use can be achieved through these tasks. As the teacher builds student awareness of how to make the projects a rich language learning experience, students can achieve a more real language use than they might in traditional classroom activities. In describing pictures of their real kitchens, for instance, Indonesian students must extend their learning beyond words labeling items in traditional Western kitchens. They acquire locally relevant vocabulary to explain such items as a stove-top oven or wok gas stove. Likewise, students who work to provide real directions to locations in real cities must learn how to talk about such realities as one-way streets, intersections to avoid during rush hour, and streets that twist and turn.

"We don't have any handouts!"

Both students and teacher may feel a bit unnerved by beginning with a task rather than a piece of paper telling them what to do. However, we found that the fewer prior decisions the teacher has made about how the task should be designed, the better. We suggest that teachers introduce the comprehensive class project at the beginning of the semester but then elicit student ideas for unit- and lesson-level tasks. Breen (1987) has argued for the advantages of learner-centered design in task-based instruction. This type of project becomes most learner-centered when plans emerge from brainstorming sessions and students take the lead in determining the shape of their projects.

"We're not learning the same things."

As students divide into groups and then further into pairs or work as individuals, they perform different tasks, encountering and using different language. For students who have been used to classroom learning and testing in lockstep, this can be disconcerting. The teacher may overcome this potential obstacle by setting aside specific times when the whole class works together. Small groups can give oral reports to the class, and all students can act as proofreaders and editors of student-created texts through class and peer-review groups. Willis (1996) suggests collaborative project development in her task framework, and this sort of learner-centered approach has led to increased student motivation to use English for a real purpose. As the project draws to a close and everyone has a copy of the work done by each group, a renewed focus on form (Willis, 1996) and question and answer sessions can provide opportunities to expand collaborative language learning.

"Will a foreigner ever really see our work?"

The cities in which I have worked have not had many foreigners. However, a lot of contact with foreigners is not necessary for these tasks to be viable. If students are aware that visitors do come to their city or school on occasion, and if they feel that the teacher (or better yet, a student representative or team) will make a concerted effort to get their product into those foreign hands, then the project can still be very authentic. Teachers should make every effort to follow through with promises that the product will be used. International schools, English schools, schools teaching the local language to foreigners, hotels, and tourist agencies may be in need of such information in English.

Benefits

A foreigner walked into one of our classes and saw posters on the wall depicting scenic sites in Indonesia, complete with descriptions and maps. "Oh, where is this?" she said. "I'd like to go there." The student who had created that particular poster jumped out of her seat and eagerly explained the attraction. She was not focused on the structure of her English, only on conveying to this visitor the beauty of her country. Nunan (1989) defines a task as "a piece of classroom work which involves learners in comprehending, manipulating, producing or interacting in the target language while their attention is principally focused on meaning rather than form" (p. 10). This student was fulfilling this definition in every way as she used language for an authentic purpose.

In this essay, I have shown how adult English learners in EFL settings can engage in authentic language use as they seek to provide foreigners with information about their cities and countries. But the ideas presented here need not be limited to this population of language learners. Children learning EFL in public school could be very motivated by the opportunity to create a booklet introducing a foreigner to their school or neighborhood. Students in a community English as a second language (ESL) program could make their favorite foods, take pictures of themselves with their dishes, and use these photos to create colorful posters highlighting international culinary traditions. A local supermarket might agree to display the posters, complete with photocopied take-home recipes. Projects such as these can be a great way for a community to get acquainted with its ESL population—and for ESL learners to contribute to their communities.

Tasks in which learners provide information for foreigners or other English speakers can open up an extremely motivating path toward language acquisition. As students give of their own knowledge rather than passively receiving information in a classroom, using a foreign language suddenly becomes for them . . . *authentic.*

———————————

Jan Edwards Dormer has taught English language learners in the United States, Canada, Brazil, and Indonesia for more than 20 years. She now works primarily in teacher education and curriculum and materials development. She currently directs the Nusantara Educational Institute in Indonesia.

CHAPTER 3

Sharing Our Culture With Visitors: English for Tour Guides

Janet M. D. Higgins

This chapter introduces a culture-based activity involving real-world tasks and materials in a Japanese university seminar called English for Tour Guides. The project consists of tasks where students use and produce a variety of authentic materials, with the distinctive environs of Okinawa University providing a vibrant background for the course.

CONTEXT

Okinawa Prefecture, the home of Okinawa University, is the southernmost prefecture in Japan. It consists of around 160 islands, and the capital, Naha, is 1,500 km southwest of Tokyo. Okinawa is closer to Taipei, Seoul, Hong Kong, and Shanghai than to Tokyo, and it attracts an increasing number of tourists from Taiwan and mainland China. However, the majority of tourists are from mainland Japan. It is a popular destination for Japanese school trips to visit the peace memorials and for senior citizens who are interested in the unique biodiversity of the islands (ecotourism is a rapidly expanding industry). In addition to its marine and terrestrial plant and animal treasures, Okinawa has a rich culture dating to the golden age of the Ryuukyuu Kingdom in the 15th century. Several of its *gusku* (castles) and sacred sites are World Heritage sites, while many buildings, activities, folk craft specialists (dance, drama, music, weaving, pottery, lacquer ware, glassware), and artifacts are national treasures. With such a rich cultural environment, there is plenty for visitors to learn about and enjoy.

Okinawa Prefecture has the largest number of U.S. military bases in Japan (70%), with bases occupying 20% of the land and a vast area of ocean and airspace used for military training (Arasaki, 2000). Military personnel are confined mainly to bases in the central and northern areas, but American personnel frequent popular tourist spots, towns around the bases, and the central shopping streets of Naha. Some of my students go on base from time to time for part-time jobs. After graduating, one seminar participant worked as a tour guide on base. However, military personnel are rarely seen near Okinawa University, and most of my students do not meet any on a regular basis.

English for Tour Guides is an elective seminar that provides second- to fourth-year students the opportunity to develop their English skills while talking and writing about their culture and the artifacts of other cultures. Many students only recognize the importance of developing such skills when they discover their need. The Division of International Communication at Okinawa University offers three majors, one of which is tourism. The seminar is particularly appropriate for students with this major, although the course is also open to students from all faculties. Typical seminar participants include overseas students (e.g., from China, Korea, and Indonesia), mainland Japanese students, local Okinawan students, and students who have spent one or more years studying or working abroad in an English-speaking environment. Their levels of proficiency vary considerably, providing interesting challenges.

CURRICULUM, TASKS, AND MATERIALS

The syllabus for this 15-week, credit-bearing course includes a variety of authentic and non-authentic materials, some of the latter from English language course books focusing on tourism and travel. Authentic materials include guidebooks, tourist brochures, television travel programs, and Internet tourist Web sites. In class, oral presentations supported by multimedia presentations provide flexibility in developing language proficiency within the English as a foreign language (EFL) classroom. The seminar also gives students opportunities to participate in field trips.

Over recent years, we have covered several projects, and I have chosen one activity—the guided walk—that I have found particularly exciting and relevant to students. Course activities are not static; they change according to the proficiency level, interests, and personality of each group of seminar participants, and the guided walk is no exception. The following is a sequence of the activities that comprise a larger thematic unit on guided tours.

The Guided Walk

The guided walk is a well-respected and popular leisure activity. It is not only fun for tourists but is a regular event in many local communities. In a guided walk, an expert or specialist leads a group on a walking tour of a locality, focusing on a particular historical, environmental, ecological, cultural, or topical theme. Many such walks and their details (time, place of departure, and the name of the guide) can be found in local community papers and tourist information. Tour guides may be volunteers with specialized local knowledge or paid tour guides. Guided walks also are available as printed maps with a route and key points of interest marked and briefly described in an accompanying text. Examples of written guided walks can be found in many guidebooks and tourist brochures. Similar kinds of material can be found on Internet tourist sites—sometimes a virtual tour is even available. Another form of the guided walk can be found on television. A local or visiting guide walks reporters or celebrities around a town, shopping area, or historical site. The video viewers become *de facto* members of the tour group. The camera closes in on the points of interest, and the viewers vicariously share the experiences with the guide.

For my purposes, the guided walk is a wonderful vehicle for authentic language and content practice. Students study background cultural materials, perhaps by reading or watching travel shows; assemble facts into interesting synopses; and then through assuming the role of a tour guide, actively communicate this information to an audience (their classmates).

My first experience with the guided walk as pedagogical tool was while working with seminar students on a project connected with local food culture. The fieldwork involved pairs of students going out into two streets adjacent to the university and photographing and collecting data (menus, costs, ambience, etc.) on three to four local restaurants. The students then wrote up their results and gave oral presentations supported by multimedia. What resulted was a walk along two streets, focusing on eateries. It was later that I realized the potential of the activity within the context of the guided walk.

The following activities support the overall goals of the project.

Guiding a Group: In at the Deep End!

The focus of this activity is basic language and gestures used in leading a group of visitors. I use a deep-end approach (i.e., going straight into the activity without any prior preparation) for a number of reasons: (a) I want to see what language the students know and where the gaps in their knowledge lie, (b) I want to assess their level of confidence in attempting the task, and (c) I want the students to identify for themselves what they need to know in order to accomplish the task.

First we go out on the campus, and I select a location. I then give one student the role of guide, and the rest of us act as the group. The student has to tell us where we are going and warn us when we are about to change direction or go off course. I encourage other students to help out if necessary, and I supply what they cannot. We then go back to the classroom and students assess their success. We brainstorm and learn the expressions and gestures we need, and then practice. The work with gestures is a lot of fun as we lose our inhibitions and learn the behavior appropriate to the practicing professional tour guide. Pointing out directions with hand and arm movements that can be seen by a group of people, for instance, needs to be done naturally and unambiguously. The language work we cover includes expressions of location and appropriate language for pointing things out, from prepositions to phrases. Phrases such as "if you look on the left," "over there on the left," and "if you look up, you'll see," are really useful and are often new to students. Most of them will have never used or heard this practical application of "if clauses" inside the classroom. The real-world application is a revelation!

To follow up, we go back out on campus and redo the initial activity, with the students themselves choosing the places where they guide the group. This practical work for each person is very short, but we aim for accuracy and confidence in using the expressions and the gestures. The student acting as guide has to hold up a pole (a pointer with a hand on the end is fun) just as many guides do, especially in Japan. I find students initially uncomfortable using this prop, but they soon get used to it. It makes the activity much more real, and we begin to look quite professional as we walk around the campus. We explain that we are guides-in-training if we are asked. We use this prop for all our off-campus guiding work, and students are expected to explain who we are as a group when we talk to people in the street or in shops and cafes.

Guiding a Group: Local Fieldwork

For our next piece of fieldwork, we focus on local Okinawan culture by going out into the streets around the university and seeking out "typically Okinawan" objects or customs. For instance, we notice the protective pair of *shisa* (lion dogs) on the tiled rooftops of old Okinawan houses, the traditional Ryuukyuuan limestone (local form of limestone) walls around the old houses, and the *Ishigantoo* stone markers at junctions to ward off evil spirits. Members of the group take turns being the guide as we walk along, pointing out these features and giving us short explanations. The focus in this activity is again to practice structure and gesture work, aiming for accuracy and fluency, with clear pronunciation, a loud voice, a lively, enthusiastic tone, and gestures to guide and direct.

Guiding a Group: Stages of the Guided Walk

Next, we study language materials aimed at managing the guided walk as a whole. These include expressions for greeting a group and introducing oneself as guide, briefly introducing the purpose and content of the walk, keeping the tour group together, interacting with the group, and concluding the walk. Appendix A provides a handout I have used for this purpose.

For our fieldwork at this stage we again go out into the local streets, but this time we create a whole guided walk. The first student introduces the walk, the last student concludes it, and the rest of the group takes turns leading us to see interesting features in the area. On one of these walks, a student introduced us to a local coffee supply shop. We lingered there, interviewing the owner and absorbing the delicious aroma of ground coffee! It was a great learning experience for us all. Although the students used Japanese in this encounter (the shop owner spoke no English), it provided welcome practice in interviewing skills, and of course, the group later discussed this information in English. This fieldwork concludes the first stage of the activity.

Guided Walks Around Lewes Old Town, England

There is limited time in the seminar to do actual fieldwork. Because we cannot go very far afield, I use authentic tourist materials in simulations. The first of these is a virtual visit to the town of Lewes in southern England, using a tourist map from the Tourist Information Centre. I chose Lewes because I have personal experience with the town as a tourist and have tourist information and a collection of photographs I took on my visit.

Founded in the 11th century, Lewes has well-preserved historic buildings spanning the centuries, a brewery and winery, and it is famous for its Guy Fawkes Night celebrations on the 5th of November. For class discussion, I use my own photographs and Internet sites featuring photographs of historic sites and the Guy Fawkes Night celebrations. I also provide students with written extracts on the history of the town pulled from the Internet. These materials provide the background required for the practical task in which each student is asked to create their own guided walk of Lewes incorporating four or five points of interest. The student guided walk must include all stages, from introduction to conclusion.

For homework, I ask students to prepare a written version of what they plan to say. They submit this script by e-mail, and I provide feedback. In the next class, they give their tour with the aim of speaking to the group rather than just reading aloud. As a virtual walk, we all look at our maps and "accompany" the guide. At this stage, I encourage the group to act as real tourists by asking questions— although it is also part of the guide's role to elicit questions from their reluctant classmates.

Guided Walks Around Fremantle, Western Australia

Western Australia comes alive through text and maps from a tourist brochure on the area around Perth, focusing on the city of Fremantle. Our final goal is the same as in the Lewes activity: to design and lead a short virtual walk. I chose Fremantle because I have excellent materials from the town and because many of my students are interested in Australia. Several of the students either have studied there (on a 1-year program or a 5-week course) or are planning to do so.

The brochure contains a map of Fremantle with a suggested city tour marked out. The accompanying text provides some basic information. This authentic written version of a city walk provides students with a model for their summaries of interesting cultural information. The Fremantle activity is more demanding in that students are expected to search through the extensive information in the brochure to devise their own tour. Again, they have to create a virtual guided walk, incorporating four to five places of interest. The rest of the group follows the map as the "guide" talks, and asks questions if possible.

The Fremantle brochure is rich in tourist language. One of the features is a set of fairly typical collocations used in tourism writing (Appendix B provides a list of examples used as class materials). In class, we explore the collocations, identifying those used in descriptions of local restaurants and the atmosphere of the town. We notice how often alliteration is involved and how many of the words are very "strong" (super, stunning, unique), and we observe combinations of nouns + adjectives and verbs + adverbs, among others. I then invite students to make use of the collocations in preparing their own guided walks.

A Television Walk: The Qualities of a Tour Guide

One activity that has proven thought provoking and enjoyable is watching an authentic Japanese TV travel program. I use a program in Japanese because I want to focus on the art of being a guide and the content of the guided walk rather than on English language skills. In the program, an energetic and very personable amateur guide leads two visitors around a historic town and her large old family house. We watch the program as a group and then reflect on what makes the woman such an entertaining guide and the walk so much fun. Students have identified such points as her ebullient personality, her interesting and unusual use of language and gestures, and her strategy of making things a mystery for the visitors and the viewers. Students concluded that the guide's personality is one of the most important factors in a successful guided walk. Students also have identified the importance of the guide's knowledge and her enjoyment in weaving tales for visitors.

REFLECTIONS

The guided walk has proven to be a rich vehicle for developing communication skills in my classroom. It has allowed me to introduce a variety of authentic materials, and while these have at times proven to be linguistically challenging to the students, they have also generated great interest, expanded students' knowledge of the world, and led to the use of richer language than is often found in and generated by English language textbook materials. In addition, the project has expanded the students' knowledge of communities in other parts of the world. As a culminating activity for this project, it would be beneficial to have the students actually guide English-speaking tourists on a walk. However, many of the groups that I have taught on this course have not had sufficient language skills, and even proficient students lack sufficient opportunities to interact with international visitors during the limited time period of the course.

ACKNOWLEDGMENT

I thank my colleague, Dileep Chandralal, for supplying the Perth and Fremantle tourist material.

Janet Higgins has worked as a TESOL teacher and teacher trainer in England, the Middle East, and the Far East (since 1991 in Japan). She has designed and taught study skills and ESP, presented papers and organized workshops internationally, and is the recipient of a number of research awards.

APPENDIX A: HANDOUT ON TOUR GUIDE LANGUAGE

A. Explain to the group **what** we are going to visit and **why** we are going to visit it (what is important or interesting about it). Examples:

- One of the unique features of Okinawa University is its water treatment system. We are going to visit the treatment plant and find out how the system works.

- Naha has produced pottery for hundreds of years. Today we are going to visit the pottery area of Naha, called Tsuboya. We are going to walk down the main street called Yachimun Dori and visit several pottery shops. We will also visit a traditional kiln. There will be time for you to buy some souvenirs.

- International Street, or Kokusai Dori, is the most famous tourist street in Naha. It is lined with souvenir shops, restaurants and cafes, and clothing shops. We will start at the southwest end and walk north eastward. We will then branch off down Peace Street, or Heiwa Dori, and visit the small streets of Naha's meat, fruit, and vegetable markets. There will be time for shopping and visiting one of the cafes.

B. Beginning the tour: Getting everyone's attention:

- Ladies and gentlemen. Here we are at the east end of the main street of Tsuboya . . .

- Ladies and gentlemen. We are now standing at the Prefectural Government Building . . .

- As you can see in front of us . . .

C. Use gesture and language to point out important features to the group:

- Please look to the right. This is an old well in use in Tsuboya for hundreds of years . . .

- If you look on the right/left you'll see . . .

- On your right/left there is . . .

- On your right/left you can see . . .

- Let's turn right/left here.

D. Draw on your group's interests by engaging them with questions. For example, this is an interesting _____ (picture/object/building/plant).

  - Does anyone know what it is/what it does?

  - Does anyone have any idea what it is/what it does?

  - Has anyone seen one like this before?

E. Always try to answer questions from the group:

  - Does anyone have any questions?

  - That's an interesting question . . . (*answer*)

  - Right . . . (*answer*)

  - That's an interesting question. I'm afraid I don't know all the details, but . . . (*answer whatever you know*).

  - That's an interesting question, but I'm sorry, I don't know the answer.

  - Okay, let's see if there's anything about it in one of my guide books . . . (*look it up in the guide materials*).

F. Be sure to indicate when the tour is over by thanking your group, such as the following:

  - Ladies and gentlemen, we've come to the end of the tour. Thank you for joining me today.

  - Well, here we are at the end of the market area in Naha. This is all we have time for today. The bus is waiting across the road.

  - Ladies and gentlemen, this is the end of our tour of . . . Thank you very much.

  - Ladies and gentlemen, I hope you have enjoyed our walk today (this morning/afternoon/evening).

APPENDIX B: COLLOCATIONS IN SAMPLE TOURIST BROCHURE

Focus	Examples
Town	X is a <u>charming destination</u> X has a <u>rich maritime</u> and <u>cultural heritage</u> . . . with <u>spectacular views</u> X is <u>an ideal spot</u> to . . . X attracts <u>huge audiences</u> . . . a <u>working harbor</u> . . . . . . can experience <u>the supreme skill</u> and <u>outrageous behavior</u> of . . . X has been <u>painstakingly restored</u>. . . . can enjoy <u>the calm, clean water and sand</u> The taste of <u>freshly caught and cooked seafood</u>
Restaurants and Food	<u>multi award winning tourist restaurant</u> <u>prime Australian steak</u> overlooking <u>the bustling boardwalk</u> this <u>unique dining and tourism complex</u> <u>romantic dinners</u> <u>creative cuisine</u> <u>funky atmosphere</u> <u>a stunning array of seafood</u> <u>great service</u> our <u>extensive menu/wine list</u> <u>fabulous location</u>

APPENDIX C: INTERNET RESOURCES

Lewes, Sussex, UK: a good site to start with is http://en.wikipedia.org/wiki/Lewes

London Walks Ltd. (2007). *London walks: Summer.* See also http://www.walks.com

The National Trust: http://www.nationaltrust.org.uk

CHAPTER 4

Oh, the Places You'll Go: Creating a Class City Guide

Laura Ramm

This highly accessible project offers second language students authentic, everyday communication experiences in the community where they live. Designed to combine in-class instruction and practice with authentic, real-world application, students learn to make requests of service-sector employees, which also teaches them about business and American culture. After practicing with in-class dialogue activities, students apply what they learn to tasks at an actual business.

The larger assignment described here is creating a class city guide, including reviews, directions, and short essays on places of interest. The finished booklet can be given to friends and family as a guide to help familiarize them with the area and serves as a record of the students' accomplishments. This lesson sequence is designed to engage students with their community and foster authentic, real-world interactions with community members.

CONTEXT

The class city guide project described in this chapter was carried out as part of the English as a second language (ESL) summer community education program at Eastern Michigan University. Because this was an adult basic education (ABE) program, I emphasized conversational English to strengthen students' oral language skills and enrich their cultural experiences. The students had various reasons for being in the United States, including work, school, and visiting family, but they all needed to access local businesses and perform day-to-day activities such as grocery shopping. Their goals were practical rather than academic; therefore, the lessons were structured to promote competency in everyday activities.

Our learners ranged in age from 22 to mid-50s. The first group to complete the project was a diverse group from seven countries with five different home languages, all placed in an advanced class. I administered a needs analysis and a background questionnaire to gain understanding of students' prior and current target language exposure and needs. All had taken English classes before, and except for one, all had been living in the United States for 1 year or more. This background questionnaire also showed that students' primary concerns were to be able to talk to community members, including neighbors and friends, more effectively. Although some writing was necessary for the class city guide, given the students' needs, their project research would be coordinated through speaking and listening activities. All students could type and had experience with the Internet, and all had computer and Internet access.

CURRICULUM, TASKS, MATERIALS

After administering the questionnaire, I developed an 18-hour, 6-week curriculum focusing on community experiences. The instructional time was short (1 hour per session, three times a week); however, the students visited local businesses as part of their daily lives, so incorporating these outside activities into the class project helped maximize class time. I chose ice-breakers for the first week to fine-tune my assessment of their language abilities, and this helped me to create lessons targeting the class project. I took a mixed approach to curriculum design as advocated by Brown (1995), which combines situational (e.g., at the grocery store), functional (e.g., interrupting, information gathering, greetings), and task-based (e.g., writing directions, reporting information) instruction to complete the larger project of the class city guide. This gave me a framework to prepare lessons, specifically for the written components of the city guide, and to include an average of one situation, function, or task each week.

Week 1: Introductions

I began by introducing students to local newspapers and magazines that give information about events and places in the community. This information can be found on Web sites, but we also have a variety of print publications that I used to model the city guide for the class project, introduce the students to locations around town, create lessons, and provide authentic materials for class (e.g., direction lessons and maps, reading tasks, and street and place names). A free local magazine that reports only on events and places in the area became our primary model.

As an icebreaker and to help the students become more familiar with the event magazine as a resource, I put together an in-class scavenger hunt (see Figure 1). I created clues and the students worked together to find addresses, event details, and locations. Other teachers have done similar activities with phone books or indexes. It is a good way to teach students how to use an index or table of contents using local, authentic resources, and the competition helps increase students' concentration and collaboration skills.

Ice-breakers are beneficial for students to get to know each other and to practice listening and speaking in English, but also for the instructor to learn

---

I Found It!

In-class scavenger hunt game with local city guide:

1. Have the students work in pairs or small groups of three or four.
2. Give each student a copy of a local city guide and ask them to identify the index, table of contents, or any other tools in the publication.
3. Give each group a teacher-generated clue sheet (see samples below) to complete as a group, and model and example clue as a class.
4. Instruct the students to work together to answer as many clues as possible within a given time.
5. Time the students to see which group finds the most answers the fastest.
6. When a group finishes, have them say their answers aloud and let the class decide if they are correct.

Alternatives:

- Before class, have the students use the city guide to create their own clue sheets. Students their trade clue sheets with each other in class and assess the answers.
- Students ask each other clues, emphasizing speaking and listening.
- If feasible, have students look for clues in the community, asking merchants about their businesses. Have them bring back pamphlets to share with the class.

Sample clues for the clue sheet:

1. What is the street address of the Visitors' Bureau?
2. Which restaurant advertises "Free Live Music?"
3. When are the operating times for the library?
4. What is the phone number for the movie theatre on Main Street?
5. Where can I go to see a play?

Figure 1. In-class Scavenger Hunt Game

about the students and assess their language abilities. Another good ice-breaker is writing postcards. By having the students interview each other about their travel experiences and then write postcards about the trips, I was able to assess sentence formation and grammar structure, and to a certain extent, composition. With a shorter semester and the focus on a writing project, this was a good way to gauge early just what they could manage.

Week 2: Paragraph Writing

Once I had an idea of students' abilities, I introduced an organizational strategy for paragraph writing called Think Sheet (see Figure 2), an idea I adapted from various resources (e.g., Harford, n.d.; Raimes, 1983; Think Sheets, n.d.).

Even though this was not a graded course, I included a rubric (see Figure 3) for this writing activity because it gave students a clear expectation for their finished paragraphs to include in the city guide we were preparing. The rubric

Think Sheet

The following is useful for paragraph writing. After completing this activity in class, or better yet, in a classroom with one or more computers, have students type the paragraphs using topic, supporting, and closing sentences. The typed paragraphs can be included in the city guide section, "Places to Go."

Topic: Decide what the paragraph will be about.

1. List places you have been in our city.
2. Select one place and write a complete sentence about it.
3. Write several sentences about this place. Include descriptive adjectives and prepositional phrases.
4. Write a topic sentence about the place to draw the ideas from your sentences together.
5. Choose which of the descriptive sentences you would like to use as supporting information, and write them into a paragraph including your topic sentence. As you rewrite, are there new ideas you would like to add? Add and rewrite as appropriate.

A second or multiple paragraphs can add relevant cultural or historic information:

1. Think of 3 or more reasons why you think this place is important within the community, and write sentences.
2. Write a closing on the place's importance.

Figure 2. Paragraph Writing Activity

provided a measure for improvement, and it helped to unify the writing for each entry in our city guide.

Week 3: Communication

Within the larger framework of the city guide, spending instructional time on greetings, interrupting, requests, suggestions, permission, and agreeing/disagreeing afforded students practice in conversational English and prepared them to interact with community members around town. Class practice centered on dialogues I prepared based on potential store conversations (e.g., locating an item, buying an item, reporting an incident, etc.). As modal verbs were essential to this activity, students had the opportunity to practice this verb form. They then worked in class brainstorming and writing advice based on their own experiences living in this city. This activity is based on a lesson sequence from *Grammar in Context* (Elbaum, 2005) in which students give advice to others. For our city guide, however, the advice was specific to the students' community. An advice column became a section in our city guide and the following categories developed out of students' shared experiences: travel, transportation, food and drink, clothes, and daily life. By integrating language functions, language structure, and the community as content, students were able to practice authentic uses for language.

Think Sheet Rubric

Scale: 1   2   3   4   5
           Poor   Average   Excellent

- Do the paragraphs focus on one place?
- Are adjectives and prepositional phrases used effectively as descriptors?
- Do the topic sentence(s) clearly indicate the specific place and its importance within the community?
- Are the paragraph(s) well supported through elaborative details?
- Are closing sentence(s) effective?
- Do the paragraph(s) contain clear topic(s), support, and closings?
- What ideas should the writer consider?

Comments:

Figure 3. Informal Writing Assessment Rubric

Week 4: Directions, Locations, and Slogans

Understanding and giving directions are essential skills in living in any community. During this week, we focused on giving and receiving directions by working in pairs to locate businesses on a local map, create directions to that location, and then record the directions by writing them out. We used free downtown maps from our visitors' bureau as well as brochures from businesses. Each student pair chose brochures at random to determine what to look for on the map. Alternatively, students could compete to see who can find locations on the map the quickest. After writing directions, student pairs traded their directions and checked for accuracy. They applied the use of directions for a later assignment when they needed to locate and visit a local grocery store.

For listening practice with directions, I repurposed an interior map from a local mall. I removed some store names and left only a few to keep students oriented. The students needed to listen to my instructions and fill in their blank maps by putting the correct store in its location (e.g., "Find the coffee shop located between the entrance and the toy store"). This activity has the potential to combine with a field trip to practice giving and receiving directions around the mall, an excellent opportunity to practice prepositions!

Another facet of giving and receiving directions is imperatives. All of the students were familiar with popular online road maps where directions are given in imperative form (e.g., turn left, head south, etc.). The students practiced imperatives in class: giving instructions, warnings, commands, and encouragement. They then created slogans and statements about the city with imperatives (e.g., Spend time in our city! Visit the Summer Festival!). They turned these into an introduction to the city guide, creating an eye-catching cover that introduced the contents and peaked reader curiosity.

Weeks 5 and 6: Community Experience at the Grocery Store

The final assignment focused on personal recipes and a field experience at the grocery store. Through recipes, students could talk about cultural experiences (two students actually made the dishes to share) and use the recipes as shopping lists for a grocery store visit. We worked together to make sure the recipes were written in English with all the appropriate ingredients. Once we had the list of ingredients, students took their shopping lists (either alone or in pairs) to a grocery store, where they completed a worksheet (see Figure 4). Students then used the worksheet and their notes to write another paragraph giving a positive or negative recommendation about the store to include in the city guide. Going to a store with a preprinted worksheet helps students stay on task and take notes. The students should include pertinent information about the store, such as hours, location, and local bus numbers that stop there. Depending on the store and their shopping lists, the students may need to ask store workers questions in order to complete the worksheet. This assignment incorporated each section of the curriculum: paragraph writing, communication, directions, and navigating the grocery store.

REFLECTIONS

The authentic, real-world situations the students encounter in this course develop communication and language skills while providing a safe environment to become more familiar with their new hometown. Because this course is taught in an ABE summer program, the students are not required to attend class and grades are not

---

At the Grocery Store

Sample items from the student worksheet

1. Include the two most important ingredients in this recipe and the prices for them.
2. Were there any ingredients this store didn't carry? What were those? What did the store manager or clerk tell you about those items?
3. Would you recommend this store as the best place to shop? Why or why not?
4. Does this store have specialty items, such as spices, fish, or imported food?
5. Include 5–7 examples of products that are not food.
6. Does this store have weekly sales? How can you find out about them?

Figure 4. Sample Site Visit Worksheet

given. The curriculum works because there are few absences and students come to class prepared to work.

Student independence is fostered through assignments in which classroom knowledge is applied to real-world situations. Unfortunately, there is not time to work on publishing the city guide, so as the instructor, I manage this process. The students act as reporters, and their assignments are the city guide content. These roles keep responsibilities clear and help us assemble the city guide within the time allowed. Even with a short course schedule, project-based learning that meets a range of learner needs is possible.

Laura Ramm became interested in teaching English while working in the automotive industry. After tutoring nonnative speaking employees in writing and pronunciation, she changed careers and now teaches ESL at Michigan State University, in the United States. She is an active member of Michigan Teachers of English to Speakers of Other Languages (MITESOL) and has a research interest in pronunciation.

CHAPTER 5

Magazine as Project-Based Learning

Hoang Thi Ngoc Diem

In the not too distant past, textbooks alone were used to teach English at Thainguyen University of Education in Thainguyen, Vietnam. Tailoring materials was not the habit of most language teachers. Sadly, apart from using prescribed textbooks and completing traditional homework, often in the form of rote exercises, students did not spend their time in self-study. Lack of access to authentic materials was one of the reasons, but antiquated teaching methods can easily be traced as the main cause. As a result, a generation of students with incomplete English competence has developed in Vietnam. But language teachers in Vietnam are slowly coming in line with international trends in language education. Questions we as teachers struggle with include: In what way can students' individual talents and habits be exploited to support their learning? How can teachers give students reasons to learn, both inside and outside the classroom? How can we increase student motivation to explore real-life environments using language as a tool? To seek answers, we have incorporated project-based learning into our curriculum to engage our learners in using English both in and out of the classroom.

Project-based learning (PBL) has proven very effective for language development (Esch, 1998; Fried-Booth, 2002; Gallacher, 2004). At Thainguyen University of Education, we designed a curriculum for our English as a foreign language (EFL) students to improve their English competence beyond the classroom in language and nonlanguage capacities, including competence in Internet technology (IT), cultural awareness, learning strategies, and analytic language skills. This chapter includes a description of PBL as a pedagogical approach. Steps in developing projects with students are described, our assessment practices sampled, and some limitations discussed in the hope that our shared experiences will be useful for other English language practitioners.

CONTEXT

We implemented PBL at Thainguyen University of Education, a regional university for the northern provinces of Vietnam. Our university is known in particular for training teachers from remote areas. The proficiency level of our first-year students in the foreign language faculty varies considerably. Students at Thainguyen University have been admitted based on different examinations and processes, namely: (a) the official national entrance examination, (b) local commitments (the local authorities select prospective staff and send them to the university for training), or (c) preparation courses (registered schools for students who fail the national entrance examination). All three of these different groups are mixed in classes and share the same curriculum and assessment criteria. Another reason our classes have mixed abilities is that the language curriculum of high schools is not unified, and often schools deliver grammar or translation-oriented classes. Few students are familiar with the communicative approach to language, and many come from rural and remote areas in the northern provinces where teachers are not adequately trained to engage learners in active and autonomous learning. Teachers typically are viewed as the main source of knowledge, and although library study is familiar to some, the Internet and English language newspapers are used only by a few. In other words, the available access and interaction with real-life English has been very narrow.

To meet these challenges, we are using methods with a learner-centered orientation (Richards, 2002), which blends knowledge and language skills. The aim of the PBL curriculum is to get students to practice English more and explore English resources both in and outside the classroom. Each project is like a workshop, where students collaborate to produce something real with the language they are learning. Completing projects requires not only knowledge and language but also skills in other subjects, such as IT, study skills, and research methods. In all circumstances, English is the main tool in language research and production (Wicks, 2000), and it becomes the main resource in the creation of a product, in our case, a magazine.

CURRICULUM, TASKS, MATERIALS

Many projects are available for students to choose from in our curriculum, like drama, overseas studies, consultancies, virtual tours, and culture quiz game shows. The "Magazine" is one of the most popular choices: As its name denotes, students are required to produce a magazine based on a succession of language, content, and IT activities. Students must meet some standard demands of the magazine format, including length and design, variety of writing styles for different sections, social correctness, and, most importantly, originality of content. Students are free to choose the theme of their magazine, but any sign of plagiarism or "copy and paste" of published materials will earn penalties in assessment.

The magazine project is supported by oral and written modules at Thainguyen University of Education as well as IT training in other university courses. The four basic language skills are taught in two modules, oral and written, in the first academic year. The main products of the magazine project are a complete printed magazine and a press conference introducing the product and project results to classmates, teaching staff, invited EFL teachers from other universities, and interested guests.

Pedagogical Approach

In PBL, students spend time outside the classroom on their own, acting as journalists, editors, designers, and producers. They apply what they have learned in practical tasks independently. What they need from the instructor is guidance, advice, technical support, and advice on best management. The teacher's role, therefore, is as both instructor and manager. Managing here means keeping control of the production process to make sure that all journalists gather information efficiently, observe rules on plagiarism, and most of all, use English language resources to learn new content and make progress in language learning.

Students do not work alone in this learner-centered approach. Teacher–learner and learner–learner contact happens during class in weekly discussions during which students correct drafts and discuss the work of the coming week. The instructor also helps any groups or individual members solve specific problems. The instructor is available to give immediate support outside of scheduled class times, such as providing digital recorders and cameras, supplying advice on survey questionnaires, and arranging dates for the press conference. Students are allowed to use the computers and access the Internet in our language laboratory with the instructor's supervision, so special times are arranged specifically for the computer lab. Though students work on their own most of the time, the instructor is not idle. During all activities, the instructor observes student progress to intensify the focus on language practice—the very purpose of PBL.

Procedure

Structuring the Product

Once grouped with peers, teams begin by outlining their magazines. A certain amount of time is assigned for designing the layout, and creativity and design detail is encouraged rather than just duplicating real magazines. When students act as "journalists," they are actively engaged with language use, and they hone their logic, planning, and critical thinking skills. Groups use the handout (see Figure 1) to frame the magazine and prepare an action plan.

The rule during the planning stages is that students themselves decide on their roles and the content of the magazine. They negotiate in groups about various aspects of the product. They are allowed to pace themselves in the production process by making their own action plan based on individual skills, capacities, and schedules. Students set their own goals for project completion, and the

Magazine Plan Handout

1. Group members:

2. Magazine theme:

3. Magazine Frame:

	Columns	Activities	Text types
1			
2			
3			

Note: You may change the topic of a certain column to suit the seasons, local or traditional events, etc., while you are completing the project.

4. Action Plan:

	Phase	Duration	Activities	Products
1				
2				
3				

Figure 1. Creating an Action Plan for a Magazine as Project

instructor's role is to make sure they practice language skills and do not exceed the time allowed. Though each magazine team has different plans, the teacher should ensure that the amount team members work is comparatively equal.

Action Plan Realization Phase

With feedback and approval from the instructor, groups prepare for the project. Some subtopics in the magazine can be changed during this phase if groups want to make use of local events, college anniversaries, festivals, or holidays, for example. During the project, students' creativity is often beyond teachers' expectations.

The project integrates all four basic language skills meaningfully as follows:

- *Speaking:* Interviewing a VIP, friend, or teacher for an article; discussing the project in groups; presenting the final product; advertising the final product to classmates and teachers; and holding the press conference with other students and invited guests.

- *Listening:* Recording and summarizing television programs or radio news from English channels to develop newspaper articles and opinion columns.

- *Writing:* Various forms, including describing and narrating a traditional festival or a local or university event, preparing tips or instructions for making something, producing catchy titles and headlines, preparing written arguments, composing free writing of personal feelings, writing short stories, composing essays that compare and contrast, predicting coming events, and preparing summaries and reviews.

- *Reading:* Referring to and extracting information from sources such as newspapers, magazine, and articles on the Internet.

- *Other Skills:* Applying IT skills, design, research (through mini-surveys), experiential learning through field trips to gather information, and so on.

At Thainguyen University of Education, projects take place over an academic year. As students complete drafts and collect materials, they build a portfolio that can be included in the magazine. Most articles are the fruit of student research, such as interviews, field trips, and writing tasks.

Editing, Designing, Proofreading, and Printing

Editing, further design, proofreading, and printing are all indispensable steps in any published work. Drafts are exchanged within and between groups for editing. Student are given a marking scheme and assessment rubric to provide their classmates with feedback. IT skills are exploited to the full for the tough work of designing and decorating the magazine. Much time is spent on this stage as our first-year students are not computer experts and computer literacy takes time to acquire. Each group is provided a certain amount of money to print some copies of the magazine for themselves, for evaluation, and for the university library.

Product Presentation

Once students complete their magazine, it is not the end of the project. The final requirement is a presentation by each group in a press conference. The instructor suggests tips for public speaking and gives presentation guidelines (see Figure 2). Group members together create a computer-based presentation, and they practice presenting with the help of the instructor, who provides tips on language use, communicative strategies, and IT use. Rubrics are distributed to students in advance so that they are aware of assessment criteria (see Figure 3).

Assessment

As students are involved in real-life activities for both end product (the magazine) and to improve their language competence, traditional testing has not been found very suitable. Assessment adjustments were needed for our curriculum. We decided to include the following two components:

Project Press Conference Guidelines

In your final group presentation, address the questions below. Each group member will be graded, so be sure that everyone has an active role. Don't forget to use computer software to support your presentation. *(Time allowance: 25–30 minutes per group)*

- What is your project? What are its purposes?
- How did you complete your project? (Give steps by time order, work distribution, plans, etc.)
- Describe your final product(s).
- Reflection/looking back:
  — What skills and other abilities did you improve?
  — What went well and what could have gone better?
  — What are your plans to continue to improve your skills? Be specific.
- Describe your personal experience working on the project (What did you enjoy most or were most disappointed by? What are you most proud of?)

Figure 2. Guidelines for the Project Press Conference

1. For *progress assessment*, portfolios are used, which are composed of students' collected materials, first drafts, edited drafts, and audio- or video-recorded rehearsals of presentations.

2. For *project assessment*, the completed magazines and the press conference are assessed.

To provide students and staff with uniform criteria for evaluation, we prepare rubrics that we give to students early in the project production stage so that they understand how they will be evaluated. We designed and have been using three rubrics, one to assess the magazine, one for the press conference, and one for student portfolios. Figures 3 and 4 provide examples of two of these rubrics. Figure 3 is an extract from the magazine rubric that we use. Figure 4 is an extract from the press conference rubric.

During the press conference, the magazines are exchanged among groups, teaching staff, classmate-readers, and any visitors. Each participant is given an assessment sheet and the assessment rubrics and encouraged to complete them. Students receive these results from the various magazine readers. Students are also asked to reflect on and evaluate their own performance.

REFLECTIONS

Students' language skills appear to be improving with the PBL approach, especially speaking and writing skills. They have the opportunity to practice various writing styles such as survey reports, reviews, and persuasive writing. A wide range of vocabulary and structures are needed for this project, and students seem more

Extract From the Magazine Rubric

Features	Excellent	Good	Fair	Poor
Purpose	All articles properly serve the magazine theme.	Most of the articles serve the magazine theme.	Some of the articles serve the magazine theme. Some are not on point.	The magazine theme is not at all clear.
Vocabulary and Expression	The magazine shows a wide range of vocabulary and expressions.	The magazine shows a range of vocabulary and structures.	The vocabulary and structures do not vary much.	The magazine demonstrates poor vocabulary and uses very simple expressions.

Figure 3. Magazine Assessment Sample

motivated to write precisely and informatively to a real audience. Also, we have observed much improvement over time between drafts, a real benefit of using portfolios.

Besides positive results in language competence, students also have the chance to discover and boost other capacities they might not even know they have, such as negotiating, working in teams, leading groups, critically thinking, planning,

Extract From the Press Conference Rubric

Features	Excellent	Good	Fair	Poor
Organization	The presentation is logical and well designed. It is easy to follow the speaker right at the beginning.	The ideas are logically arranged, but it is not outstandingly attractive.	The ideas are quite logically arranged, but the speakers should have been able to make it better.	The presentation is a mess and I cannot follow it. I cannot figure out what it is about.
Public Speaking Techniques	Excellent use of the techniques of gestures, eye-contact, and other body movement.	Good command of nonverbal techniques, but some improvement is needed.	Student performance is OK, but he/she forgets to use these techniques sometimes.	Students don't apply public speaking techniques.
Notes, visual aids, facts or examples	Student shows careful preparation in the use of visual aids.	Visual aids are used but not always appropriately.	Student uses few visual aids and not very well.	Visual aids are not used in the presentation.

Figure 4. Press Conference Assessment Sample

and conducting surveys. Although all students appear to increase their IT skills, students from remote areas who had never even touched a computer before they entered the university also accumulate sophisticated technology skills during the project, including word processing and page layout using a computer and preparing computerized presentations for the press conference.

What has surprised and pleased the teaching staff most is students' attitudes toward learning. We have found that

- Our students find the magazine project beneficial and fun.

- Members love working in groups in and outside the classroom, and group members make more of an effort to arrive on time to class.

- Groups submit projects on time, and individuals submit portfolios on time.

- Many students have hidden talents as journalists, editors, designers, or project managers.

- All students increase skills in processing and synthesizing information.

- Cooperation results in superior products.

- Everyone is thrilled to see the final product appear in print.

- Students appear more confident in English communication and appear more motivated to learn, even in language-focused practice.

- Individual self-study is becoming a routine habit.

We have also noted some limitations of the project-based work. One shortcoming is caused by a lack of technical support. Students reflect that they could do much better with the design work if they had more chances to use the computers (not every student owns a computer at home), access to software, or more modern facilities with better access. Despite these limitations, the magazine project can even work in classes with limited technology resources. Students' creativity has the chance to flourish as handwriting, drawing, and handmade illustrations also can be used to create and enhance a unique magazine.

Project-based learning has been very powerful and practical in helping students apply what they are learning to create an end product. The project not only reproduces a real-life learning environment but also encourages the authentic use of English from negotiations with classmates to the production of original news stories. The magazine project has helped teachers in our faculty to break free from traditional teaching techniques and create a more fun, motivational, and engaging environment using a learner- and learning-centered approach.

Hoang Thi Ngoc Diem teaches at the Foreign Language Faculty of Thainguyen University of Education, in Thainguyen, Vietnam. She holds an MA in English and is an active contributor to the Vietnam-Netherlands Higher Education Project. Her interests include curriculum development, culture studies, and particularly, project-based learning.

CHAPTER 6

Language Training à la Carte

Peggy Allen Heidish

Before Kim arrived in the United States for a PhD program, he had imagined that he would adapt easily to graduate school abroad; he had been a top student at an elite high school and university in his home country. As soon as he started classes, he was dismayed to find that he had to struggle with English; his years of English training had not prepared him for the high level of fluency expected of graduate students at a competitive U.S. university. Students in his department typically put in 60 hours a week of work, but Kim needed to spend considerably more time because he was not a native English speaker, and due to cross-cultural differences, he often misunderstood what was expected of him. Lectures were a special challenge because he was trying to learn complex material presented in a second language. Both reading and writing assignments took him more time to complete than native speakers, and he often worked late into the night.

Participating in his research group was another challenge because he could not always follow the discussion. He was embarrassed by his inability to express his knowledge in English. Moreover, again due to cross-cultural differences, Kim was misperceived in his department. For example, his advisor felt he lacked initiative because Kim, following the mores of his own culture, did not express his ideas openly in discussions and meetings.

Because of gaps in his academic English, Kim was concerned not only about keeping up as a student but also about developing the very high fluency level needed to be a teaching assistant in the future, a requirement in his department. How, Kim wondered, would he survive these next few years? He needed support . . .

Kim's situation is not unique. Many international graduate students arrive in the United States with years of English language training and strong Test of English as a Foreign Language (TOEFL) scores but with linguistic and cultural gaps that hinder their ability to handle many of the communication demands of graduate work (e.g., participating in class discussions, interacting in interdisciplinary research teams, writing in the appropriate style for the U.S. academy, communicating as teaching assistants). These gaps also may prove to be detrimental after graduate school, if students choose to begin their professional lives in the United States. Far too many talented and highly trained international students find themselves stuck under a "glass language ceiling" both during their academic career and once they enter the workforce. If universities want to prepare international students to become successful members of their professional communities, it is important to provide language and cultural support during the course of a graduate degree.

Offering a language and cultural support program for nonnative-English-speaking (NNES) students at a given university would be easier if all of these students arrived with a homogeneous set of needs, but they do not. The reality is that international students arrive with great variation in their backgrounds and needs, including the following:

- **Language differences** (e.g., native language, literacy levels in English and native language, level of English training available in their countries, experience with academic English): For example, one student may have a strong command of academic vocabulary but have pronunciation issues, while another may lack academic fluency but may do well in social conversation. Many students may be experiencing English as the language of instruction for the first time, while others (e.g., from India, Hong Kong) have used academic English for years but still need language support to succeed in the U.S. academy.

- **Disciplinary differences:** Depending on the academic program they enter, some students are expected to be highly verbal, regularly presenting in seminars and possibly even working as teaching assistants teaching classes or labs. On the other hand, others may have little need to communicate orally but need to develop stronger writing skills.

- **Cross-cultural differences:** Educational systems around the world have different assumptions about the role of "student." For example, some may have been trained to listen quietly to lectures, while others learned to actively participate in class discussion.

Consequently, a one-size training program cannot fit all.

Many universities allow matriculated students to attend English as a second language (ESL) classes through an on-campus intensive English program (IEP); however, not all universities have IEPs, and many that do require the students to pay additional tuition. An increasing number of universities now provide training for international teaching assistants (ITAs; Kaufman & Brownworth, 2006), but most do so through a workshop in the summer before students start their graduate programs or semester-long ITA classes. However, there are few options for full-time graduate students if they are not ITAs, or if an IEP is not feasible (e.g., lack of time or funding, or if the student is too fluent to benefit from general IEP classes).

CONTEXT

At the Intercultural Communication Center (ICC) at Carnegie Mellon University, we have developed an alternative model of language training that provides support for all graduate students (potential ITAs or not) who are nonnative English speakers. By allowing students to choose from a wide selection of short workshops, seminars, and individual work, our innovative model provides flexibility and in-depth training and allows the institution to offer a quality program in a cost-effective way. This highly successful model, in place for over two decades, gives students the opportunity to attend the workshops that focus directly on the skills they most need to develop.

The language support program at Carnegie Mellon began in 1985 when the numbers of NNES graduate students had reached a critical mass (20% of the total student population). The university community was forced to confront a variety of communication issues, including the ability of NNES students to communicate in research teams and with advisors, write in the style expected in the U.S. academy, and be comprehensible as ITAs. The students' diverse language and cultural needs indicated that no single ESL course would work for this group; instead, the center evolved to create a unique support program based primarily on allowing students to focus on those skills most crucial to their academic success. This individualized approach became the hallmark of the ICC and gave us the flexibility to evolve a program tailored to the needs of the Carnegie Mellon campus (Heidish, 2006). This chapter describes how this model developed and now functions, and hopefully will enable others to adapt the model to meet the particular needs of their own institutions.

CURRICULUM, TASKS, AND MATERIALS

The Genesis of our Curriculum

What started as a tutoring program has slowly and organically grown to fit the specific needs of both the Carnegie Mellon student population and the graduate departments in which they are expected to thrive. The program developed as we recognized new needs that arose. For example, when we realized that many of the graduate students coming to tutoring shared some common gaps in their experience with spoken academic English, we added a workshop, "Academic Speaking and Listening." A year later, recognizing that many of the potential ITAs needed explicit training for both language and pedagogy to teach in the U.S. academy, we added a 6-week class for ITAs (Althen, 1991). We also hired and trained undergraduate tutors to provide individual practice giving mini-presentations. The next year, we added individual writing appointments; students could bring academic writing assignments and get feedback on both language usage and discourse style.

By 2008, the program had grown to include over 33 different classes, workshops, seminars, and individual sessions each semester (many with multiple sections) and now provides support to over 400 students each semester. This flexible format has proven to be very beneficial in a number of ways:

- **Ease of scheduling:** Rather than being wedded to semester-long classes, our short courses (e.g., 2-hour seminars, 3-week workshops) allow us to easily schedule sessions throughout the week (day and evening), and additional sections of any class can be added if needed to meet student demand. Not only does this make it easy to work with our staff availability, but it also allows for a program that will most likely accommodate student schedules.

- **Adaptability:** Unlike the situation in many language institutes, our staff members are not hired to teach one or two specific classes but rather to teach in any of our services. There is consistency between all classes in terms of our overall goals. If we decide to add or drop a seminar or workshop, instructors can easily change their course load. And because there are so many small sessions, it requires little effort to subtract one module and replace it with another.

- **Cost effectiveness:** A relatively small staff can provide a wide variety of services. Our center currently has three full-time instructors (including the director), three part-time instructors, and several tutors. Despite this small staff, we are able to offer 8,000+ class hours each academic year.

Defining our Mission

In the past two decades, the number of international students at Carnegie Mellon has increased from 350 to over 2,680, roughly 15% of the undergraduates and over 40% of graduate students. This diversity makes the campus a rich multicultural environment, but the language and cultural differences create many communication challenges. To meet these challenges, the goals of our program have broadened over the years to include not only helping ITAs develop the skills needed to communicate effectively (the original focus of the program) but also to help all NNES graduate students succeed in their academic programs (Heidish, 2006).

Although our international students have spent years studying English and preparing for standardized language exams, they have not necessarily developed "robust academic fluency," that is, the depth and breadth of language needed for success as graduate students. We developed this concept of robust fluency by working with both faculty and students to capture the authentic communication challenges faced by our NNES students (Heidish, 2006, p. 171). For example, students must be able to participate in class discussions, ask and respond to questions, write clear and comprehensible papers appropriate to the U.S. academic writing style, understand and master complex material presented in lectures and in readings, interact with peers in research teams and group projects, and understand the U.S. communication styles. Some students will also work as teaching assistants, a task that requires an even higher level of fluency. Many NNES students find that while they may be "fluent" in certain contexts (e.g., social conversation or writing informal e-mails), they lack the full array of language skills to communicate in all of the situations requiring academic English.

"Hooking Them In" by Developing Student-Centered Motivation

"But how do you get students to want to attend a program that is mainly non-credit?" is the question we are most frequently asked by colleagues from other institutions. This was a challenge we had to grapple with in the early days of our program. Our response was to find ways to help students develop internal motivation by connecting language work to their personal and professional goals, and this process begins when we meet students at Carnegie Mellon's International Student Orientation each August. Students have the opportunity to take an individual 20-minute placement interview with one of our instructors. This interview, a kind of language "counseling and advising" session, gives students a realistic assessment of how their language strengths and weaknesses might impact their academic success; students leave with a written plan for long-term study. By offering customized support through the initial interview, we are able to target each learner's specific needs and are also able to get students to "buy in" as active partners in their own ongoing language development, both in and out of the classroom.

Once students start to use our support services, we help them maintain motivation even while they are dealing with the demands of their graduate programs. We continually look for ways to tap into each student's personal motivation (e.g., their desire to pass the ITA test, give effective presentations, or become a successful professional) in order to keep them working on the problems we have identified, such as pronunciation, fluency gaps that hinder their ability to communicate, or a lack of understanding of U.S. academic discourse styles (Oreto & Carlson, 2006).

Students become active participants in their own language development not simply by attending a workshop or tutoring appointment, but by becoming members of the program's learning community. In addition to the initial written plan of study, students receive continual feedback and counseling after workshops and during tutoring. For example, at the end of several of our longer classes, students give videotaped presentations. The instructor then meets individually with each student to review the video, offer detailed feedback about language as well as cultural understanding, and guide students in identifying and taking ownership of problem areas in their language. The teacher or tutor also advises students on future workshops they should take to improve their language skills.

Our Techniques

The goal for all of our workshops, classes, and tutoring sessions at the Inter-cultural Communication Center is to help students develop the skills they need to succeed in their academic programs (this includes, but is not limited to, ITA skills). There is no set order for workshops; choice depends on students' sched-ules and individual needs, thus the term "à la carte." As students move from one service to another, they cycle through the same core set of skills that build robust fluency. Our à la carte selection of classes, workshops, seminars, and tutoring provides training and practice with some or all of the following:

- linguistic competence (e.g., pronunciation and grammar)

- academic fluency (e.g., presentation skills and field fluency)

- cross-cultural adjustment (e.g., cross-cultural differences in educational systems, academic discourse styles and expectations)

- ITA skills (e.g., teaching by simplifying or giving examples)

- writing appropriately for the academy (e.g., avoiding plagiarism)

We make liberal use of multimedia resources in our program. For example, we frequently videotape student presentations for individual feedback on issues such as pronunciation, grammar usage, and fluency. In addition, we often use commer-cially produced educational videos as models of pronunciation, academic English, and presentations techniques. Many of the same materials are used, although in different ways, in a number of our classes and workshops, so students get the chance to cycle through the materials many times. In this way, we tap into one of the crucial principles of language learning and cross-cultural adaptation: repeated exposure and practice over time. In all of our classes, no matter what the topic or focus, we consistently look for ways to foster the development of robust academic fluency.

Structure of Classes: Optimizing Time for Language Work

Graduate students work under intense time constraints, so one of our goals in designing the program was to provide maximum training in a minimum amount of time. Our students are able to focus on skills in which they are weak or skip areas in which they are proficient, and concentrate on developing the set of skills that will be most beneficial for their particular situation. Our format accommo-dates a variety of schedules and department requirements (e.g., whether a student must serve as an ITA in the first year or can wait several years) and differences in training needs.

Our menu of options each semester includes the following:

- a 7-week credit class, Language and Culture for Teaching (for ITAs)

- noncredit workshops (generally 3 hours weekly for 3–5 weeks)

- 2-hour seminars, which can be offered multiple times each semester

- weekly drop-in sessions for specific skills and individual tutoring for either speaking or writing skills

Appendix A provides an overview of language training that demonstrates the breadth of work available. An up-to-date list of program services is available through Carnegie Mellon's Web site: http://www.cmu.edu/icc/calendar/index.shtml

Course Content

To give the reader a better understanding of how we structure our classes, the following provides an overview of three of our noncredit workshops and sample activities are provided in Appendices B, C, and D:

1. **Presentation Basics** prepares NNES students to deliver effective oral presentations. Many of these students lack both the experience with public speaking—even in their native languages—and the language skills needed to give presentations in the U.S. classroom. Students focus on developing a broad range of skills, including the ability to: (a) communicate clearly with an audience in academic English; (b) employ linguistic features such as stress, intonation, and nonverbal cues to clarify and emphasize information; (c) consider various organizational strategies; (d) assess their own speaking strengths and weaknesses; and (e) feel comfortable in the role of presenter (5 weeks, 15 hours total).

2. **Preparing for the Oral Qualifier** (sometimes called *Qualifying Exams* at other institutions) addresses the dynamics of oral exams in U.S. universities, helps students develop language skills for effective interaction with examiners, and introduces strategies to help compensate for language weaknesses and cultural differences; useful for both doctoral and master's students who face oral exit exams (2-hour seminar).

3. **Advanced Grammar Monitoring** is for students comfortable using academic English but who still make a significant number of grammar mistakes while speaking. Students expand their knowledge and understanding of spoken English grammar and of the kinds of errors graduate students typically make. They also learn to monitor (identify and correct) grammar errors while speaking. This workshop is a springboard to additional grammar monitoring work in tutoring sessions so that students can make a long-term change in their English language skills (6-hour workshop).

Authenticity

Everything we offer must relate to our students' academic lives; all of our services focus on skills and language immediately applicable for students at our institution. Our advisory committee, made up of faculty and support staff from the various colleges, keeps us up-to-date on issues and challenges facing our students. For example, when we learned that a number of international students were doing poorly on PhD oral qualifiers, we put together a pilot for one of the seminars described above, "Preparing for the Oral Qualifier." Based on positive student feedback, we then added it to our list of seminars.

Our individualized program allows many opportunities to get feedback directly from the students, which helps us constantly revise and develop our services. To illustrate, many of our students attend conferences or work in multidisciplinary groups, and many have trouble participating in small talk about their research interests. In response, we created a seminar, "Elevator Talk," in which students learn how to simplify technical topics in their fields for a wide variety of audiences, a linguistic and cultural challenge for many of our students.

We work hard to create authentic classroom activities that mirror the communication tasks our students will be required to master, giving them chances to practice the language of their fields. For example, in the "Advanced Fluency Challenges" workshop, one very successful fluency-building exercise simulates a competition for research funding. Students work in teams to sketch out a research project, prepare arguments, and then elect a spokesperson to present their case to the "funder" (in this case, the ICC instructor). The fact that students come from a cross-section of departments helps them practice and develop the fluency to communicate with people outside of their fields, a skill we emphasize in all of our classes.

Many of the videotaped materials we use come directly from the students' own fields. For example, in "Language and Culture for Teaching," a credit class for ITAs, the instructor uses videos of lectures by Carnegie Mellon professors as well as commercial educational videos to help students develop teaching fluency, organizational language, vocal stress and intonation, and a culturally appropriate teaching style.

The most authentic source of language comes from the students themselves. We create a partnership in which they are the experts in their various fields, while we are the experts in providing feedback and guidance on language. For example, students frequently give practice presentations from their fields that we either videotape or critique on paper. We then review these presentations with the student to give detailed feedback on a myriad of issues such as clarity, pronunciation, question handling, and presentation style. The conversation during the feedback session itself is a fluency-building exercise that uses the student's own field as the material.

Recordkeeping

Without effective recordkeeping, we would not be able to give students or their departments a sense of coherence as they move through the program. We keep detailed records for each student in our program by recording every hour of tutoring and class work in a database. At the end of their graduate work, students can request a "transcript" from our center detailing all of the work done during their time at the university (see Figure 1). Many students have found this document useful to show to sponsors or to add to their portfolio when applying for jobs, post-docs, or further graduate work. Having this transcript provides an additional incentive to help students conceive of their work with our program as integral to their graduate degree and their professional preparation.

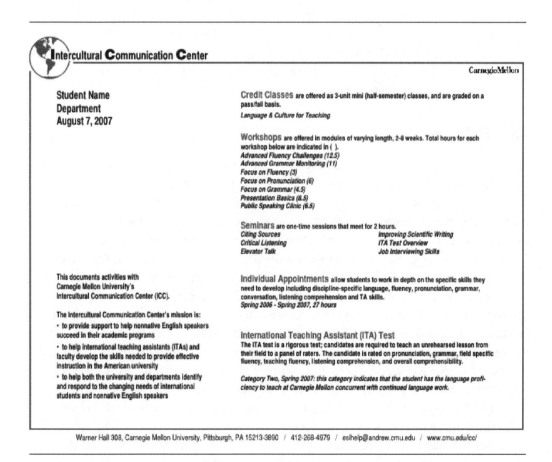

Figure 1. Sample Student Transcript from the Intercultural Communication Center at Carnegie Mellon University

Student Success

Let us return to Kim to see how he moved through the ICC program:

> ... An ICC interview during orientation assessed Kim's fluency with academic
> English and gave him an individualized program of ICC work to help him develop
> fluency to meet the demands of his graduate program and prepare for his job
> as a teaching assistant. The interview also gave him a realistic estimate of
> how long he would need to develop that level of fluency.
>
> In the second year of his PhD program, Kim took the ITA test. He passed
> but continued to attend ongoing ICC work during his ITA assignments to help
> support his teaching (see Figure 1 for an overview of Kim's work with ICC).
>
> During the last years of his PhD studies, Kim still found a need to use the
> services at the ICC: these supported him through his preparations for the
> oral qualifier and in writing his dissertation. When it was time for him to enter
> the job market, he once again faced cross-cultural barriers in the interview
> process. The job interview workshop at ICC helped him prepare for this new
> communication challenge, and he included his ICC transcript in his portfolio to
> document his language and cultural competency for future employers. Kim was
> hired by a top research company in the United States.

REFLECTIONS

The à la carte model has been highly effective and successful at Carnegie Mellon, and we believe that the same basic model could be adapted to work in other institutions, large or small, as well as in workplace language programs. However, for such a program to flourish, it is important to consider the administrative structure of the institution, the student body, and the language instructors themselves.

We have been fortunate to work at a university that encourages innovative programs, and, more importantly, gives sufficient autonomy and financial support to those programs. The à la carte model would have difficulty flourishing at a highly centralized institution with a complicated bureaucratic approval path. In addition, the university administration funds our program, seeing it as an investment in both educating international students so that they can take their place in an increasingly globalized world and assuring the highest quality education for our undergraduates by preparing ITAs to be fluent and culturally adept instructors. For this type of program to exist, the institution must be willing and able to fully fund it like other support services.

Our instructors appreciate the opportunity to use their creativity to adapt classes and materials to the needs of the students. However, we have found that some ESL professionals are more comfortable teaching clearly defined semester-long classes, so our model does not resonate with all teaching staff. In order to create and use materials that reflect authentic academic language, à la carte instructors must be able to invest time in understanding the communication challenges of a variety of students and have a teaching style that accommodates constant revision of classes and materials (Heidish, 2006). Also, given our relatively small program, all instructors serve as "ad hoc advisors" at the end of workshops and in tutoring appointments; a larger program might need to assign specific advisors to each student.

Our students, highly motivated, disciplined, and with clearly defined professional goals, readily avail themselves of our support services. Noncredit language classes may not work as well with students who have less personal motivation to continually develop their communication skills.

Peggy Allen Heidish is director of the Intercultural Communication Center at Carnegie Mellon University in the United States, where she coordinates programs for NNES students. She also supervises ITA testing and training, consults with international faculty, works with graduate departments on issues related to international students, and develops workshops to increase cross-cultural understanding on campus.

APPENDIX A: OVERVIEW OF LANGUAGE TRAINING AVAILABLE EACH SEMESTER AT THE ICC

(detailed descriptions available at http://www.cmu.edu/icc)

Credit Courses
- Language & Culture for Teaching
- Building Fluency for Presentations

Workshops
- Advanced Fluency Challenges
- Advanced Grammar Monitoring
- Presentation Basics
- Public Speaking Clinic
- Speaking & Listening

Seminars
- Becoming a Better Language Learner
- Conversational Styles
- Critical Listening
- Drama Techniques for Academic Presentations
- Elevator Talk
- Hallway Talk

- ITA Test Overview
- Job Interviewing for International Students
- The Multicultural Classroom
- Preparing for the Oral Qualifier
- Pronunciation for Advanced Speakers
- Reading Strategies
- Small Talk
- Writing: Citing Sources
- Writing: Communicating Data Effectively
- Writing: Improving Scientific Writing
- Writing: Intro to Academic Writing
- Writing: Using Articles Accurately

"Focus On" Series

- Focus on Fluency
- Focus on Grammar
- Focus on Pronunciation

Individual Appointments

- Tutoring
- Self-paced Appointments
- Writing Clinic

APPENDIX B: SAMPLE ACTIVITY FROM PRESENTATION BASICS

First mini-talk: Describing an object from your field

Today we are going to work on robust presentation fluency by learning how to clearly describe an object from your field. We will begin by watching and analyzing a videotaped lecture by a Carnegie Mellon engineering professor describing an object from his field. Then each of you will have the chance to describe an object from your field. Remember to

- Give an introduction to the object, what it is, and its use/importance in the context of your field.

- Say what the object is, and what it looks like, if appropriate.

- Describe the parts of the object.

- Say what it is used for.

- Give a conclusion that reminds the listeners of two or three things that they should remember (e.g., main function, importance, difficulties or dangers in using the object).

Part 1: Focused viewing

Have students watch video presentations with guided exercises to help students identify key aspects (both language and techniques) of the presentation followed by instructor led discussion.

Part 2: Student practice

Choose an object from your field to describe to your classmates. This object can be a piece of lab equipment, a system, software, etc. Choose a method to describe the object, referring back to the ways described above. Remember that your audience probably has very little idea of what the object looks like or what it is used for. Prepare a 5-minute explanation.

APPENDIX C: SAMPLE ACTIVITY FROM THE ORAL QUALIFIERS SEMINAR

Oral exams are challenging for all graduate students but pose a special problem for you as international students due to language and cultural differences. This seminar addresses a wide range of topics and techniques including the following:

1. underlying purpose of oral qualifiers
2. common expectations of U.S. examiners
3. possible cultural variations on professionalism
4. culturally appropriate ways to present information and respond to questions

Nonnative English speakers often find it difficult to express their personal connection to their research during the oral exam. The activity below will help you develop the awareness and fluency to do so.

Write about your motivation for your PhD research. If you do not yet have a well-defined research topic, you can write about your motivation for entering your field.

One of our engineering departments recommends students ask themselves the following questions as they prepare for an oral qualifier. Take 15 minutes to write your responses, and then share with others in small groups:

- What is your work about?
- Where did your ideas come from?
- Why did you choose this particular method?
- Why does your work matter?

APPENDIX D: GRAMMAR MONITORING SUPPLEMENTAL ACTIVITY

In conjunction with the Grammar Monitoring workshop, students can work individually with an instructor. Below are guidelines for the instructors:

Grammar monitoring is most useful for students who have developed an intermediate or advanced level of speaking but make grammar errors when speaking because they have stopped monitoring themselves. Students still struggling with fluency are probably making errors because they must focus primarily on "performance" and are not ready to monitor. Grammar monitoring is not useful for these students and may even be counterproductive.

In monitoring, look at two kinds of errors:

- recurring errors, that is, missing endings, tense, articles, etc.

- errors that confuse meaning: more serious errors that change or distort the meaning

Techniques:

- Videotape a short (5–10 minute) presentation.

- Review the video with the student; pause after every significant error (do not be afraid to pause frequently).

- Encourage students to find their own errors. If they cannot, give cues as needed.

- Write down the incorrect phrases; some students can recognize an error only when they see it in written form.

Authentic Language: Skills, Content, and Culture

Using Authentic Texts to Facilitate Culturally Relevant Extensive Reading Programs in Tajikistan

Lori Fredricks

Extensive reading, or having students read a variety of self-selected texts over a period of time, has been shown to be beneficial for increasing language awareness and proficiency in numerous ways, including increased reading and writing abilities and gains in vocabulary (Day & Bamford, 1998; Elley, 1991; Gradman & Hanania, 1991). With an extensive reading approach, teachers act as facilitators by modeling a love for reading and creating an environment in which reading is more about pleasure and less about traditional reading assessments. Language teachers and researchers have focused on the value of extensive reading to assist students in developing a reading habit or a passion for reading that extends beyond the classroom (Krashen, 2004; Tinker Sachs, 2001). Readers' choices and participation in discussions and other activities are central to the approach. One of the facilitator's roles is to help students learn to view reading as fun, engaging, and related to their daily lives. Another is to provide a range of reading resources and materials to assist learners in meeting their linguistic and cultural learning goals.

As a proponent of extensive reading, I have been working to expand English language resource centers in Dushanbe, Tajikistan and establish reading clubs (of 10 or fewer members) open to any upper intermediate to advanced adult English as a foreign language (EFL) readers. These reading clubs differ from classes in that participation is completely voluntary, participants need not be currently enrolled in a university or college, and members receive certificates rather than grades. Members were offered a library of texts from which to select, including culturally relevant texts, or texts that learners can relate to because of shared cultural values, experiences, traditions, and practices. This familiarity can motivate students to read more frequently, compare their experiences during discussions, and comprehend texts more easily because of their background knowledge. Through interviewing, surveying, and observing students involved in extensive reading, significant themes have emerged that explain why these learners select particular texts. This study has resulted in a selection of criteria that are dynamic, continuously updated, and hopefully beneficial for establishing new libraries and programs for extensive reading.

CONTEXT

Authenticity and Texts

Authentic texts—which are usually written for native speakers—and simplified texts or graded readers are both potentially useful for extensive reading. Day and Bamford (1998) highlight the advantages and drawbacks of authentic texts, noting that many teachers and students believe "it is the very difficulty of texts that makes them worthwhile as learning tools" (p. 54). Authentic texts are thought to be "interesting, engaging, culturally enlightening, relevant, motivating, and the best preparation for reading authentic texts" (p. 54). However, authentic texts may also discourage readers when they are beyond the learners' comprehension. When this happens, readers focus on decoding language rather than meaning, and their confidence may decrease. Day and Bamford (1998) suggest that judging whether or not a text is authentic actually may be more a matter of purpose of reading rather than text design or linguistic complexity. When texts are intended to communicate meaning, reading for meaning is more authentic. Thus, even texts labeled "simplified" or graded can provide readers with authentic, engaging reading experiences, which may complement their experience with language textbooks. As a result, teachers should make both simplified and nonsimplified texts available for extensive reading. The range of selections reinforces the idea that students should determine what they are prepared to read as well as what they prefer to read.

Another key factor in developing reading resources and encouraging learners to read is students' possible connections with the available texts. For instance, students who like literary texts may be inspired to read novels and short stories that represent cultures similar to their own, while others may prefer texts about characters and themes that are vastly different from their own experience. Learners should also be supported in reading a wide range of text types. Most extensive reading practitioners focus primarily on classical or contemporary novels. Although fiction is engaging and motivating for many readers, students frequently enjoy nonfiction as well. Facilitators can easily locate nonfiction texts that either parallel the themes of student-selected fiction texts or that serve as the main focus of a reading club, such as one focusing on current events or biographies. Some students, particularly younger readers, may enjoy other types of fiction such as graphic novels or comic books, which also provide valuable linguistic input and opportunities for discussion. As every group of students and each educational setting is unique, it is best to provide learners a variety of texts and text types representing content rich in diverse cultures and themes.

Reading Resources in Tajikistan

Reading club facilitators should consider what reading materials students have been exposed to in relation to content and authenticity. Resource developers must consider local conditions and employ every available resource in gathering extensive reading materials. In Tajikistan, I have found the curriculum in most schools has changed little in recent years, with a continuing lack of funding for new textbooks and other reading materials. At most universities, students represent dynamic, mixed-gender groups of various ethnicities including Tajiks (the majority), Uzbeks, and Russians. Since the breakup of the Soviet Union, students have studied English through a grammar-translation approach, usually using Tajik (Persian/Farsi with the Cyrillic alphabet) or Russian as the primary language of instruction. Though few English language texts are available in universities and public schools, several resource centers have recently been established, mainly by nongovernmental organizations (NGOs). These centers provide students and local residents access to a wide range of English reading resources and the Internet.

Although some local English teachers are developing culturally relevant English textbooks that have Tajik characters and themes, most course textbooks are older and contain mainly Russian themes and stories. Some students may have Tajik courses that require reading Tajik/Persian literature, such as *The Masnavi-i Ma'navi* by Jalalu'd-din Muhammad Rumi (2005), but they rarely encounter this type of reading in English. When investigating what types of texts students prefer for both resource centers and reading clubs, they frequently suggest materials that are culturally relevant or related to their worldview and lifestyle in some way.

CURRICULUM, TASKS, MATERIALS

The following are criteria I developed, based on students' input, for determining which literary texts are culturally relevant. Facilitators and teachers of extensive reading in other settings may wish to apply these criteria to their own settings.

Text Selection: Issues to Consider

In Tajikistan, which has limited funding for education, the text selection process is centered on expanding English resource centers, principally sustained by grants. Grants have been procured from several different sources, including embassies and the U.S. Department of State. Through the U.S. Department of State

English Language Fellow and Fulbright programs, I received funding for multiple copies of several fiction and nonfiction texts, which I use in teaching and loan to my students. In the event that a group exceeds the number of copies, students share texts with a partner. Each group can read a different text, and those texts are then rotated depending on group interests and preferences. Reading groups meet weekly to share their opinions of the texts, discuss plot and character development, and answer each other's questions about linguistic elements such as vocabulary and grammar. As their facilitator and a member, I initially structure the discussions, gradually prompting members to lead our talks themselves by initiating their own debates and voting on texts.

Perhaps the most important step in setting up an extensive reading program is deciding what materials to include. It is impossible to predict exactly what texts participants will prefer before meeting them and discussing their reading interests. Further, some learners may prefer to read texts about cultures that are dissimilar from their own. Thus, I do not suggest including only texts that can be deemed culturally relevant. Instead, I propose that including culturally relevant texts in the overall selection will afford students a broader set of choices that will allow content to reflect the groups' goals and preferences. If a facilitator is relatively new to teaching or is unsure of criteria to use to determine cultural relevancy, I have found the following very useful in text selection:

- regional proximity or texts about cultures within the same part of the world

- religious, traditional, and linguistic similarities

- ethnic diversity

- social class

- gender

Regional Proximity

It may not always be possible to locate much English language fiction about a particular culture; there may be few translations of local writers' works or the available literature in English may be limited. In working with Tajik students, I have discovered that there is a good deal of classical literature (considered both Tajik and Persian) that has been translated into English. However, there is little contemporary literature in English about Tajik characters. In such cases, it is useful to look for novels and stories about nearby countries in the same region, which, in my case, includes Iran and Afghanistan. For my region, I have found appropriate pieces of nonfiction and fiction might be *Reading Lolita in Tehran* (Nafisi, 2003) and *The Kite Runner* (Hosseini, 2003).

Religious, Traditional, and Linguistic Similarities

Reading themes with similarities to their own experience in terms of religion, traditions, and language have been most salient for my students. For instance, my students have often mentioned enjoying reading about Islamic practices from different cultures that parallel their own, including cultural practices of marriage ceremonies and burials. My students also enjoy reading about characters whose roles in society are comparable. Some of the novels, for example, have older characters who are respected for their opinions as elders and who give advice on crucial decisions, mirroring their own cultural practices. Many of the students prefer novels and short stories that mention shared holidays and sports, such as *No Rooz*, the traditional Tajik/Persian New Year, and *Buz Kashi*, an ancient sport with horsemen who compete during *No Rooz*. When authors describe these elements in their stories, they regularly use terminology (such as *Allah-o-Akbar* or "God is great," and *Assalam-O-Aleikum*, the greeting used by Muslims) that is common to various Islamic cultures. My students are often encouraged by the familiarity of these bilingual interjections.

Ethnic Diversity

Arguably, many—or perhaps most—countries in the world are ethnically diverse. In Tajikistan, for example, in addition to the Tajik majority, there are Russians, Uzbeks, and other minority groups. These cultures influence one another, and group members sometimes intermarry, creating a complex blend of cultures. Thus, texts that touch on issues of ethnic and family interrelations are sometimes exciting for students who live in ethnically diverse communities. My students have been intrigued by *The Kite Runner* (Hosseini, 2003) because of the range of ethnic groups in the story including Tajiks, Pashtuns, Hazaras, and Uzbeks. The relationship between Pashtuns and Hazaras is highlighted through the two main characters, a Pashtun boy and his Hazara friend and servant. When discussing these boys, we analyze how ethnic differences also affect relations in our own communities. Investigating this potentially sensitive topic through fiction allows for a comfortable format for our discussions.

Social Class

With an extensive reading approach, considering culture means more than a broad definition of culture inclusive of religious beliefs, traditions, and languages. Facilitators of extensive reading should also consider the lesser discussed aspects of cultural identity such as gender and social class. Readers in a recent group were initially enthusiastic about *Reading Lolita in Tehran* (Nafisi, 2003) because the novel is about a professor and her female students in Iran. Unfortunately, they did not identify with the author, who is also the narrator of the text, because of her status as a wealthy person. The novel bore strong similarities in the broader sense of culture because Iranians and Tajiks share common history, literature, and language. My students, however, viewed the author as identifying more closely with European or American values and lifestyles that afforded greater material luxury than they had experienced. Thus, the element of social class is an important consideration in text selection as readers may feel social distance or dissonance.

Gender

Many readers use gender in determining text selection. In reading clubs that have more female members, male students may feel alienated by being outvoted during text selection as they may prefer texts with male characters. Consequently, male students may tend to participate less. Recently, most of my students selected *Shabanu* as their favorite text of the year, a female story (Fisher Staples, 2003). Though both male and female students enjoyed the suspense of the story and similarities to their own lifestyles, the discussion of controversial issues such as arranged marriage sometimes made the male students uncomfortable. Controversial topics can generate student participation and lead to thoughtful discussions, but facilitators must carefully gauge when students feel divided or withdraw from the discussion. One way of creating a balance when groups are uneven in terms of gender is to offer texts that have both male and female main characters, or are written both by men and women.

Extensive Reading Club Ideas

Many extensive reading programs require students to read their own individual texts, which they may read at home or in class. Readers may give reports to a partner or the class, including a summary and their opinion of the text. This method of at-home reading coupled with retelling has often been used in reading clubs in Tajikistan due to the scarcity of reading materials. Though beneficial for developing presentation skills, readers may become more engaged when reading a shared text and discussing and debating their opinions of the themes and events they encounter together in reading groups. Facilitators can break down texts into chapters or sections, providing plot summaries prior to reading, rather than having students tackle entire texts on their own. Such an approach allows group members to explore texts together and contrast their interpretations and responses.

A facilitator can easily create a great number of activities that encourage student involvement when discussing and analyzing a common text. Writing activities have been popular with my students. Students read reviews in online or printed sources (in English or Russian) of books they have selected and use these reviews as models to write their own. We discuss these student-generated reviews in class and post them on our Web site to aid future participants in text selection.

Readers have also written questions for an informal conversation with an author. For instance, members who read *Hatchet* (Paulsen, 1996), wrote questions that had emerged throughout the club sessions, including: "Did somebody whom you know ever face such a situation like Brian (your hero)?" and "Why did your pilot die from a heart attack (because as I know pilots should pass doctors before going to fly)?" We then predicted the author's responses and sent him the questions via e-mail.

When reading texts about a culture or country that differs from those of the author, I like to encourage readers to debate the issue of authenticity, to question what it means to represent another cultural group and whether an author can genuinely do so. Some students have been surprised to learn that Fisher Staples is not actually from Pakistan but had been inspired to write *Shabanu* (2003) while living there. Though they are not from Pakistan themselves, they concluded that she represented Islamic practices well and that the story felt real to them. Thus, extensive reading activities may be used to explore "authenticity" in terms of the purpose of the text, the relationship to readers' culture(s) and experiences, and the author's ability to make the characters and story feel truly genuine.

Whereas reading clubs may emphasize meaning and cultural authenticity, class reading of extensive texts can further incorporate activities that explicitly focus on language. Specific procedural roles can be used to offer students a framework for language exploration. For example, one reader can act as a "vocabulary detective," selecting and defining new terms found in the readings. Another reader may be the "discussion leader," developing intriguing questions (after exposure to teacher or student-generated examples) to guide the discussion. Other students can be assigned specific characters they must describe or segments of the text to summarize. Roles can be switched from session to session for variety. Additionally, learners can work on grammar by reading an altered summary of a text to find and correct grammatical mistakes, thus heightening grammar awareness while continuing to focus on meaning.

Whenever possible, students should be encouraged to bring their own reading materials to the discussions. My students recommend books, fiction and historical nonfiction, that we add to our reading lists. Others find articles related to group topics by using the Internet in cafés, libraries, centers, or their workplaces. Though the supplements and suggested texts, like most of our readings, are authentic materials, students report little if any difficulty with comprehension. This may be because they read for meaning rather than attempting to understand each individual word, or because they are motivated by interest in the content and their own active role in adding to our curricula. In either case, students are effectively integrating a variety of textual resources into our club readings. The readers say that these materials broaden and deepen their background knowledge, and the familiar elements ease their comprehension.

REFLECTIONS

Facilitators should elicit feedback from participants about the activities as well as the content of the club readings. It is important to understand which activities readers prefer and why. Some learners may feel most comfortable with more structured activities, while others may prefer to let the discussion proceed more organically, with students taking random turns. Student feedback is important in determining reading-related activities. Teachers can always ask a colleague to observe the sessions or ask students to write reflections on the content and tasks at home, which can be done through journals or blogs. Learning about and implementing new activities also contributes to increased student motivation to read and engage with the texts.

Facilitators can almost never predict precisely what texts readers will enjoy most. Even when teaching within their own cultures, teachers find that each group of readers is unique. However, creating an ever-expanding library based on student choices and preferences will likely offer future participants a selection of texts that motivates them to read more extensively as well as more deeply and personally. Resource libraries and reading programs also send learners the message that their needs and interests are highly valued. I further hope that reading in English about cultures and communities similar to their own will prompt their sense of ownership over the language. They may increasingly come to view English as their language, one in which they can read and write about their own rich lived experiences.

Lori Fredricks is a doctoral candidate in the language and literacy education program at Georgia State University in the United States. She has worked in Dushanbe, Tajikistan as an English Language Fellow and a Fulbright grantee. After graduation, she plans to continue promoting culturally relevant extensive reading programs in both EFL and ESL communities.

CHAPTER 8

The English of Math— It's Not Just Numbers!

Kathy Ewing and Bill Huguelet

Despite broad differences in their math or English backgrounds, college-bound students of widely varied first languages share the identical need for explicit English language instruction to recognize, manipulate, and communicate math terminology in English. For a simple experiment, try to orally describe the following formula in a second language:

$$3,116 \div 9a^2 = b^4 - 10.4 \times 6c^3$$

If you found that task difficult to accomplish, you are not alone. Attempting to articulate math problems usually frustrates most second language learners, yet teachers commonly assume that nonnative English speaking students will have little trouble with math comprehension because of the erroneous belief that math is exclusively numerical. We have found this assumption to be incorrect. The language of math (e.g., discussing equations, explaining word problems, and using jargon) is rarely included in any English as a second language (ESL) or English as a foreign language (EFL) curriculum. As a result, students struggle in their introductory college or university math courses as they simultaneously attempt to acquire math concepts and language.

This chapter addresses these shortcomings by describing two English for specific purposes courses, one in Muscat, Oman on the Arabian Peninsula, and the other in Seattle, Washington, in the United States. Specifically, we identify the problems facing ESL/EFL math students, present our curricula and materials for our students in both ESL and EFL contexts, and provide our reflections on challenges and the need for further curriculum development.

CONTEXT

We began our research independently on opposite sides of the world at North Seattle Community College (NSCC) and at Sultan Qaboos University (SQU) when we each noticed that our English language students were constantly struggling in their math classes. By conducting research on students and math professionals at our institutions, we found extraordinary parallels in the students' deficiencies in the language of math, despite the vastly dissimilar contexts.

NSCC students need to complete math courses as part of the requirements for most degrees, whereas at SQU, students in the sciences, engineering, medicine, agriculture and commerce must complete several math courses as part of their degree programs. In both institutions, the language of instruction is English; the textbooks and materials also are in English. Most students at SQU enter the university after graduating from high schools where content courses are taught in Arabic. An entry placement test allows students with strong English skills to enter the university math courses directly. The vast majority do not pass this English test, however, so an intensive English program (IEP SQU) is provided to help bridge the language gap. The maximum time allowed for students to study in the IEP is 1 year. Students at NSCC face similar requirements: They must pass an English placement exam in order to enroll in regular college courses. If their English is weak, students must attend and pass NSCC IEP classes before continuing their education at NSCC; however, they do not have a time limit for completing their language courses. The profiles of NSCC and SQU students are summarized in Table 1.

To inform our curriculum development work, we interviewed math professors at NSCC and SQU with questions, including: What are the greatest math

Table 1. Student Characteristics

Description	North Seattle Community College (2003–2004)	Sultan Qaboos University (2005–2006)
Gender	men and women	men and women
Age	18–55 years	18–22 years
Native language	Spanish, Farsi, Japanese, Korean, Bulgarian, Mandarin, Cantonese	Arabic
Education (highest level)	partial high school to university degrees, some college ESL	high school, some students had some university EFL courses
Math education	high school to university	high school only
Math attitudes	high anxiety to strong confidence	disinterested to strong confidence
Income level	very low-income to "comfortable"	very low-income to wealthy
Funding for education	some government assistance for education and living expenses	education and living expenses fully funded by the government
Employment	small private businesses, fast-food workers, stay-at-home mothers, unemployed, or full-time students	no employment (full-time students)

needs of your students? What difficulties did they have last semester, and how did you address them? What specifically do you want your students to be able to do in order to succeed in your math courses? Do you have specific examples of language problems that your students have had? At both institutions, virtually identical frustrations were expressed: Students cannot understand or use basic math terminology, and students cannot ask questions about math when they seek clarification. Math professionals at NSCC and SQU further identified weak reading skills as a factor in students' difficulties with word problems.

At both NSCC and SQU, high failure rates in math courses prevent students from graduating from college or pursuing their career goals despite the fact that many had mastered college math in their first language. At SQU, this was surprising because most students entered the university with high math scores and strong confidence in their math abilities. This paradox resulted in the search for an explanation and remedy. Prior to entering university math courses, we asked students to orally produce a series of numbers, to verbalize simple equations, and to explain elementary word problems. This student-based research revealed three main trouble spots:

1. **Math jargon problems:** ESL/EFL students misunderstand, do not understand, or are unable to produce key words and phrases, including those in word problems.

2. **Cultural reference problems:** Math textbooks and faculty frequently use cultural references that distract or overwhelm the students.

3. **Strategy problems:** ESL/EFL students have difficulties solving word problems, even when they understand all the vocabulary.

Although some strategy problems are also conceptual (native speakers have the same problem), ESL/EFL students clearly have contributing language complications.

Math Jargon Problems

College and university math professors expect their students to know basic math terms and to be able to use them without hesitation. Math teachers have a great deal of required content to cover in class and have no time to spend explaining or teaching basic math terminology. However, students in Seattle and Oman could not use or understand elementary math vocabulary, so they were left to work out meanings while they studied advanced concepts. Specifically, students in each of our studies lacked jargon awareness in several areas:

1. Although most of the students could produce *plus* and *minus*, few knew *multiply* and *divide*.

2. Almost none of the students who did know these basic terms were able to use *by* or *into* with the verb *to divide*. For example, "8 divided by 2

equals 4" is not the same as "8 divided into 2 is 4." The latter, of course, is incorrect. Another common error was for students to say, "8 divided 2 is 4." Without a crucial preposition, this math problem is completely bewildering, as the listener does not know which number is the divisor.

3. SQU students did not know how to say fractions, decimals, exponents, or large numbers such as 111,011.

4. Fundamental geometry terms such as *angle* and *area*, and more specific terms like *right angle*, were unknown.

5. Homophones (and near homophones) caused students great difficulties understanding the rapid speech of lectures and comprehending word problems:

angle/ankle	many/money
area/era	meet/meat
before/four/for	one/won
column/calm	pair/pear
divisor/advisor	quotient/quota
eight/ate	remainder/remain a/remain the
exchange/change	son/sun
factor/factory	sum/some
flower/flour	tens/tense
give/keep (for Arabic speakers)	two/to
in/an	vary/very
know/no	weigh/way

Although it is clear that a math teacher would be unlikely to use certain words in place of others (e.g., *ankle* in place of *angle*), the confusion and difficulty lie in the distraction to the students as they take valuable seconds away from listening to the math instruction in order to sort out the correct meaning.

Other jargon proved challenging because of a general as well as specific, content-based meaning. The following words are usually first learned in other contexts with different meanings. For example, *table* is usually learned as a piece of furniture where we place items or where we eat. However, in math, a table, of course, is similar to a chart. Similarly confusing words include:

area	power
even	rational
group (noun and verb)	root
last	shaded
left	square
lighter (adjective vs. noun)	steps
measure	times
order (noun and verb)	trade
place	value

Cultural References Problems

Textbooks in both North America and Oman are U.S. publications. Publishers try to make the books relevant to young students in the United States; therefore, they include great numbers of cultural references like U.S. geography, stock markets, and baseball. The metric system is used in some math textbooks, but the nonmetric system is still prevalent. The teachers at NSCC further frequently use cultural references in their lectures, and the teachers at SQU, although usually not American, are also accustomed to using the references from the textbooks. However, one professor at SQU, an Egyptian, successfully instructs his students to change all U.S. geographical names to *Point A* or *Point B*, and to change unfamiliar measurement terms (e.g., miles, inches, quarts) to *units* in order to enable the students to focus on the math and not be distracted by extraneous information.

Strategy Problems

The strategies for solving word problems involve reading skills as well as analytical competence. All math students must (a) recognize the goal of the problem, (b) identify the given information, and (c) construct and solve an equation. This may be difficult for even native speakers, but second language learners must first understand the language and then work out the problem. Students at both NSCC and SQU had difficulties with the vocabulary and phrasing of word problems as well as confused commas with decimal points. Four examples of such misunderstanding follow:

1. 1 out of 10 = 90%. Every student in two classes at SQU erroneously believed that "one out of ten" referred to the "nine" that remained after the "one" was extracted.

2. $8.642 \times 10 = 86.42$ or 86,420? In the majority of countries around the world, the comma and period—or "dot"—have different math functions than those in English. Therefore, for many students, $8,642 \times 10 = 86,420$ (commas used for thousands) and $8.643 \times 10 = 86.42$ (dots used for tenths) are extremely problematic. In fact, except for Mexico and Peru, all of Latin America uses commas and dots differently from English countries. Similarly, except for the United Kingdom, Ireland, and Switzerland, all of Europe uses commas and dots as Latin America does. Historically, Middle Eastern countries used a system of slashes to mark math figures, but they have since incorporated the commas and dots of the majority of Europeans. Most of East Asia, including the People's Republic of China, has the same usage as English speaking countries (Wikipedia, n.d.).

3. "How many are left?" is interpreted as the items that were removed instead of those that were remaining. Both NSCC and SQU students

believed the question, "How many *are left?*" referred to how many of the items or people had been removed or had left an area. Even after having this explained in detail, students had considerable difficulty remembering that "How many are left?" was the same as "How many remain?"

4. ". . . in all?" This short phrase created great confusion with SQU students. They simply did not understand the concept. Compounding this particular comprehension difficulty was the common question, "In all, what was left?" or, even more confusing, "In all, how many are left?"

CURRICULUM, TASKS, MATERIALS

Recent cognitive science research has shown the value of repetition in memory and learning, which is especially useful in language and content learning. Curran (2000) demonstrates that memory, familiarity, and recollection arise from distinct neurocognitive processes, thus aiding learning and retention. Although numerous studies focus on the crucial need for repetition in second language learning, classroom practice of the past two or three decades has employed little repetition, perhaps to avoid the appearance of old drill-and-kill methods. However, the very nature of frequency "actively contribute[s] to retention of words" (Ruchkin et al., 1999, p. 345) and influences neural organization (Federmeier & Kutas, 1999). Griffin and Bock (1998) argue that we retain words in memory according to "phonological encoding by word frequency" (p. 313) or, the more phonological input, the more the brain stores words and phrases by sound. Repetition also applies in literacy learning, as demonstrated in *The Rereading Effect* (Rawson, Dunlosky & Thiede, 2000). These researchers state that "rereading improves metacomprehension accuracy" (p. 1004). Even physiologists find that through repetition, the very control center of our cells, the mitochondria, adapts and is actually physically altered (McArdle, Katch, & Katch, 1994). For these reasons, we integrated repetition through games and other activities to maximize student learning of the language of math.

In Seattle, Washington, United States

NSCC offers Math 070: Basic Math for ESL and Limited English Proficiency (LEP) Students in preparation for taking basic math and basic algebra courses. Math 070 consists of (a) daily classes (1 hour each weekday), (b) pair work and board work, and (c) weekly tests, including oral components. (For a list of course topics, see Table 2.) Every class includes oral practice both in pair work and at the white board in front of the class. Although teachers may be hesitant to have students perform the latter because of potential student embarrassment, all students struggle equally with the English of math, so they are sympathetic and patient with each others' mistakes as well as supportive of the teacher's public corrections. Because they learn from one another, the classroom atmosphere

Table 2. NSCC MATH 070 Basic Math for ESL and Limited English Proficiency (LEP) Students

Week 1	Introduction, problem solving, and whole numbers
Week 2	Common fractions: addition, subtraction, and multiplication
Week 3	Fractions: division and combined operations
Week 4	Decimal fractions: operations
Week 5	Review, catch-up
Week 6	Decimal fractions and common fractions, percentages
Week 7	Averages, estimates, ratios, and proportions
Week 8	Measurements: length, mass, volume
Week 9	Measurement instruments, paycheck calculations
Week 10	Review
Week 11	Final exam

has always been pleasant. In order to make the math relevant and interesting for students, we include active math problems, such as having students calculate the circumference of their automobile tires or compute areas of rooms or buildings at the college. And as a school tradition, the college flagpole has been measured in a variety of ways.

Basic math concepts and vocabulary are covered simultaneously in Math 070, including ample practice with word problems. Students are tested at the end of the week, including a pull-out oral component. While the class takes a written test, students are asked to explain orally to the instructor one of the math problems from the test, which we have found takes about 3 minutes per student. Because our classes are usually small (approximately 15 students), we can select various problems and generally cover one or more problems per student.

In Muscat, the Sultanate of Oman

At SQU, a math course such as the NSCC model was not deemed possible because the existing IEP curriculum is very full. Instead of developing a full course, the SQU Language Center administration authorized the development of self-access, online materials (see Figures 1 and 2). In the engineering and medicine programs, students must complete some or all of the units. Each unit contains a variety of math problems and multiple vocabulary learning tools, including audio segments, in order to facilitate acquisition (Nation, 2001).

Built into the self-access materials are explanations of wrong answers with hints to find correct ones, repeated opportunities to try again, step-by-step

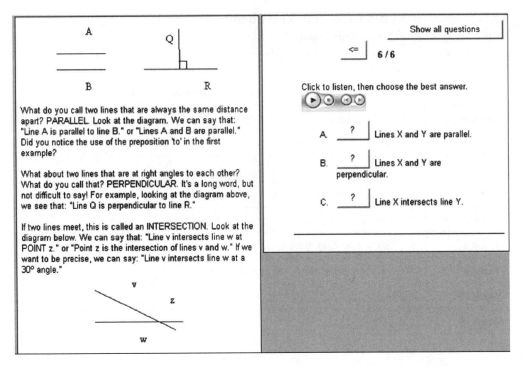

Figure 1. Unit on Lines With Example Question

guidance on accurately reading and solving word problems, and tests with aural components.[1] Figures 1 and 2 provide samples of these self-access materials. Other topics include: numbers and number listening practice (especially large numbers); basic functions, such as addition, subtraction, multiplication, and division; fractions and decimals; exponents and roots; geometry, such as lines, angles, triangles, circles, and so forth; and word problems. The software provides various features, including

- glossed key words

- definitions through a mouse click

- sound files to hear the pronunciation of the words

- problems requiring students to answer with new vocabulary

- questions, primarily multiple choice and matching

- questions requiring students to listen before answering

---

[1] This self-access course is designed for use with educational management software programs such as Blackboard or WebCT. To request free copies for noncommercial use, write via post to Bill Huguelet, P.O. Box 43, PC 123, Muscat, OMAN.

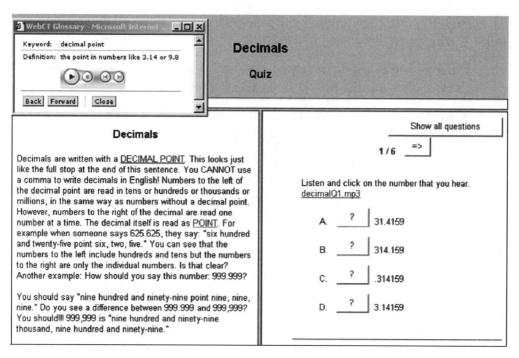

Figure 2. Unit on Decimals With Popup Glossary

Sample Activities for Communicative Practice of Math Language

Most communicative activities can easily be modified to substitute specialized math vocabulary, numbers, and equations to create a fun math vocabulary activity. The following are samples of the types of activities we have developed for our learners on both sites, and for traditional classroom instruction as well as online delivery. The goal of our instructional practices is to give students many opportunities to produce and understand math words, numbers, equations, and so forth. Game-like elements make the activities enjoyable.

Running Dictation

This idea, adapted from Davis and Rinvolucri (1988), has the teacher prepare a set of identical papers containing numbers or equations, which are taped to the wall in different parts of the classroom. Students are divided into pairs, a "runner" and a "writer." After a start cue, all the runners go to the papers, read silently, and try to remember as much of the number or equation as possible. Make sure to post the paper in a way such that runners cannot stand at the posted paper and shout the information to their scribes. Runners must return to their partner and dictate what they remember, which the writers take down. Runners may need several trips before everything is written down accurately. When all pairs have finished, the teacher elicits the correct version, which goes on the board.

The goal is to perfectly reproduce the paper while practicing oral and reading skills. Variations on this game include

- Different sets of papers are taped up. When a pair finishes the first one, they change roles with the runner becoming the writer and vice versa.

- A short word problem can be used instead of numbers or equations. When the problem has been transcribed, the pair then tries to solve it.

- If the class is too crowded for comfortable movement, or the teacher does not like the confusion of students walking around, the items can be written on the board. All the writers sit with their backs to the board. Runners face the board but dictate from their seats.

Facts About X (Research and Ask)

In the previous class, students are assigned a research topic on a theme (planets, animals, countries, properties of nanotubes, etc.) Each student has a different topic, but the theme is the same. For example, if the theme is countries, each student would be assigned a different country to research. Our resources are limited, so we make the best use of such available sources of information as almanacs and various encyclopedias. With Internet access, students can also use sites such as Wikipedia. One SQU class used the CIA World Factbook (n.d.) for demographic data.

As homework, students find and write answers to a set of common questions. For the theme "countries," students have generated the following questions: How many people live there? How big is it? What is the gross domestic product? How many tons of carbon are produced per capita? In class, then, an empty chart can be put on the board with students copying it into their notebooks. (Copies of blank charts can also be distributed. See Figure 3.) In groups of about five, students ask and answer questions to complete the chart. Active listening and speaking is required.

Question	Country 1	Country 2	Country 3	Country 4	Country 5
Population					
Land area					
GDP					
Carbon/capita					

Figure 3. Sample Chart

BINGO! and Tic Tac Toe

These games can be used as a summary activity at the end of class when the board is full or as a stand-alone review. When the board is full of numbers and words, even complex equations from the day's lesson, students draw a 3 x 3 grid in their notebooks. In each of the nine squares, they write an item from the board. The teacher then calls out the items in a random order, keeping track of what has already been called. Students mark their grids, and when a student has three crosses in a row, he or she shouts, "tic tac toe!" The student must then read back the three items to confirm accuracy and provide speaking practice. As the game continues, the teacher can add challenge by disallowing those three items. BINGO follows a similar principle by having students cross off items as they hear them. When someone has five in a row, they shout BINGO! The student must then correctly read back the five items to be declared a winner. This provides listening recognition practice.

Trivial Review

In Trivial Review, students sit in small groups with a piece of paper and a marker. The teacher calls out (or shows) questions based on recent lessons. Each group negotiates to write an answer without using notes or books. After a specified time elapses, the correct answer is given. Groups then hold up their answers, and if correct, the group gets a point. Items can be simple review or complex story problems. Examples of questions given after a geometry unit include: What is another way to say a 90 degree angle? What is a four-sided figure with only two parallel sides? What is the area of a room that is four meters by five meters? What is the Pythagorean theorem? What is the longest side of a right triangle called? Review such as this reinforces the math concepts and practices using key terms in listening, speaking, and writing.

$20,000 Pyramid (Speedy Math)

This game requires quick responses to simple math problems within a time limit. Each student receives a set of three or four teacher-prepared game cards, each with a list of six to ten simple math calculations. In pairs, one student reads the problems on his or her card to another (but must not show the card). The listener gets one point for each correct computation. The goal is to get through the list within the time limit. After one card has been completed, roles reverse so that the listener becomes the speaker and vice versa. The student with the highest number of points wins the game. Triads or a second pair can act as referees, keeping time and counting points. We have found that this game works best when we keep the problems very simple, focusing on four basic functions, simple fractions, percents, simple exponents, and roots. The first time we play this game with a class, we find it helpful to model it with a volunteer. To save the teacher from writing up all the cards, we have had one group write cards for another group to use, or one class do a set for another class. Because students also have to supply the correct answers, this provides productive repetition.

Measure It!

Everything in a room can be measured and areas and volumes calculated. It is not necessary to have rulers or measuring tapes. It is possible to use any measurement unit, such as one textbook-length or one arm span. In this case, area and volume can be described as square or cubed units. We often go beyond the classroom for this activity with students measuring almost anything, then reporting back to the class. For example, different groups might measure the area of the campus, the amount of classroom space or laboratory space, the area of campus car parks, roads, sidewalks, sports facilities, or even tires or hubcaps on vehicles. A master chart of campus space allocation can then be created and comparisons made, such as the ratio of parking lot area to classroom space. Students may be surprised at the results.

What Is the Average Student?

Working in pairs, students are given (or choose) some aspect of student life that can be quantified, such as height, age, number of siblings, and library hours per week spent. Pairs quickly come up with a grammatically correct question to ask in seeking their piece of information. Students then mill around and ask other students in class or in the extended campus community. When the surveys are complete, each pair calculates averages. For example, the average number of siblings could be 2.4. The averages are then compiled on the board or an overhead projector with all students comparing themselves to the average in each category. They determine the number of categories in which they are average or very close. An "average student" can be determined as the one closest to the average in the most categories.

REFLECTIONS

Our research and curriculum development has opened up new lines of communication among English and math faculty. In follow-up interviews with math faculty, we found that some professors perceive students' problems in math as conceptual rather than linguistic. At the same time, other math professors were adamant that the students' problems were wholly English language related. For the average ESL teacher, math was not a priority. Teachers we interviewed dismissed math with such statements as, "I am hopeless in math." ESL/EFL teachers and program designers seem to believe—and even express relief—that math is the one course where language is not a factor. Because of this erroneous assumption, the overwhelming majority of teachers interviewed expressed the opinion that poor math concepts—not language—were the cause of students' difficulties in math courses. Such discord among teachers of both math and English has hindered efforts to add a math language component to IEP courses on both campuses. Because the self-access course implemented at SQU is currently not a required part of the curriculum, it is difficult to assess its effect on students' performance in math classes. Indisputable empirical evidence is needed to convince administrators and faculty before changes will be made to the English curriculum.

Because we believe that the language of math urgently needs to be addressed in academic ESL/EFL programs, we feel a dedicated ESL math course, such as the one at NSCC, may be the best option when a large number of students are preparing for technical studies. Even when such a course is not possible or appropriate, learning and practicing math language may well be a valuable use of regular classroom time in any English for academic purposes program. This need not be at all boring for students or threatening for teachers, as we demonstrate here. A self-access course such as the one developed at SQU is an alternative, but for full effectiveness, it may be necessary to require it of students.

Math is the basis for almost all science study and thus for all science-related careers, in addition to a multitude of other university pursuits. For this reason, English teachers and academic ESL/EFL programs can no longer ignore the language component in math studies. Educators must provide effective support for integrating math into the language curriculum in order to help our students achieve their academic goals. Research on this at the university level currently is in progress.

Kathy Sedoff Ewing holds a BA in linguistics, an MA in TESOL, and a PhD in education from the University of Washington in the United States, and serves as a lecturer and materials developer at Sultan Qaboos University, Muscat, Sultanate of Oman. As an oral language specialist, she has extensive international teaching experience with university students, interns, laborers, interpreters, professors, diplomats, and engineers.

William Huguelet earned an MA in TESOL from the University of Texas at San Antonio in the United States. He has been an EFL teacher, materials writer, and curriculum designer since 1982, working in Asia, Europe, and the Pacific. He is currently a lecturer and course coordinator in the English for engineering program at Sultan Qaboos University, Muscat, Sultanate of Oman.

CHAPTER 9

Readers' Theater: Turbo-Charged Language Acquisition

Gary Carkin, Sarah Dodson-Knight, Alexis Gerard Finger,
Silvia Rodriguez Spence, Nigel A. Caplan, and Judy Trupin

Picture this: a group of English language learners wearing different hats that represent different characters, holding highlighted scripts, and sitting on stools in front of their peers. They are working with an authentic text and have spent days or weeks rehearsing the script, using English in authentic ways to negotiate meaning and decide how to present a play. But they have not had to learn their lines or memorize movement because they are using Readers' Theater—a turbo-charged way to bring dynamic language use to English language learners.

As a tool of language acquisition, Readers' Theater has traveled from the world of professional theater to mainstream and English language classrooms. Defined generally as the oral performance of literature (drama, poetry, or prose), Readers' Theater performances occur without elaborate material support. There are few props, limited costumes, no makeup, sound effects, or lighting requirements, and most importantly, no memorization of lines. Learners perform the text with a minimum of movement, relying on the power of the spoken word to ignite the imagination of the viewers (Bafile, 2003).

Readers' Theater is an ideal technique for engaging students with authentic texts while at the same time lowering their affective filter (Krashen & Terrell, 1983). The technique does not require innate acting talent on the part of the students—or their teacher—or unreasonable risk-taking. As the actors' scripts are always in front of them, the performance is challenging without being terrifying (Bafile, 2003), especially as the actors are the students working together with classmates. Preparing, rehearsing, and performing texts for Readers' Theater increases students' reading comprehension, ability to read aloud with expression, vocabulary, and awareness, and gives them confidence and an appreciation of drama as literature. In turn, these improvements and skills result in energized and eager students who really listen to one another as actors and as audience members; students work together to create meaning as they interpret and react to literature with meaning as key (Kao & O'Neill, 1998; Kozub, 2000; Laughlin & Latrobe, 1990; Prescott, 2003; Smith, 1984).

Readers' Theater versions of existing plays may increase students' integrative motivation, the desire to understand and fit into the culture where the target language is spoken. Stern (1980) demonstrates the affective benefits of using drama in language classes, because play scripts permit students to engage actively with the target culture, "helping them develop a sensitivity as to how speakers of the language interact with each other. It familiarizes them with the cultural appropriateness of words and expressions to specific settings and social situations" (p. 79).

Perhaps the most valuable benefit of Readers' Theater is the extended context that using a script brings: Students spend many class sessions working with one text to be able to perform it for an audience (Bafile, 2003), allowing them to truly engage with the text. Learners use English to discuss the text and its meaning and adapt it to a Readers' Theater script, then to rehearse it. All the while, through authentic collaborations, learners use practical functions of language such as making suggestions, hypothesizing, following directions, expressing alternatives and disagreement, and much more (Wessels, 1987). Moreover, they benefit from this repeated exposure to vocabulary and grammar in a meaningful context (Nation, 2001, pp. 67–68).

Readers' Theater allows students to become someone else. Students performing in a play wear a mask, literally or figuratively. No longer a shy and stumbling second language speaking student, the actor takes on a new role and thus takes moderate risks, playing with the language and achieving what might not be possible sitting at a desk in a classroom (Stern, 1980). Readers' Theater truly is turbo-charged language: Enhanced context and repetition make language work easier. Readers' Theater is an intense—and intensely rewarding—experience that students and teachers value for language learning.

CONTEXT

There are several approaches to second language acquisition that include the use of drama and role play, including suggestopedia (Lozanov, 1978) and total physical response (Asher, 2003), but it is the theoretical framework of Vygotsky (1986), the Belarusian psycholinguist, that most informs the use of Readers' Theater in second language acquisition. Simply outlined, Vygotsky views language (and second language learning) as the process of producing speech "from the motive that engenders a thought to the shaping of the thought, first in inner speech, then in meanings of words, and finally in words" (p. 253). This might be illustrated through the following (see Table 1).

The speaker (actor) starts with a clearly felt motive, something as general as wishing to tell a story, or as specific as an underlying motive for a particular line.

Table 1. The Communication Process Modeled After Vygotsky (1986); Text From Carkin (2005)

Text	Motive	Subtext/ Inner speech	Image	Feeling	Speech
Betsy: I'm so tired of writing. And nothing comes together right!	Tries to get some attention and sympathy from Pat.	Hate this. No good at it!	crumples paper	desperation	I'm so tired of writing. And nothing comes together right!
Pat: Just keep trying, Betsy. You're bound to improve.	Tries to cheer Betsy up and give her confidence.	Oh, now. It's not so bad. Everyone improves.	of a happy and confident Betsy	confidence	Just keep trying, Bet. You're bound to improve.

In working with drama, the character's motive or intention is a necessary step to determine the subtext, the motive-thought or intention. This in turn generates inner speech (subtext), which evokes image-sense and feeling and leads to a mental search for words related to the meaning. Once organized, words are then patterned according to grammar and discourse and used in speech.

The reverse occurs for the hearer. The received speech can be used to stimulate a reply or nonverbal response. The receiver hears the speech, detects meaning, and feels emotion as a result of recognizing meaning, thereby generating thought and forming a new motive or intention. The pattern is repeated again and again in the back and forth of rehearsing a play, thus building language in context and in depth. The natural psycholinguistic process of motive to speech to new motive is authentically replicated in Readers' Theater.

CURRICULUM, TASKS, MATERIALS

Literature-Based Readers' Theater

Authentic and effective Readers' Theater scripts can be developed from any genre of literature (see Appendix for helpful online resources). Three tried-and-tested sequences for adapting literary texts are presented below, in order of complexity: first poetry, then short stories, and finally plays (see Figure 1 for tips on selecting literary texts).

Poetry

A good place to start developing a curriculum that leads to an expressive Readers' Theater performance is haiku. Haiku's imagery is direct, uncomplicated, intense, and concrete. Because haiku is short, it lends itself well to oral readings. Haiku helps learners develop their oral reading skills by forcing them to slow down and

Criteria for Selecting Literary Texts for Readers' Theater

Choose:

✓ themes that match the interests of your students and audience

✓ material with vocabulary that your students can manage well

✓ material with characters that are clearly defined

✓ material that lends itself to dialogue between characters

✓ material that contains many characters for large classes

✓ material that can be expanded to accommodate more student roles if needed (perhaps by increasing the number of narrators or dividing large roles in appropriate places)

✓ material that contains strong dramatic conflict or tension

✓ material that can be performed in 15 or fewer minutes. Short pieces allow for a sense of completion, and longer pieces can be done as confidence and knowledge of Readers' Theater increases.

Figure 1. Selecting Texts

dwell on the meaning the words create in the mind's eye. Meaning gives rise to a feeling that will, in turn, affect the tone of voice and the delivery of the poem. Focusing on image-feeling connections, where vocal work develops from image to feeling and through vocal tone, the performer builds expressive use of his or her voice to avoid mechanical performance.

Almost any haiku can be used, but the work of American haiku poets Nick Virgilio and Carol Montgomery (Ross, 1989) offer immediate images. Students should take time to envision the poem. Each word has meaning and significance, and the teacher needs to make sure that students experience every word fully. The clearer the image, the stronger the feeling evoked, and it is the feeling that supports the expression in the voice which will, in turn, convey meaning to an audience.

For Readers' Theater, be it poetry or prose, each image or group of words can be divided, with one, two, three, or more students responsible for expressing a particular word and image. Such segments are typically called *breath groups,* and as such, the breath supports vocalization of the image-action contained in the phrase. Having multiple performers express different phrases allows not only variety, but also supports the language acquisition process as each performer must listen keenly to what has been said before in order to become part of the total flow of imagery, feeling, tone, mood, and meaning.

Two of Robert Frost's poems are especially useful for Readers' Theater with language students: "Stopping by Woods on a Snowy Evening" (1923) and "The Road Not Taken" (1916). In using Frost's verse (or any poem, for that matter), the pedagogical value for language learners lies in developing an eye for imagery and the expression of that imagery in word-breath groups, ("Whose woods these are," "I think I know"), and learners can be divided and assigned parts accordingly. Varying the number of performers for each image-word-breath group enhances the tone, mood, and general dynamic of the performance. Learners must be given time to experience the imagery of the poetry in order to convey feeling and meaning in oral performance.

Short Stories

Short stories rendered into scripts can make a Readers' Theater performance truly memorable for both performers and audience. The short story selection should be appropriate to both learners and audience. For adult learners, the whole range of English literature is at hand, but selections must be made with care based upon language level and learner interests. Stories written by James Thurber—such as "The Unicorn in the Garden" (1940) and "The Little Girl and the Wolf" (1939)—work well because they often are short and succinct, suitable for performers as well as viewers.

To adapt a short story for a Readers' Theater presentation, we follow these six steps:

1. We read the story together, identifying and discussing difficult vocabulary.

2. We discuss the main idea, theme, or purpose of the story, and the characters and their relationships. We encourage students to express how the material relates to their own lives. We point out details of the story that students might have missed, explaining cultural references and attitudes and beliefs.

3. Collaboratively, we choose a narrator (there can be one or many) and students choose the character they would like to play. Often students choose characters that have some personal growth value to them, which provides good energy and motivation for performance. If more than one student wants the same role, we ask students to select three possible roles that they would like to play and choose between them. We find the most success when the approximate length of the roles is more or less equal.

4. Collaboratively, we rework the stories to produce a Readers' Theater script, beginning by turning the dialogue into speech. We summarize portions of the text as needed not only to shorten the length but also to make it appropriate for the learners' vocabulary, level, or sophistication. The outcome is dialogues, monologues, and soliloquies, all suitable for oral reading. Directions for physical movement are written into the script to remind us of students' actions and also to supply a record for future productions of the same material. We produce a copy of the script for each student for rehearsal and performance.

5. We rehearse the material, adding limited movement and any simple props or costume features (like hats) that might be suggested by the script. We work toward clear speech, meaningful intonation, and appropriate characterization through voice and movement.

6. Students perform for a selected audience once the material is smooth and well paced. By now the group should operate as a unit, picking up cues and functioning as a whole to tell the story in an intelligible way.

Short story reading, scripting, and performance engage students with a range of language skills and increase their confidence in speaking English and interest in literature.

Plays

In a traditional dramatic performance, one step in character development involves creating movements that reinforce the dialogue and enhance the excitement on stage. Because movements help clarify a character's intentions and behavior, much time is spent on planning them and on memorizing lines so that performers are free to move around the stage. As a result, student actors may become so preoccupied with their movements and with learning their lines and delivering them that their intelligibility and vocal expression may suffer. However, in Readers' Theater, memorizing lines is not necessary. Students may hold their scripts or place them on a lectern for reference. This frees students to channel their energy into perfecting their pronunciation and developing colorful vocal expression and phrasing that will effectively convey their character's authentic thoughts and feelings.

Because Readers' Theater requires performers and audiences to use their imagination even more so than traditional theater, it is best to select a play or an excerpt from a play containing characters who express themselves vividly, relationships that are clearly defined, and a story line that is easy to follow. One-act plays, scenes, and monologues may be easier to adapt for a Readers' Theater performance than full-length plays, depending on the time available. Still, there is no need to reject a popular play because of its length. Teachers and students have the creative freedom to alter, delete, or add:

- lines of dialogue

- monologues

- minor characters and stage directions

- scenes or acts

- a narrator

- a chorus

A particular play may be chosen for many reasons. The Readers' Theater activity may be used to prepare students to attend a professional performance of that work (or view it on DVD) if at all possible. As an alternative, the play might be associated with an upcoming holiday or a political or social issue that is in the news.

We have adapted two and three act plays in several ways. When time is short or the language level of the students is relatively low, a student narrator can summarize the plot and introduce one or two scenes that other students perform. Alternatively, different groups of students can perform selected scenes from the same play, with a narrator making the connections between scenes. In high intermediate and advanced language classes, students can perform the play—with some modifications—from beginning to end, perhaps as a semester-long project. In each of these approaches, narrators should also be used to relate any necessary description, exposition, and transitions between scenes so that the audience can follow the progression of events (Ratliff, 1999). Stage directions are useful additions to a script and aid in potential staging and production phrases of play performance.

Creating the script is manageable if critical factors such as the students' language proficiency, interest in the activity, record of reliability, creativity, and independence are considered. When time is very limited or students are inexperienced in working in groups or creating stories, the instructor can write the initial script and elicit suggestions for modifications during the first class reading. If students enjoy writing and time permits, they can write their own script.

Before students are empowered with the responsibility of rewriting literature, they should be given an opportunity to discover or review the basic structure of drama. Students need to understand how all actions are connected to be able to make these clear to their audience. The basic components of a play (adapted from Nagleberg, 1948) include

- **Exposition:** The setting and background information of the characters and their relationship to each other and the situation.

- **Rising action:** The building of suspense, incidents, and events that dramatically intensify the characters' behavior and situation.

- **Complication:** An incident or situation introduced that heightens the suspense and prolongs the conflict or problem.

- **Climax, or turning point:** The highest point of the dramatic action when characters or circumstances change for better or worse.

- **Falling action:** The events that follow the climax leading to a resolution of the conflict.

When students apply these components to an actual play, they better understand their own characters' roles within the development of the play.

The following is one possible procedure for preparing for a Readers' Theater performance of a play:

1. The instructor introduces difficult vocabulary from the play using sample sentences.

2. The class reads the play together aloud and then answers comprehension and discussion questions. If time constraints preclude reading the entire play together, the instructor can write a detailed synopsis, show a movie version, or ask the students to read it (or segments of it) for homework.

3. Students select the most important scenes, keeping in mind the plot of the play and the basic structure of drama. The class works in groups to analyze the scenes with each group suggesting which lines are essential and which could be condensed or cut.

4. Each group reads a scene to the entire class, and classmates recommend transitions between scenes such as narration or character monologues.

5. The class creates a list of all the characters that have been retained or created, including narrators. Parts are selected as in the short story example above, at the instructor's discretion, or by drawing names from a hat.

6. Students analyze their character in terms of appearance, background, personality traits, distinctive features, temperament, and relationships. They also analyze their character's goals and motivation. This can be done as a writing assignment to integrate writing into the project.

7. Students analyze their character's lines for meaning, intention, and emotion. They paraphrase their lines to help understand the meaning of the words.

8. Students practice reading their lines for intelligibility, expression, and emotion. They insert stress, intonation, and phrase markers. They then record their lines and submit the audio recording and script to the instructor for feedback on form and suggestions for alternative deliveries.

9. Students practice learning their lines by reading them silently to themselves and saying them aloud when looking at the audience or the character they are addressing.

10. Eye contact with audience or fellow characters, type of stage, positioning of the performers, use and appearance of scripts, lighting, props and sets, costumes, and music as well as body movement can all be considered from the simple to the elaborate, depending on time available. Music may also be used to enhance the mood for performers and audience (Finger, 2000).

11. Students rehearse the entire script and individual scenes that are challenging and require more practice. They are encouraged to provide each other with feedback through concrete suggestions. The instructor takes notes during each rehearsal and provides feedback at appropriate times.

12. The performance is videotaped for several purposes. When it is played back, students have the opportunity to evaluate their own performance by discussing what was effective and what could be improved. The very act of videotaping the experience also affects the students' perception of the importance of the activity and provides evidence of accomplishments.

An alternative is to have students choose characters from the play and then create their own character monologues. The goal of the monologues is to reveal the plot through the thoughts and feelings of the character.

Readers' Theater to Support Textbook Materials

Textbooks also can provide rich and readily available sources of material for adaptation for Readers' Theater. They are likely to be level appropriate, include grammatical and rhetorical structure focus, and contain ready-made activities. In the case of skill-specific texts (e.g., writing textbooks), adapting content to Readers' Theater creates a truly communicative language experience by drawing on students' other skills (i.e., listening, speaking, and reading). For example, story telling can illustrate cause and effect development (as in *Tapestry Writing 3* Weidauer, 2007, p. 97). We first follow the textbook's prereading, reading, and postreading strategies and questions. In class, we discuss the plot (actions and timeline), characters, and vocabulary. We divide the class into as many groups as there are characters, with one or more students playing the narrator role. (When more than one student plays a role, they may either take turns or deliver lines together.) Each group draws a character mind map that includes personality description, relationship to other characters, and actions taken. Groups collaboratively write dialogue for their characters that fit the authentic role and actions in the story, creating situations where the character can be revealed through dialogue and actions. As students write their scripts, they share and revise as needed through comparison with the original textbook story. Together, the groups share suggestions with the class and then rehearse prior to performance.

Case studies in English for specific purposes (ESP) textbooks, such as *Business Communications: International Case Studies in English* (Rodgers, 1998), may also be adapted to Readers' Theater by extending the role-play activities suggested in the text. Suitable case study topics include those that have an emotional aspect or human element. Cases dealing with unethical business behavior, customer dissatisfaction, intercultural issues, and management-employee conflicts can be effectively presented as Readers' Theater. Adapting ESP case studies involves an additional element to working with a traditional textbook reading: creating the "story" itself. Although the textbook provides the facts in the case, students must develop the script based on an analysis of the case and on stakeholders' individual viewpoints. For instance, in a case dealing with environmental pollution, company management, environmentalists, workers, residents, and government officials would have differing viewpoints. The class can develop a Readers' Theater script based on the interaction of these viewpoints. The focus is on teamwork as the groups discuss case issues and create the script. Stakeholder teams have two distinct tasks: (a) analyzing the case, and (b) writing the script, both requiring full participation by all members to be accomplished successfully. Checklists or rubrics identifying the skills required of an effective team member serve as a guide to encourage students. Introducing the concept of teamwork as a professional skill that requires practice can motivate students to participate in case discussion, script writing, and performance.

Each team becomes responsible for one stakeholder in the case study. Teams research their stakeholder, the case, and the key concepts and share their findings with the class. Each group analyzes the issues from the stakeholder's viewpoint and considers solutions to the problem. Students prepare a script in which everyone has several lines to deliver. The forum for the Readers' Theater presentation is determined by the case itself. A question and answer period after a performance adds an element of reality, especially when the audience has been studying the case or has a genuine interest in the subject. As a follow up, each group may be asked to write a report of the issues and proposed solutions, with individual students writing about the process of creating and performing the script and discussing how they can apply the skills learned to a business setting.

Using textbook material dynamically as the basis for Readers' Theater activities enriches the language experience for students and provides both teachers and students a creative venue for authentic communicative language learning.

REFLECTIONS

Readers' Theater has evolved from an activity used to increase reading comprehension skills in primary classes for native speakers of English to a technique that English language teachers can use in many different teaching contexts. It is as appropriate for ESP learners using nonfiction texts as it is for students studying poetry, short stories, and drama in English. Readers' Theater ranges from simple (students reading from existing scripts in front of their classmates) to elaborate (students developing their own script from an original text to perform for their entire school or community after repeated rehearsals). It is equally valuable for young learners and adults, beginning and advanced, and all those in between. However, because not everyone is familiar with drama techniques in the language classroom, a teacher may at first be hesitant. Additionally, very timid students and those without previous drama experience may show resistance. These challenges are easily overcome. Teachers should reassure themselves that they do not have to be experienced actors in order to help students read a text aloud with expression. Teachers also can explain the benefits of this technique to administrators and supervisors and then invite them to see the power of a Readers' Theater performance in person.

To counter student apprehension, teachers introducing Readers' Theater can begin with physical and vocal warm-ups (such as stretches and tongue twisters) and include simple drama-related activities like thematic role plays throughout the class (see e.g., Burke & O'Sullivan, 2002; Maley & Duff, 2006; Wessels, 1987). If students become accustomed to getting up and moving around the classroom, as well as reading and improvising in front of their peers, they will be more comfortable engaging in Readers' Theater. Teachers can ensure that the shyest students play smaller roles in the production or take on a stage manager or other helper role that will require them to use English while developing the script and in rehearsals, even if they remain silent during the performance.

Readers' Theater is a versatile medium for language development appropriate for all age levels. This technique introduces a sense of authenticity in the classroom because it communicates true emotion, meaning, and realistic language use to a larger audience, whether through poetry, prose, or dramatic dialogue, allowing language learners to build and then test their communicative ability in front of a real audience. That they are understood and appreciated by the audience is both the goal and the reward of the lesson.

The authors are all members of TESOL-Drama, the membership e-group within the TESOL association dedicated to the discussion and promotion of drama in the profession.

Nigel A. Caplan is an ESL specialist at the University of North Carolina at Chapel Hill in the United States. He has presented at regional and international TESOL conferences and published with the University of Michigan and Oxford University Presses. At the time of writing, he is teaching at Michigan State University's English Language Center.

Gary Carkin is professor of TESOL at the Institute for Language Education, Southern New Hampshire University in the United States. A professional actor, Dr. Carkin's specialty is teaching English through drama. He currently teaches in the intensive English program as well as in the graduate TEFL program. His Web site is http://garycarkin.tripod.com/garycarkinsesleﬂdramalog/

Sarah Dodson-Knight taught French and ESL at the university level and high school English in France before coordinating a reading enrichment program at Lafayette Public Library in Lafayette, Colorado in the United States. A long-time member of TESOL-Drama, she has produced many plays with her language students and the children at the library.

Alexis Gerard Finger is the senior lecturer in the English and philosophy department and a communication specialist in the English Language Center at Drexel University in the United States. She has authored four textbooks, including The Magic of Drama *(2000, Full Blast Production.) She specializes in international teaching assistant training and using drama to teach oral communication skills.*

Silvia Rodriguez Spence is associate professor of TESOL at the Institute for Language Education, Southern New Hampshire University in the United States. Recipient of a 2007–2008 Fulbright Scholar Award, she has taught a professional development course for English teachers at the Universidad Autonoma de Yucatan, Mexico.

Judy Trupin is an ESOL adult educator and curriculum developer. A professional performer, director, and choreographer, she performs her original theater pieces for adults and children and has worked as a teaching artist in schools. She is assistant program manager of the Queens Library Adult Learner Program, New York City.

APPENDIX: INTERNET RESOURCES

Overview and Support for Readers' Theater

Carrick, L. (2001). *Internet resources for conducting Readers Theatre*. Retrieved February 17, 2007, from http://www.readingonline.org/electronic/elec_index .asp?HREF=carrick/index.html

NWT Literacy Council. (n.d.). *Readers Theatre how to kit*. Retrieved February 17, 2007, from http://www.nwt.literacy.ca/famlit/howtokit/theatre/theatre.pdf

Shepard, A. (2003). *RT Tips: A guide to Readers Theatre*. Retrieved September 28, 2007, from http://www.aaronshep.com/rt/Tips.html

TESOL Electronic Village. (2007). *Online workshop on Readers' Theater*. Retrieved February 17, 2007, from http://groups.yahoo.com/group/EVO_drama_2007/

Walker, L. (n.d.). *Readers Theatre: A reading resource, a teaching tool, a performance vehicle, and a chance to play with language!* Retrieved February 18, 2007, from http://www.loiswalker.com/catalog/teach.html

Williams, S. (n.d.). *Readers Theatre*. Retrieved February 12, 2007, from http://www.thinkingscripts.co.uk/ts/rt1.html

Guidelines for Creating Scripts

Pizarro, D., & Buchanan, R. (n.d.). *Creating a Readers Theatre script: Onion tears*. Retrieved February 12, 2007, from http://www.aspa.asn.au/Projects/english/ rtonion.htm

Shepard, A. (2003). *Tips on scripting.* Retrieved February 17, 2007, from http://www.aaronshep.com/rt/Tips1.html

Rehearsing and Performing

ReadWriteThink. (n.d.). *Readers Theatre.* Retrieved February 12, 2007, from http://www.readwritethink.org/lessons/lesson_view.asp?id=172

Walker, L. (n.d.). *Staged reading rehearsals: Twelve teacher guidelines.* Retrieved February 12, 2007, from http://loiswalker.com/catalog/teach7.html

Free Readers' Theater Scripts

Chiff.com. (n.d.). *Theater scripts.* Retrieved September 28, 2007, from http://www.chiff.com/art/theater/scripts.htm

McCormick, K. (n.d.). *Readers Theatre scripts.* Retrieved September 28, 2007, from http://bms.westport.k12.ct.us/mccormick/rt/rtscriphome.htm

Shepard, A. (2003). *Aaron Shepard's RT page.* Retrieved September 28, 2007, from http://aaronshep.com/rt/RTE.html

CHAPTER 10

Inexpensive, Effective ESP Material Development for the EFL Classroom

Marvin D. Hoffland and Oswald Jochum

This chapter focuses on an inexpensive, highly effective method of developing English for specific purposes (ESP) materials in an English as a foreign language (EFL) setting by using authentic marketing materials from a local high-tech company. It is now common practice in many global companies to produce marketing videos and annual reports in English and these are usually readily accessible and available for educational purposes at no cost. The authors share their experiences in designing authentic materials for university degree programs that focus on information technology and electronics at the Carinthia University of Applied Sciences (CUAS) in Austria, as well as in a corporate training setting.

We adapted selected marketing material—a promotional DVD and the 2003 Annual Report—from Semiconductor Equipment Zubehör–accessories (SEZ Group), an international high-tech company based in Villach, Austria for a comprehensive course in which students learn techniques to describe charts and graphs, company structures, and marketing terms (business English); and technical vocabulary involved in semiconductor production (technical English). By utilizing real-world marketing materials from a local company, students' typically are more engaged because they already know the company, or at minimum, have heard of it through the local media.

CONTEXT

Our materials were originally designed for native German speakers in the second semester of a 3-year bachelor of science degree program in medical information technology (medIT). One of the challenges of developing materials is that the students' language abilities range considerably, from advanced basic/lower independent language user (A2/B1) to higher independent/proficient language user

(B2/C1) using the Common European Framework of Reference for Languages (Council of Europe, 2007a; see Figure 1). This wide mix of student language levels may be explained by the fact that our student population at the CUAS is made up of graduates from different secondary schools and thus different backgrounds. Austrian primary education is from 6–10 years old. At the age of 10, Austrian families must choose between two lower secondary schools, the lower level *gymnasium* and the *hauptschule*. Usually at the age of 14, Austrians students choose between the higher level gymnasium (academic secondary school), higher technical secondary college (HTL) and the higher business secondary college (HAK). In all three secondary school forms, students have 8 years of English; however, based upon our precourse assessment tests, their language capabilities vary considerably. Students from the gymnasium and HAK usually score much higher than HTL students, but this varies by secondary school as well.[1]

Another challenge is developing materials suitable for the specific needs of the medIT curriculum, which includes courses in programming, electronics, and electrical engineering as well as business administration and anatomy and physiology. The English component of the overall curriculum should not focus exclusively on technical and academic English but also on business, medical, and social English. The task is to find materials that incorporate all of the aspects above to meet the students' ESP requirements of being able to communicate in English in medical, technical, and business settings. Many up-and-coming technicians "only want the English they need." There are a number of excellent textbooks that provide instructors with very good exercises, texts, and audio and video examples to meet the business English goals. However, based upon our students' reactions, they often find it hard to relate to these texts—especially the audio and video, as

	C2 (Mastery)
Proficient User	
	C1 (Effective Operational Proficiency)
	B2 (Vantage)
Independent User	
	B1 (Threshold)
	A2 (Waystage)
Basic User	
	A1 (Breakthrough)

Figure 1. The Common European Framework of Reference for Languages (adapted from Council of Europe, 2007b, p. 26)

---

[1] According to educational guidelines of the Austrian Ministry of Education, a graduate from any form of higher secondary school should have a language ability of B2, an advanced independent user (Bundesministerium, n.d.). Additionally, the term *higher* is used to differentiate between the two levels of secondary school (10–14 vs. 14–18) and should not be confused with the *higher education* meaning of university-level studies.

the characters are usually actors and the situations are contrived to stress certain vocabulary and phrases that are part of a thematic unit. In other words, students do not find the material authentic, which makes it even more difficult in the EFL setting to answer the perpetual student question, "Why do I need English?"

The goal is to develop materials that combine different ESP aspects (e.g., business and technical) and include abstract texts and real-world vocabulary that students can relate to, thus increasing their motivation. One approach is to use authentic marketing materials from local companies. Annual reports, marketing handouts, DVDs, and so forth are for the most part very professional, utilize target business vocabulary, and contain excellent graphs and images as well as provide a specific focus on technical English (or other ESP areas). Moreover, these materials are authentic and because the company in our case is Austrian, our CUAS students naturally want to know more about it. We have also found that by highlighting features of a major local company and potential future employer who uses English in their marketing and business reports, we reinforce to our students the concept that English is important and relevant to them. Additionally, companies usually provide their marketing materials at no cost and have no problem if the materials are used for educational purposes.

Naturally, there are also limits to the usefulness of marketing materials as authentic materials. Compared to standard textbook lessons, which include texts, exercises, defined learning objectives, and audio and video material, the task of adapting authentic company marketing material into a course plan using specific language learning objectives can be quite daunting. To say the least, the time and effort needed is quite substantial. However, the time, effort, and perhaps most importantly, the cost of obtaining appropriate ESP materials to meet the students' future language needs can far outweigh the time and effort needed to develop or adapt your own material.

CURRICULUM, TASKS, MATERIALS

Authenticity and Curricular Goals

In the medIT degree program, major language learning objectives in the second semester course (Technical English II) are learning business structures, describing charts, graphs, and trends as well as focusing on vocabulary associated with electronics. The primary priority is placed on the business vocabulary, but by introducing the technical vocabulary into this lesson, we can achieve more realism by showing the students how companies use language in their marketing materials.

Specifically, the business English goals for this 2–3 week lesson (at the CUAS, a typical course meets for two 45-minute sessions per week) are to focus on different company structures (e.g., Corp., Inc., Ltd., subsidiaries), company titles (e.g., CEO, CFO, managing director, vice president), charts and graphs (e.g., pie, bar, stock), and trend vocabulary (e.g., peak, recovery, rise). Definitions for this vocabulary can be taken from standard online dictionaries or standard textbooks. Specific technical English goals are an introduction to semiconductors (front-end and back-end production), wafer processing (e.g., wet processing, batch, etching), and descriptive vocabulary (e.g., yield, particle contamination, fabs).

Not many technical English books that are designed for the language learner focus on semiconductors. Moreover, technical materials can be so complicated that the language instructor can be easily overwhelmed with the daunting challenge of moving from ESP to content-based teaching, in this case, trying to teach semiconductors. When faced with the challenge of more technical areas, many English instructors will either try to teach just vocabulary or avoid the subject as much as possible. This is where adapting authentic real-world ESP materials can come to the rescue.

Teaching With Authentic Company Documents

We have adapted the SEZ Group's annual report and promotional marketing DVD with their permission to meet the language learning goals described earlier. One of the advantages of utilizing the SEZ marketing materials is that the language used is focused on a wide international audience with both technical and nontechnical backgrounds. Thus, complex technical concepts are explained but in such a way that even a lay person can grasp it. Because these materials are designed for potential investors, of course, excellent business language is used.

In the company's annual report, actual terms and titles are placed next to photos of real people who have appeared regularly in the regional Austrian media. Students acquire a real feeling for an actual management board and come to realize that one employee can hold two titles (such as executive vice president and chief marketing officer). This reinforces concepts and provides authentic examples of the business definitions that were introduced earlier in the course. Additional lecture activities could also include mapping the SEZ organizational information into organizational charts. Harding (2007) describes an activity that focuses on introducing and discussing working organizations and then applying them to specific examples. One could easily adapt Harding's activities to relate to a real company or organization.

The SEZ Group's annual report profiles their business units, so students can see that an international organization can use both British and American business unit types (Inc. vs. Ltd.) as well as the German types (AG, GmbH). Especially in the European EFL setting, the discussion between American English vs. British English can be quite heated and may be reflected in different textbooks. Large corporations organize their structures to match consumer needs; thus, companies such as SEZ tend to prepare their promotional materials with an international audience in mind using a much more global style. Asking students to come up with their own ideas to explain why SEZ Japan is an Inc. whereas SEZ Korea is Ltd. has led to a number of interesting discussions. Because SEZ is a local company, many students have relatives and friends who actually work at the company or are familiar with it and can provide interesting insights. Additionally, annual reports contain a number of good business terms (e.g., branch office, business unit, types of business activities) that support the discussion as well as the students' understanding of business structures.

Students can relate to SEZ's business charts from the annual report and the promotional DVD much better than, for example, a pie chart that describes fictitious company X's sales of computer games by distribution. Moreover, companies' marketing materials usually have a more professional "slick marketing" look than the average textbook chart, which also has the potential to peak students' interests. These charts in addition to their professional feel also are more authentic because they are up-to-date, reflect actual marketing data in the semiconductor sector, and utilize business terms as well semiconductor vocabulary. Exercises related to these charts can include partner work to describe the information presented. Students can also write short paragraph descriptions using the vocabulary they have learned. Trend analysis and the ability to describe charts and graphs are important aspects of the English that our graduates will use in their future careers.

The following is an excerpt from SEZ annual report that provides a concise explanation of the company's vision and a part of its mission statement (see Figure 2). From a language point of view, there is a nice mix of business terms (e.g., leadership, supplier, mission, global customers), common production and manufacturing terms (e.g., processing solutions, lifecycle, manufacturing, yields), and ESP vocabulary specific to the semiconductor industry (e.g., singlewafer, wet-processing, IC, semiconductor). The marketing action verbs (extend, enable, optimize and boost) are also introduced to students, in most cases for the first time. As mentioned earlier, the objective is to use authentic materials that combine both technical and business concepts to peak students' interest and thus hopefully aid their learning.

THE SEZ VISION

SEZ will extend its global leadership and become the industry's most complete supplier of single-wafer wet-processing solutions throughout the IC manufacturing lifecycle.

THE SEZ MISSION

Product

Our mission is to enable the manufacturing of advanced semiconductor devices by delivering superior single-wafer wet-processing solutions that help our global customers optimize process results, enhance device performance and boost manufacturing yields.

Figure 2. SEZ Annual Report 2003 (p. 5), "SEZ Vision and Product Mission"

The review and introduction of vocabulary from the SEZ Annual Report leads well into the multimedia portion of this lesson unit—the SEZ video. The SEZ promotional DVD utilizes both technical and business marketing jargon and is an excellent tool for listening comprehension as well as introducing and reinforcing vocabulary. The primary audience for this promotional video is existing and potential business partners, investors, and customers. The video is somewhat bombastic (sound effects, music sound track, and many visual effects) as it is intended to run continuously on large screens at the company's booth at large international trade shows and expos. Because the DVD is used at trade shows in Europe, the United States, and Asia, images and on-screen text are integrated quite professionally to support the spoken English script. The following screenshot (see Figure 3) provides a fill-in-the-blank exercise we designed based on an excerpt of this 8.5-minute video. The corporate culture section focuses on business vocabulary, whereas the technology section focuses on semiconductor and technical vocabulary.

There are many ways to approach this exercise. One way is to play the DVD in its entirety, then distribute the handout and pair students together—ideally a stu-

---

Corporate Culture 2:25

Uniting the company's more than ____ _____ is a unique[4] _____ driven by a powerful set of guiding principles and business ethics.
Time after time, SEZ has offered
   1. Highest _____ and the superior technology at lowest
     _____ ____ _____.

   2. On demand _____ _____ service and support to our
     _____ _____ customer base.

   3. Employee excellence through _____ planning,
     continuing education and_____ programs.

And remain ahead of the curve with _____ technology and
marketing strategies plus sound _____. management

Word bank
productivity
localized
600 employees
career
cost of ownership
global
innovative
corporate culture
training
fiscal[5]

Technology 4:06

With an increasing demand for _____ ,
[there] comes a need for more advanced processing technologies to
_____ high-end consumer _____.

4:26 Chip Application Market Graph

Its single wafer processing equipment is used to _____ and
_____ wafers in the chip manufacturing cycle

The sophisticated cleaning that SEZ provides is vital to combating costly yield[6]-killing particle _____ .

Word bank
consumer
electronics
clean
manufacture
devices
condition
contamination[7]

Figure 3. Excerpt of Handout to Accompany SEZ Image DVD (Designed by the Authors)

dent who is stronger in English but has little technical knowledge with a student with the opposite strengths—to fill in the text using the vocabulary provided. Next we play the DVD again so students can check their answers and fill in those answers they did not know. To assist the students with this exercise, the authors have matched the number of blanks to fit the word (one blank) or the phrase (two or more blanks). Additionally, terms that may be unfamiliar to the students have been footnoted (see 4–7 in Figure 3) to provide definitions in English and German.

Students view the video again or fast forward and pause at specific frames to highlight technical and business concepts. Eight and a half minutes may seem too long of a segment for students to listen to multiple times, but the amount of text is relatively short and is clearly separated into eight sections of about 15–20 seconds each. Most DVD players allow you to place time tabs so you can easily jump forward to the desired section for review or small group discussion. Thus, if your language learning objectives are more concentrated on business subjects (such as chart analysis), you can go directly to that section. For example, there is a pie chart that breaks down the "chip application market" on the DVD. By pausing here, students can work together and discuss the many different uses for computer chips. Afterwards, one or more groups describe the pie chart in front of the class.

Images from the "technology" text on the DVD clearly illustrate concepts so that students and teachers can relate terms like *particle contamination* and *clean and condition wafers* to the actual objects. Students with a more technical background are often familiar with some of the technical vocabulary needed to describe these images, which motivates them to participate more even though their overall English abilities may be weaker than their peers. A useful speaking interaction language task is to have those more technically inclined students explain to their less technically inclined colleagues the images we select from the DVD. This provides a good basis for language negotiation: The "techie" students provide more of the content (e.g., the technical vocabulary and the setting), and the students with higher level English provide more of the language rules (e.g., grammar and syntax).

Our experience has shown that using authentic company materials resulted in higher student motivation, and in this specific case it also appears to have evened the playing field among the different levels of language and technical abilities.

REFLECTIONS

Our language learning materials were effective because students could relate to the practical examples (personal, professional, regional, or corporate context) and were able to apply the acquired skills using relevant vocabulary in a variety of classroom situations. More and more companies in Austria have to use English as a *lingua franca* because of globalization, and our Austrian EFL students seem to realize that this fact will affect their future jobs. Additionally, both of our bachelor programs are highly specialized technical programs. Thus, we as language teachers are faced with the challenge of offering authentic ESP situations and materials to meet the specific language needs of our students.

Can this approach of adapting authentic materials be adapted to other ESP settings as well? This depends on the language program's goals and what is expected of the language learner. In Europe, many countries have universities of applied sciences (UAS)—also called university colleges—which differ from traditional universities in that the degree programs are much more specialized (a degree in medIT vs. a degree in computer sciences). English is extensively integrated into the UAS curricula, whereas English at the traditional university is normally offered as an elective. In these cases, an authentic material approach can be easily adapted into a variety of different specialized programs.

Using authentic company marketing materials, the language instructor can easily develop lecture plans to fit their students' needs. Using selected sections of the company's annual report such fits well in a reading comprehension exercise, whereas product data sheets are excellent material for reading for technical terminology. Fill-in-the blank exercises using marketing DVDs or Internet audio files are excellent ways to practice listening for terminology. After the unit on SEZ, our students choose their own companies in the medical industry, gather their own authentic materials, and present their company in a 15-minute presentation. This allows the student to role play as the company representative; in our case, students need to explain at least two graphs and charts from the company's promotional materials.

As a final note, based upon the overall positive feedback from our students and the corresponding motivation we have seen when using authentic materials, we have adapted other multimedia material from the Carinthia Chamber of Commerce and Human Technology Styria, a consortium of companies, universities, and the provincial government of Styria involved in the medical technical sector. With these authentic materials in hand and a little ingenuity on our part, we strive to meet the diverse language, technology, and business needs of our learners.

Marvin D. Hoffland is a senior lecturer of English at the Carinthia University of Applied Sciences in Klagenfurt, Austria. He teaches ESP/EFL courses in business, medical, and technical English. His degrees include an MS in economics and a BA in German and economics.

Oswald Jochum holds a PhD in social psychology and an MA in anglistics and cultural studies. He is a senior lecturer of English at the Carinthia University of Applied Sciences in Villach, Austria and teaches ESP/EFL courses in the area of business and technical English. He also is the managing director of GlobeSkills.

Authentic Connections: Community Partnerships

CHAPTER 11

Exploring the Global Landscape Through Language and Service Learning

Beth Kozbial Ernst and Megan Allen

International students studying at U.S. universities often find it difficult to connect with their new community and truly interact with other community members. The purpose of our project is to get English language learners out of the classroom and involved in the community to learn more about American culture and to communicate on a more authentic level through volunteering. By integrating service into language courses, teachers can encourage students to participate in the community and then reflect on their experiences through journal writing and oral presentations. Community service is a common practice in many cultures, and students often see such experiences both as a benefit to the community and an opportunity to become active members.

CONTEXT

We incorporate service learning in our intensive English program (IEP) at the University of Wisconsin–Eau Claire in the United States. Our learners' ages generally range from traditional college age to the early 40s. Most learners are 18–23 years old and come from a variety of countries, cultures, and backgrounds; most are working at the intermediate or advanced level. Upon completion of the IEP, some of our learners will enroll in degree programs (undergraduate or graduate), and some will return to their home countries either to finish a university degree or begin or continue a career. Many have already performed some sort of community service within their own communities in countries such as Venezuela, Japan, or Korea.

CURRICULUM, TASKS, MATERIALS

Integrating Service Into the Language Curriculum

Before introducing service learning, we thought about where we could make improvements to the English as a second language (ESL) program. We noticed that our students often remain isolated, primarily speaking their native language with others from their home country. We wanted to provide them with authentic opportunities for real communication with a genuine purpose to practice their listening and speaking skills with native (and also nonnative) English speakers. Through this type of authentic community-based communication, "students have the chance to interact naturally, in 'real time,' to achieve a particular goal, which will be 'far more likely to lead to increased fluency and natural acquisition' than controlled exercises" (Willis, 1996, p. 18 as cited in Guariento & Morley, 2001). Finally, we wanted to encourage learners to venture off-campus and learn about U.S. culture while at the same time improve their English language skills in a real-world setting.

We began the project by introducing service learning into an advanced level multiskill ESL course. The class discussed the importance of service learning in their own countries and cultures, their past volunteer experience, and its value in the United States. The Ninety-Sixth Yearbook of the National Society for the Study of Education's book *Service Learning* (Schine, 1997) includes a chapter on "An International Perspective on Service-Learning," which gives an overview of service learning movements in a variety of countries in Europe, Africa, Asia, and Central America as well as Canada, England, and the United States. We used this resource in class to provide a good background for global discussions on service learning.

After these informed discussions, students filled out interest surveys (see Appendix A), and the instructor worked with individual learners to match each with an organization in the community needing volunteers. The survey asks students to explain their past experience with volunteering, what their interests are, and in what areas they may be interested in working. This will help give the instructor ideas of where the learners may enjoy volunteering as well as where their personal skills may best be used. With the instructor's guidance, students choose a site from a list of possible organizations and attend an orientation. In most cases, the instructor guides the students on how they should dress and what safety precautions they may need to take when they attend the orientation. Although many such issues are covered during their orientation, the instructor often needs to address these issues with individual students depending on their service site. For added support, instructors can accompany students to their volunteer sites the first time they go. Matching students' skills and interests with specific community services eager to have volunteers can be a time-consuming organizational task for the instructor, but the payoff in terms of student participation makes it time well spent.

We require that students volunteer 1 or 2 hours each week at their site and submit a reflective journal of their service-learning experiences to the instructor every other week. Near the end of the project, the learners prepare and present an oral presentation about their site and experiences, reflecting on what they learned about language, culture, and interacting with the community.

Ideas for Service Sites and Tips for Teachers

Many nonprofit agencies and some businesses welcome service volunteers. The following are some examples of service organizations with which to collaborate:

- nursing homes

- senior centers

- homeless shelters

- soup kitchens and food pantries

- hospitals

- rehabilitation centers

- museums

- early childhood centers

- education centers for children with special needs

- community agencies (Red Cross, Salvation Army)

- town agencies (parks, halls, gardens)

- teen centers

(Adapted from Rizzo & Brown, 2006)

After teaching service learning in several of our courses and collaborating with several agencies suggested above, we have developed the following tips for organizing service projects for ESL learners.

Prior Preparations Needed for the Service Project

- Visit your local college or university Web site to see if the campus has an office of service learning. Such offices offer a variety of resources to teachers and students to aid in developing service-learning projects, as well as lists of possible placement sites. Service-learning offices can assist students in setting up their own service-learning agencies.

- If such a service is not available, make contacts within your local university or college—such as the education department—to see if there are students willing to help with implementing a service-learning project. Some institutions require students to engage in a certain number of hours serving the community and helping instructors implement service experiences for their classes can fulfill such a requirement.

- If no such support is available, the instructor can provide the students with a list of contact information for possible organizations where they can serve.

Locating Agencies and Businesses for Service

- Look through the classified ads for organizations seeking volunteers.

- Look in the local phonebook for a list of social service agencies or volunteer opportunities (Wade, 1997).

- Check at your local public library, town hall, county health and welfare council, or local United Way for other opportunities (Wade, 1997).

- Go to your local Chamber of Commerce or organization of local businesses to find volunteer needs.

- Use service-learning clearinghouses to locate service sites and learn more about community service. Examples of two include: http://www .servicelearning.org/, administered by the Corporation for National and Community Service, and http://www.learnandserve.org/, both associated with the U.S. government's USA Freedom Corps.

- Compile a list of interested organizations and keep in contact with them so that you can contact them for future collaboration. Make sure to follow up with any agency or business that has hosted a student volunteer to thank them for their involvement. Keeping community connections positive means more success for future classes.

- Check out these additional informative service-learning Web sites: charityguide.org which is a directory of service-learning project ideas; rootsandshoots.org, a Web site founded by the Jane Goodall Institute, which connects youth from around the world in community service projects; and, finally, goodcharacter.com, a Web site geared toward K–12 teachers. It provides free teaching guides and service-learning project examples currently in use in classrooms.

In-Class Preparations for Service Encounters

- Teach students how to contact and communicate with the organizations so that they can set up their own service-learning partnership, if necessary. Role-playing the initial contact with the service organization in the classroom can be a great way to ease the students' anxiety and ensure that they communicate clearly and receive the information they need in order to begin.

- Teach active listening skills and appropriate questioning techniques to ensure that students can follow and remember directions at the service agency or business. Role play giving instructions and asking for clarification.

- If transportation or logistics are a problem, seek service-learning opportunities within the school or close by. Alternately, build into class activities planning for public transportation or cooperative carpooling.

Journaling as a Reflective Tool

We integrated journal writing into the service project to encourage the students to reflect on their experiences and learning. Journal entries were one way we could read and understand on an ongoing basis what the students were getting out of their service learning. Rhoads & Howard (1998) argue that including reading and writing about service experiences provide opportunities for reflection and growth. They suggest following three steps when reflecting on a service experience: (a) describe one's own role in the experience, (b) analyze the experience, and (c) describe the impact of the experience. Students used this framework as a model to organize their journal entries.

When reading the journals we focus mainly on our students' ideas, but we also encourage them to make their ideas and writing understandable to the reader. We use the rubric in Appendix B to assess the journals. This rubric is very flexible. Instructors can easily alter the categories according to the purpose they envision for the journal writing. Furthermore, if the service-learning activity is in a class with a primary focus on speaking, the instructor can ask students to submit audio journals rather than written ones.

REFLECTIONS

Before students start volunteering in the community, we have found that it is important to discuss what community service is and the value it has in American and other cultures. It is also important that students understand the goals behind the activity—to listen, speak, read, and write English at a higher proficiency level; to collaborate with community members for the benefit of others; and to reflect on their experiences through journal writing.

Service learning can easily be integrated into courses in numerous ways. For older and more advanced English speakers, the instructor may expect students to research and create their own volunteer partnerships with local organizations. Class time spent researching possible sites and role-playing the initial telephone and person-to-person contacts all serve to prepare the advanced learner for such roles. Instructors can vary the requirements on how often and how long students volunteer each week as well as the journal and presentation expectations, and teachers can pair students up or even take the class together to perform some community service, such as a river, beach, or park cleanup day.

Younger learners can also benefit from service learning. Teachers can incorporate service-learning opportunities for the whole class to participate in together. There are several categories of service-learning projects ideal for integrating into the K–12 curriculum to expand younger learners' experience with social justice issues, such as intergenerational concerns, environmental dilemmas, hunger and poverty, school as community, and animal treatment (Wade, 1997). When working with younger students, find one organization or project that the entire class can participate in as a group. Contact the school administration before beginning a service-learning project in the event that parental permissions are required. Send a letter to parents including the rationale for the project, special clothing requirements (as needed), and assignments that the students will complete (including optional assignments to get the family involved). Ask parents to be involved with the transportation and supervision, if possible. Parents can be a valuable resource in developing a serving-learning project to enhance students' success in schools (Wade, 1997), and the project work has the potential to connect families and their communities.

Beth Kozbial Ernst teaches in the ESL program at the University of Wisconsin–Eau Claire in the United States. She also serves as the ESL coordinator. Her interests include experiential learning, curriculum development, service learning, and mentoring preservice ESL teachers.

Megan Allen is an undergraduate student at the University of Wisconsin–Eau Claire. She is majoring in elementary education with minors in TESOL and Spanish. Upon graduating, she hopes to teach English to students in a Spanish-speaking country.

APPENDIX A: SERVICE-LEARNING SURVEY

Name: _____

Major: _____

E-mail address: _____

Previous volunteer experience: _____

_____

In what areas are you interested in volunteering? (Choose your top 3 choices with 1 being your first choice, 2 your second, and 3 an acceptable alternative)

___children	___education	___environment
___animals	___health care	___history
___senior citizens	___housing	___youth
___other: _____		

Available days and times: _____

_____

Goals for Service Learning: _____

_____

APPENDIX B: ASSESSMENT RUBRIC FOR SERVICE-LEARNING JOURNALS

Category	4	3	2	1	0
Content	Clearly describes experience at service-learning project site in detail	Describes experience at service-learning project site with some detail	Describes experience at service-learning project site with minimal details	Brief or vague description of experience at service-learning site	Illegible or otherwise unintelligible response (e.g., off-topic)
Analysis	Detailed description of 3 or more things observed/learned from the service-learning experience	Description of 2 or 3 things observed/learned from the service-learning experience	Brief descriptions of 2 things observed/learned from the service-learning experience	Brief description of one things observed/learned from the service-learning experience	Illegible or otherwise unintelligible response (e.g., no analysis)
Organization	The structure clearly establishes relationship between/among ideas/events	The structure establishes relationship between/among ideas/events	The structure is minimally comprehensible	The overall structure is incomplete or confusing	Unintelligible response (e.g., not prepared in journal format)
Grammar/Spelling	Writer makes few errors in grammar or spelling, which do not hinder the reader's ability to understand	Writer makes several errors in grammar and/or spelling	Writer makes numerous errors in grammar and/or spelling which may hinder the reader's comprehension	Writer makes many errors in grammar and/or spelling, which hinder greatly comprehension	Unintelligible response
Length	One or more pages	¾ of a page	About ½ page	About ¼ page	Less than ¼ of a page

CHAPTER 12

Creating a Technical Career ESL Program Through Community Partnerships

Gilda Rubio-Festa and Rebeca Fernández

The Technical Career Ladders (TCL) program at Central Piedmont Community College in Charlotte, North Carolina in the United States tracks program participants, enrollment, retention, goal completion, employment, and continued study. Although these variables are an important measure of program effectiveness, the stories students tell us about the changes in their lives as a result of obtaining high-demand skills and a credential are equally important measures of the TCL program's success.

The program creates a pathway through which adult English as a second language (ESL) students can enter curriculum certificate programs, prepare for entry-level work in a high-demand industry, set the groundwork for pursuing advanced job training in that industry, and ultimately, pursue a postsecondary degree. It challenges the idea that authenticity is a purely local, classroom-based tool used to prop up student motivation.

The TCL program is founded on the notion that authenticity extends beyond classroom activities into relationships and partnerships in real-world contexts and situations. By crossing the boundaries of our language departments into other instructional and administrative divisions of the community college and beyond (i.e., into the community itself), we facilitate students' transition out of ESL, elucidate the college process, and prepare them more fully for economic self-sufficiency and civic involvement.

In this chapter, we discuss what drives the TCL program and reflect on challenges and lessons learned when attempting to make the college experience relevant to our ESL population. Students understand that what goes on in the TCL classroom is truly authentic, not just in that it uses relevant, real-life tasks, but in its resolve to go a step further and deliver on the promise that these methods can truly diminish barriers and enhance adult immigrants' participation in the target society (Condelli, 2003).

CONTEXT

> When asked to report his experience with Technical Career Ladders, Edwin, a former student, proclaimed "This program changed my life." After graduation, he went to work for a utility company. A year later, he returned as a degree-seeking student to the community college to pursue further education. While in school, he worked part-time as a lab assistant in the electrical lab. He had the technical skills and the cultural competence to work effectively in the community.

The TCL program was developed in collaboration with local industry, disciplines at our community college, and the college's adult ESL program. The program began in late 2005 in response to the workforce needs of the community. During that time, Charlotte, an urban center in the Carolinas, had a thriving economy strongly driven by its financial industry, the second largest in the United States. In the past decade, the city's total population has grown by 20%. Its Hispanic immigrant population expanded by 600%, and unemployment hovered around 4%. At the end of 2008, despite an 8.3% unemployment rate due to the global recession, TCL continued to grow, with increasing numbers of students enrolling and additional certificate areas participating in the program.

The major provider for ESL services in Charlotte is Central Piedmont Community College (CPCC). It has six campus locations serving approximately 70,000 students a year and offers adult basic skills, degree programs, diploma and certificate programs, and corporate and continuing education programs. On average, the adult ESL program serves over 4,000 students a year from a range of educational backgrounds and with skills in various occupations or training in professional careers. Our students generally are employed and indicate that they are studying English to get a job, get a better job, or be able to participate in their community. Reasons for dropping out of programs or not attending include changing work schedules, parenting responsibilities, and lack of reliable transportation. Like most community colleges, CPCC has an open-entry admission policy and affordable tuition.

The demographic shift of the past decade caught CPCC and other community colleges across the state by surprise, and most were unprepared to meet the needs of a population that historically had not lived in this region. The adult ESL program responded to ESL immigrant needs by expanding its offerings to include life and work skills curricula with special courses devoted to civics themes. TCL courses are an extension of these new offerings for advanced-level students setting their sights beyond the adult ESL program. In addition, we offer a distance-learning component that allows students to take video or Web-based courses without having to commit to a fixed class schedule. In order to develop courses and specific curricula that are relevant to students' evolving needs, our program requires skilled professional ESL instructors. With the recent influx in our immigrant population, CPCC faces a critical shortage of qualified English to speakers of other languages (ESOL) instructors. We have addressed this shortage by continually searching for grant funding to support highly qualified full-time instructors.

CURRICULUM, TASKS, MATERIALS

We developed the TCL program by drawing on research and practices from adult learning theories, workforce development, corpus linguistics, and content-based instruction to meet the special challenges adult ESL learners encounter within and beyond the classroom. Educators need to draw on adult ESL students' "nonacademic assets," the personal strengths and qualities that allow immigrants to survive in their newly adopted country (De Maria, 2007, p. 18). We need to demystify the process of going to college and create paths that make accommodations for adult learners to help them meet their educational goals. For many English language learners, the connection between education and jobs is either tenuous or inaccessible, but the TCL model establishes an infrastructure that allows students to make connections among education, employment, and economic advancement (Crandall & Sheppard, 2004).

The TCL program at CPCC is based on a career pathways model that creates a bridge from basic skills programs to education programs in high-demand industries (Alssid et al., 2003). The program assists English language learners' transition from the adult ESL program into curriculum programs by giving students the option of pursuing certificates in one of six technical careers:

1. Applied Electrical Technology (Basic Machining Certificate)

2. Construction Technology (Fast-Track Carpentry Certificate)

3. Applied Technology (Print Shop Certificate)

4. Engineering Technology (Basic Machining Certificate)

5. Motor Sports Technology (Automotive Technology Certificate)

6. Office Systems Technology (Basic Office Skills Certificate)

In a period of 16–24 weeks, students take 12 credits of courses in a high-demand technical area, a work readiness course, and a linked ESL support course. The articulation between basic skills and the participating technology departments allow students to follow a linear progression leading to a certificate (see Hughes & Karp, 2006) that includes multiple entry points depending on the student's academic skills, language proficiency, and individual goals. The TCL program operates around four major components that pave the way to career advancement: (a) outreach and recruitment, (b) assessment and registration, (c) academic support–curriculum, and 4) follow up.

Outreach and Recruitment

When we launched the TCL program, we partnered with our college's marketing department to create a media campaign to generate interest in the program. We created a special TCL Web site (http://www1.cpcc.edu/esl/career-ladders/technical-career-ladders-for-ells), and we offered live informational sessions throughout the college and in the community. In partnership with our workforce development board, we set up a desk with weekly office hours at the local JobLink Career Center, a U.S. Department of Commerce-sponsored career planning, training, and placement service located in many states. The TCL program is further promoted through local media outlets, including radio shows, the local English language newspaper, and Latino newspapers.

Assessment and Registration

Students who express interest in the program after the information sessions are referred to the assessment and registration process. We developed an ESL-specific assessment protocol in collaboration with discipline area partners in the college that each student completes before entering the program. The protocol includes a standardized reading assessment, an informal writing sample scored holistically by ESL instructors, an educational background questionnaire, and an interview with the technical career area department chair. We defer to the department chair for final decisions on acceptance. To date, all students who have been recommended by the adult ESL program have been accepted. Students who do not meet the screening requirements of the program are directed to other adult ESL course options appropriate to their level. In general, low reading scores are the primary reason why interested students do not immediately enter certificate programs. To help boost these students' reading scores and language skills, we designed a content-based preparation course to provide an orientation to technical careers while focusing on improving students' language and academic skills.

Cooperation with our discipline partners diminishes educational barriers as we assist students through the registration process and in locating financial support from a private community donor, which provides tuition, books, and materials for each participant. This fund, initially established for any student applying for a certificate program in any technical area at the community college, has now been expanded to include funding specifically designated for our learners.

Academic Support—Authentic Curriculum

The notion that adult learners need to be able to connect learning to experience is well documented (Condelli, 2003). Education cannot be a purely abstract academic endeavor when one is sacrificing personal time and family obligations and postponing financial gain in order to pursue it; it must be authentic, grounded in the world outside of the language classroom, and it must produce visible results. In order to be effective, support programs must also address the educational and intrapersonal barriers that limit economic advancement for new immigrants. The TCL curriculum, regardless of the training area, includes such considerations.

The TCL curriculum is guided by an English for specific purposes (ESP) approach, which is founded on the theory that the learner needs drive curriculum development. Learner need is seen as "the reason for which the student is learning English" and provides the primary justification for employing a variety of methods (Dudley-Evans & St. John, 1998, p. 3). In our case, students in TCL learn English in order to succeed in certificate courses, pass licensure exams, obtain a job, or pursue further education. The needs-based activities that help them accomplish these goals use topics or themes from the certificate area as the vehicle for developing both micro-level (e.g., syntax, semantics, lexis), and macro-level language skills (e.g., identifying main idea, analyzing organizational structure, evaluating arguments; Dudley-Evans & St. John, 1998).

In developing TCL language support courses, we began by analyzing the curriculum and content courses. A designated full-time ESL instructor was released from her normal teaching load to work on development of the courses. The funding to support this program required that certificate programs be offered exclusively in high-demand industries. Initially, we contacted departments at CPCC to discuss the possibility of collaboration. Now, programs are calling us to discuss how they can be included in the TCL program.

The curriculum development process begins with a meeting between the certificate course faculty from CPCC departments and the ESL instructor and developer (see Figure 1). In accordance with the standard ESP needs assessment process, we ask faculty to identify dominant themes that characterize their field. They also share syllabi, written assignments, and core texts. The curriculum developer observes two types of learning situations in the certificate programs, usually a lab and a lecture session, in order to form hypotheses about the language demands for the adult English language learner. These hypotheses guide the draft of an initial curriculum plan, including the syllabus for the support courses. The initial plan provides a roadmap for instructors who are asked to pilot, with an open mind, and continually modify the course to fit the specific needs of the student cohort in any given term. Teachers are also asked to document and, if possible, keep a journal about their experience working with the curriculum plan, certificate area faculty, and adult ESL students. The teacher's comments and modifications to the course serve as the basis for further revisions. Each time the course is taught, therefore, it is informed by an accumulation of data and experiences from its previous incarnations.

The curriculum plan includes skills-based projects focusing on authentic tasks that simulate activities or skills students are required to demonstrate in the certificate program. Corpus-based activities may be developed from materials provided

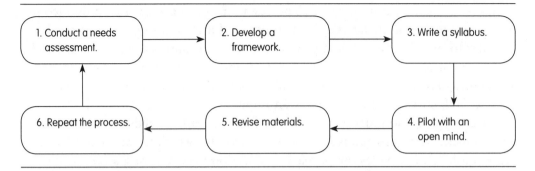

Figure 1. Basic Components of the Technical Career Ladders Curriculum Development Process

by certificate faculty that allow students to analyze language structures in the context of their training area (O'Keefe et al., 2007). We also introduce personal corpus-based analysis as an effective strategy for approaching unfamiliar language when reading and working through the course texts (Cobb, 1999).

Computer skills and learning independently through online course delivery is also an essential practice that enhances the authentic nature of TCL courses. Teacher-generated online activities have been most effective in increasing precious learning time for adult learners (Crandall, 2007). The learning modules for the online component include an introduction to computers, learning skills and strategies, reading comprehension and listening skills, improving writing and language structures, and an introduction to the certificate course itself. Using a content-based approach, material from the certificate area is woven into discussion forums, multiple-choice tests, journal assignments, grammar or discrete language skills exercises, and Internet references to the field (see the Appendix for a sample of materials for the electricians group). Providing many materials online has facilitated flexibility and materials access to our learners, who have many demands on their time.

Curriculum development in TCL courses factors in the importance of giving adult ESL students "a chance to practice new behaviors in a non-threatening environment to enhance their intercultural sensitivity and coping skills" (Bhagat, 1999, p. 362). The curriculum draws from various language teaching methods and approaches as it works to balance skill building, ESP, and content-based activities with reflective critical inquiry tasks. For some students, these tasks result in the realization that reaching their goals may take longer than planned; for others, it means that dreams they might have otherwise dismissed are suddenly now within their reach. The stakes involved in the program and its direct implications for students' lives outside of the classroom often forces them to battle with a host of intrapersonal issues rooted in fear and yearning for change. Because the English language instructor does not pass or fail students, teacher and students are able to confront personal and academic concerns in the safe space of the

English language classroom. The willingness to take on a variety of roles and the commitment to see students through the entire certificate process (Sifakis, 2003) is thus paramount when selecting teachers for TCL courses.

Follow-Up

A graduation ceremony is organized to recognize student accomplishments, and in some content certificate programs, students also attend a job fair organized specifically for technical career occupations. An exit interview is conducted to track the post-training destination of graduates. This level of close guidance serves to make educational opportunities and processes more transparent to students. The major success of the program is measured one student at a time. We end the semester with the ceremony where community leaders and senior-level college administrators are invited to participate. A small reception follows for students and their families. These students are now on their way to realizing their career paths.

REFLECTIONS

As ESL learners try to access and navigate our educational institutions, existing administrative structures and fragmented registration procedures present many barriers for them. Content instructors who are not trained in working with English language learners and curriculum design appropriate to learner's lives and realities further contribute to the obstacles learners face in accessing and achieving academic success (Scribner, 1999). ESL learners frequently turn to an ESOL practitioner to serve as their first point of contact for help in navigating the system.

Many ESL instructors serve as cultural brokers, social workers, academic tutors, language interpreters, and advocates (Szelényi & Chang, 2002) as we try to make education as accessible to ESL learners as it is for the mainstream community. Given the large numbers of immigrant students entering the community college system and the vast needs they present, the responsibility for preparing our ESL students in educational institutions should now become the shared commitment of all.

One of the key components of the TCL is the community approach to working together to provide a program that holds learners, college administrators, faculty, staff, receiving employers, and advocacy organizations accountable for equitable access to educational opportunities, and ultimately, success in meeting learners' educational goals. A strategy we use in garnering this support is to work with faculty, staff, and administrators who are already aware of English language learners' special needs and have an interest in addressing them. Student support services and other service providers have been helpful, first by coming to an understanding of needs, mission, and availability of resources and then by collaborating to develop solutions sensitive to these students. We have also established administrative support by informing colleagues through presentations, reports, and meetings on the current social, economic, and political events that impact our learners' lives and how they relate to our college mission and strategic plan. As Kasarda and Johnson (2006) suggest, we extend our influence in the community by serving on community committees, attending presentations, and using our personal social networks to keep English language learner contributions to the community in the forefront.

Our program came to fruition through (a) our commitment to reflective teaching practices, (b) an institution that supports innovation and excellence in workforce development, and (c) our personal desire to make an impact on immigrants' lives in our region. Our biggest challenge remains securing continued funding for scholarships and support for permanent full-time staff. We have been diligent in connecting our work to other college initiatives so we can be in a position to benefit from internal funding opportunities. Another challenge is establishing mentoring opportunities with employers. Recruitment and outreach require tremendous resources and expertise, but effective recruitment and ongoing support are essential to ensure the educational and occupational success of recently arrived immigrants.

Gilda Rubio-Festa, director of international community and outreach at Central Piedmont Community College, oversees program planning and curriculum development of the adult ESL program. She received her master's in TESOL from Teachers College, Columbia University, New York in the United States and taught ESL in the New York community college system.

Rebeca Fernandez, instructor and curriculum developer at Central Piedmont Community College, develops and trains instructors on content-based and English for specific purposes curriculum materials for the adult ESL program. Fernandez trained at University of California-Los Angeles in the TESL and applied linguistics program and is currently working on completing an EdD from the Harvard Graduate School of Education.

APPENDIX: ESP MATERIALS FOR ELECTRICIANS

Drawing on the input from Electrical instructors, the support course focused on underlying skills needed to succeed by developing authentic tasks (Ellis, 2003). One of the first skills students needed was to become familiar with the use of abbreviations and acronyms while reading diagrams and charts. Also, ESL students needed practice with pronunciation and sound/symbol relationships. Because this was the first college-level course for many of the students, tasks were developed to practice direct and indirect language learning strategies (Oxford, 1990).

Word Toolbox Group Project

Team Work Plan

Groups will develop a vocabulary journal for electrical occupational vocabulary and abbreviations, which can be used as an on-the-job resource or study guide for future electrical courses.

Resources

- Electrical Wiring Commercial (1999)—Unit 14: Lamps for Lighting

- Electricity glossary at http://www.nooutage.com/glossary.htm

- Google search engine at http://www.google.com

- Electricity vocabulary at http://www.bbc.co.uk/skillswise/words/vocabulary/wordsforwork/electrics/index.shtml

- Free online dictionary at http://dictionary.reference.com/

Skills Focus

- searching the Internet

- categorizing vocabulary

- listing and understanding abbreviations

- working in a team to complete a project

- reading and taking notes

- labeling a diagram

Directions for the Project

1. In a group: Label the following picture of the lamp using these words: shade, cord, base and describe how the lamp operates.

shade, cord, base

2. Individually: Look at **Unit 14—Lighting Terminology**. Complete the chart with the correct abbreviations.

Lighting Terminology	Abbreviation
Candela	
Lumen	
Color rendering index	
Lumen per watt	
Kekvin	

3. In a group:

1. Discuss

   a. Do you need to understand all of the electrical vocabulary used in the textbook or do you need to know key words?

   b. How do you know which vocabulary words are key?

   c. Do you need to know how to spell and pronounce key electrical vocabulary?

   d. What are the best ways to learn key vocabulary?

   e. What resources can you use to help you understand key vocabulary?

2. Skim **Unit 14: Lamps for Lighting** and choose five electrical vocabulary words or phrases your group considers to be important to the occupation.

   a. Do a Google search to see how these words are used.

      1) Go to http://www.google.com

      2) Put the word in " . . . " quotations in the search box.

      3) Select two or three sites and skim for the word.

      4) Notice how it is used.

   b. Put these words in your vocabulary journal. Your group can design your journal. An example follows.

Example: *Vocabulary Journal*

Unit Title: Lamps and Lighting				
Word/phrase	**Description/ operation**	**Abbreviation/ units**	**Visual**	**Noticing the word in context (Google search)**
1. *Incandescent lamp*	*Type of lamp used in commercial buildings*	*Lumen (lm) Watts (w) Voltage (volts)*		*Incandescence Incandescent bulb*
2.				
3.				

CHAPTER 13

Climate Change and Other Hot Topics on Campus: Project-Based Learning

Marianne Stipe and Lora Yasen

Discussion of global climate change is at the forefront of hot topics on U.S. college campuses, in the community, and around the world. This common concern can provide the content for integrating real-world issues into the curriculum of English language classes. Our chapter details project-based learning involving a group of Japanese university students studying on a U.S. college campus discussing important environmental issues with their peers and experts in the community. English as a second language (ESL) student goals while in the United States often include finding opportunities on campus and in the community to converse in English with native speakers. However, some seem hesitant to seek out these opportunities on their own and end up limiting themselves to learning from the textbook and classroom communication exercises orchestrated by their instructors. They often leave their study abroad program without taking full advantage of the opportunities around them for authentic language experiences. Project-based learning focusing on topics of world concern is one way to draw students out of the classroom and into the wider community.

CONTEXT

The Environment as Project

At Tokyo International University of America (TIUA), in Salem, Oregon, in the United States, we search for ways to go beyond the textbook—both in and out of the classroom—to provide structured and unstructured authentic communication opportunities for our students. For this project we integrated content and language with two shared groups of students in listening/speaking and reading/writing courses (15 hours of weekly instruction combined). The language level of these study abroad students from Tokyo International University, Japan, ranged from low-intermediate to low-advanced. We used English for speakers of other languages (ESOL) textbooks with chapters on the environment, which coincided with a planned regional sustainability conference hosted by our U.S. affiliate (Willamette University). Our students could participate in this regional conference by giving poster presentations on sustainability. The posters were one product in our project, with the following assignments as stepping stones toward poster presentations: (a) creating definitions, (b) preparing reactions to cartoons, (c) participating in a cartoon carousel, (d) conducting Internet research, (e) conducting community interviews, (f) preparing the poster, and finally, (g) the capstone, presenting their posters in the university-sponsored regional conference.

This project required close collaboration between instructors to facilitate schedule changes and accommodate guest speakers and other group activities. Through daily discussions, instructors enriched the curriculum and created opportunities that would not be possible in single classes. This integration of the curriculum gave the students opportunities to increase their language skills in preparation of the project. We started planning from the end product and worked backward to map out a 3-week thematic unit. We decided on sections for the posters and student research by dividing environmental sustainability into the four different themes designed for the regional conference: education, environment, equity, and economics.

We prepared a series of tasks for students utilizing a scaffolding technique that involved practicing language skills we had already covered in classes as well as covering new skills to be developed both before and during the project. Each project step included reading/writing and listening/speaking assignments to meet our curricular goals. Although the assignments were structured and the communication opportunities with native speakers were arranged, the outcomes and resulting learning were left open ended. Students were ultimately responsible for the information gathering, direction of research, group dynamics, synthesis of concepts, conclusions, and presentation of results in their poster presentations. Stepping out of the traditional language textbook and classroom engaged our students in authentic language, communication, and content learning.

Project-Based Learning

Project-based learning (PBL) is an interdisciplinary, student-centered approach to teaching focused around student-generated projects. According to Thomas (2000, pp. 3–4):

1. Projects should be central to the curriculum.

2. Projects should focus on a driving question (Blumenthal et al., 1991) or an ill-defined problem (Stepien & Gallagher, 1993). Students complete activities that facilitate discovery of questions and answers.

3. Projects require students to do constructive investigation, gaining new knowledge and skills while pursuing answers.

4. Projects are student-driven. PBL gives students more autonomy, choice, and responsibility than traditional classroom experiences.

5. Projects must be realistic and authentic.

Our unit on sustainability encompassed all five criteria. First, it was central to the curriculum and related to chapters on the environment in our textbooks. The driving question was: How are Japanese and American views on sustainability similar or different? Students practiced language skills and gained content knowledge as they worked through assignments to investigate answers to this overarching question. The culmination of the project was to present the findings in an authentic situation: the regional conference on sustainability.

CURRICULUM, TASKS, AND MATERIALS

The following steps were built into our project-based curriculum focused on environmental sustainability. By keeping the end goal of the poster presentations in mind, students worked toward professionalizing their language for presentations, which required expertise in both oral and written skills. The regional conference made the experience especially meaningful and authentic.

Definition Practice Assignment

We began project work with a worksheet—not a lecture. Students were asked to find definitions of sustainability from different sources. Students worked to "discover" definitions of sustainability in pairs, in groups, and as individuals both in and outside of the classroom. It would have been faster for us to simply write a definition of sustainability on the blackboard and ask the students to memorize it for the next vocabulary quiz, but perhaps students would not have completely understood the concept nor remembered it for long. In PBL, when students are asked to discover information on their own, they are more likely to learn concepts thoroughly, remember the information, and have a vested interest in the content as well as the learning process (Blumenfeld, 1991).

For our project, students asked both Japanese and Americans for their definitions of sustainability (see sample instructions for students in Appendix A). While one student asked questions, a second took notes. For Japanese definitions, students interviewed fellow students and Japanese staff members. American tutors, roommates, university staff members, and high school students also provided definitions. Students in a local high school Japanese language class were part of our learning community, and our students returned from one high school visit with a variety of definitions. They found that some of the high school students did not know what *sustainability* meant, and they also discovered that differences in definitions existed not only between but within cultures.

For literacy development, students practiced using dictionaries and the Internet to find definitions. Dictionary work included applying grammar skills in finding parts of speech and word forms. In many cases, students had to infer meaning based on the definition of *sustain* since dictionaries did not always include *sustainability.* Critical thinking skills were involved in finding both the dictionary and the Internet definitions as students realized that online definitions differed depending on the focus or bias of the Web site. For example, some definitions focused on the environment while others focused on people, or both. Students talked about these differences in small groups and developed conclusions based on their own research. Together they wrote a paraphrase of an Internet definition. Paraphrasing is difficult, but through explicit instruction and peer practice, students applied this essential academic writing skill.

Cartoon Reaction Assignment

Reading about editorial cartoon techniques, such as the use of symbols and irony, and analyzing several cartoons together with the class helped students' understanding of the analysis process. We discussed cultural differences, and then students wrote a successful interpretative analysis of one of the cartoons for homework. The second phase of the assignment had students elicit reactions from five Japanese and five Americans to a Japanese editorial cartoon on sustainability (with English captions) from the High Moon Cartoon Collection (Tatsuki, 2003–2008).

To prepare for interviews, students learned how to analyze editorial cartoons by comparing two on climate change (one Japanese and one American), and then wrote an interpretive paper analyzing one. Beginning with a simple comparison and then moving to a more detailed study of cartoons provided a scaffold for student learning. After completing the analysis assignment, the students were ready to elicit reactions and discuss cartoons with Japanese and American community members. These informal interviews were conducted in pairs with one student asking questions and the other taking notes. Afterward, in class, the students worked together to write a compare and contrast essay on the reactions of American and Japanese informants to the cartoon.

Cartoon Carousel Assignment

For more speaking practice, students were given new cartoons on climate change to study individually. After completing an initial analysis, each student prepared a short speech to explain the themes and symbols in the cartoon. Students and instructors listened to explanations in a carousel format with each student repeating the explanation several times and answering questions to small groups of students who rotated through the carousel. This timed, in-class activity is similar to a poster carousel discussed in a study by Lynch and Maclean (2001) in which they found immediate task repetition led students to change and improve their spoken English. Our students did not perceive the activity as repetitious or boring because they were explaining something of interest, and they had a different audience to interact with each time. The repetition seemed natural because they were discussing a topic they understood. In pairs, students then wrote essays highlighting features of their cartoons using descriptive language and comparative language.

Internet Research Assignment

Students conducted Internet research on environmental sustainability focusing on one of the conference areas assigned: education, equity, environment, or economics. Internet research provided background information and highlighted relevant terminology. Students used a worksheet to analyze the sources for reliability, expertise, bias, opinion, and fact (see Appendix B for a sample worksheet). Through their research, students discovered subtopics such as alternative fuel sources, sustainable agriculture, and glass recycling. Next, students discussed in small groups what Japan is doing in regard to their topic, what our university is doing, and what the U.S. community (city and state) is doing to develop sustainable solutions to environmental problems.

Turning the learning process over to the students, as we did with this assignment, involved some risks. Some groups were very capable and ready to choose topics and do research independently. Others had disagreements among members on what topics were relevant or significant. Extra time was often needed to work through such issues within the groups. The assignment could have been adapted and specific topics assigned for research to make things progress more smoothly, but it would not have been as meaningful to the students, who were in the process of discovering their own ideas and appropriate resources. Giving up some time and efficiency was worth the increase in effective student-centered learning through negotiated learning.

Community Interview Assignment

As part of the listening/speaking class, students were asked to interview a member of the community to get information about their topics. This activity reinforced the language skills we were working on in the class while giving the students the opportunity to learn about their topic in an authentic situation. Although we set up the interviews, the students were responsible for generating the questions and taking notes on the conversations. This assignment allowed us to create a dynamic learning community in our classrooms. Dynamic learning communities allow a variety of positive outcomes such as the ability to

- adapt a project topic to local needs

- develop projects over time, to cross traditional content areas

- allow a variety of viewpoints

- involve expert community members in the learning process

(Wilson & Ryder, n.d.)

We involved experts in the field of sustainability and climate change to broaden our learning community by arranging for people from the university, governmental agencies, and private business to meet with the students to answer questions specific to each group's topic. For example, an engineer provided information about alternative fuels, a facilities manager discussed recycling and green buildings, and a business owner answered questions about electric cars. Some of these interviews occurred in the classroom; others were conducted in the field.

Japanese students may have particular problems conducting interviews with native speakers, such as deferring to the group member with the highest language skills or the senior member of the group, which means fewer opportunities for the rest of the group to participate. Japanese students often ask indirect questions because they want to be polite, and they may miss cues such as when to enter into the conversation or when to interrupt with a comment, a new question, or a clarification. With formal interviews, students may not understand some answers because of anxiety about asking the next question rather than listening to the speaker. For these reasons, we added preparation steps to our interview assignment to include the following language practice: (a) polite modals for questioning; (b) phrases and strategies to seek for clarification or repetition, to interrupt, paraphrase, and check for understanding; (c) question narrowing from general to specific; and (d) strategies for getting the intended response.

To review polite modals, students generated a list with sample phrases to begin questions, such as, "Could you tell me . . . ?" and, "Would you mind explaining . . . ?" Our students are very familiar with English grammar, so this aspect of our lesson tapped into their prior knowledge. Earlier in the course, we had practiced language for clarification, repetition, interrupting, paraphrasing, and checking for understanding, and the interview task promoted review and consolidation of these pragmatic functions. The formal interview was an opportunity to experience genuine communication with community members. Students learned how to take a question and rewrite it several times to make it more specific. They generated sample interview questions and worked in groups to predict the kinds of responses they might hear. Another new skill for our students was using interview strategies to elicit the intended response (see Appendix C for a model).

After preparation activities, students studied guidelines for completing the community interview assignment (see Appendix D). This process prepared them for the interview and note-taking. Later, students compared notes to make sure all the pertinent information was included, and then they prepared written summaries.

In both the cartoon carousel and the community interview activities, we utilized "successive cycles of performance" (Lynch & Maclean, 2001, p. 159), which is defined as "recycling" the same material several times in immediate repeated presentations. Each performance cycle may be slightly different as presenters modify their speech based on audience feedback. Thus the speaker becomes more comprehensive and accurate with the content and linguistic patterns. (See Figure 1 for our cycle.) In the carousel, explanations were repeated several times to different listeners and in the interview, questions were repeated and refined. Repetition of this sort helped our students develop the necessary confidence to conduct interviews effectively.

Capstone: Poster Presentation

Prior to the sustainability unit, we had modeled poster presentations on a number of different topics, so this was a familiar mode of presentation for our learners. Groups of students circulated around the room while we presented posters with short explanations, and we encouraged students to ask questions and make comments. This experience simulated their final assignment: the poster session to be presented at the regional conference. The students saw how native speakers

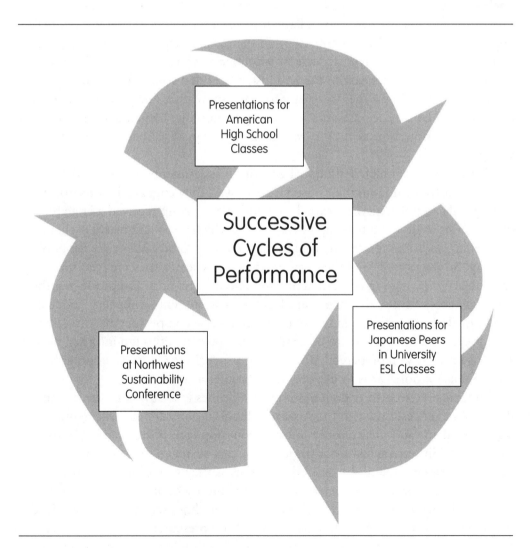

Figure 1. Curriculum Integration of Presentation Skills

of English improved their dialogue with each repetition. They also saw how presenters handled questions, incorporated answers from previous questions, and interacted with their audience. They observed how the audience moves around and that talk is generally back and forth during a poster presentation.

By the final week of the unit, groups had collected the following items for their posters:

1. definitions of sustainability from Japanese and American viewpoints

2. cartoon reactions from both Japanese and American viewpoints

3. summaries of interviews with experts in the field on sustainability

4. detailed information on sustainability from Internet research

Each writing assignment was typed into Microsoft Publisher using the Quick Publications template, which has a large font size and is customarily used in making posters or signs. The students typed in their assignments and added graphics and borders. After several drafts, students printed the pages in color. The desktop publishing software was easy to use and instantly added color, design, and a professional look. The pages were easy to read and ready to be pasted on a poster board for the conference presentation. Using technology helped make the knowledge construction process clearer by organizing the materials visually (Brown & Campione, 1996).

The students completed a number of writing assignments, so they had to decide what to include on their poster. In this way, they engaged in selection and editing skills to pull together textual elements. Each group received a large piece of newsprint to design a mockup of the poster, which peers and teachers checked for spelling and other errors to ensure that the final product was ready for public viewing. Students explained their plan to the class. Clearly, they enjoyed spending time on artwork, adding additional pictures and information, and producing the posters collaboratively, all while using English. The students generally produced a high quality end product and were proud of their accomplishments. Students then prepared a brief speech to present with the poster. Although informal, poster sessions must be well prepared. After writing a speech, students listed only the main points on note cards to use during the conference.

Students practiced their presentations many times in a carousel format with different audiences, first with the American high school students. At the high school, students and their teachers moved from poster to poster, talking both formally and informally with our students. By this we mean that students not only gave their presentation and answered questions as they would do at a conference, but they also engaged in conversations with the high school students about how they could improve the presentation. The American high school guests provided useful feedback to help our students improve their presentations. Comments like, "You need to look at the audience more," or, "Don't talk so fast" were given in a very nonthreatening way as these students were friends and partners in language exchange. Each group of our students gave the presentation several more times in class for more practice and feedback.

The final culminating activity required each group to give the poster presentation in a public forum. In 2006, we participated in the Northwest Sustainability Conference, "Creating Synergies: Community, University and Business." By the time our students presented at this conference (see Figure 2), they could use notes appropriately, maintain eye contact with the audience, and use the visual aid (their poster) well. Groups repeated their poster presentations several times during the 2-hour poster session and answered questions as the conference attendees from campus and around the northwest rotated around the room. Overall, the students were quite polished speakers for their first experience giving poster presentations at a real conference.

REFLECTIONS

Thomas (2000) states that PBL enhances the quality of learning and leads to higher levels of cognitive development. We found this to be true with our ESL students. They were actively engaged and vested in their projects. They displayed

Figure 2. TIUA Students Present a Poster at the 2006 Northwest Sustainability Conference

a high degree of ownership and were very motivated. The integrated curriculum allowed students to improve English skills, whereas the group work created an opportunity for student collaboration and community interaction. The project also made it possible to better meet the needs of a wide variety of skill levels and learning styles.

Students appeared to make gains in communication and task management. We feel that this project on climate change and sustainability was successful because often hesitant Japanese students demonstrated comfort conversing at length with native English speakers. Studying global issues provided content knowledge, and successive cycles of performance allowed students to gain confidence and language skills.

Project-based learning can be used in other courses and with other topics. The *Project Based Planning Form* from the Buck Institute of Education (n.d.) illustrates how to begin with the end project in mind and work backward to plan all the tasks students need to master. The carousel presentation format that we used can be integrated into almost any course. Our colleagues have used the idea of a carousel poster presentation in several different classes by having students prepare a poster or slide presentation related to a topic in class. Students work individually or in pairs or teams. They set up the posters or computers around a large room and invite guests to move around the room listening to the brief presentations and looking at each other's work. It is an interesting and quick way to see student products and allow speaking and presentation practice while highlighting student design and technology skills. PBL allows us to extend the curriculum beyond the textbook and provide authentic communication experiences for our students.

Marianne Stipe is an assistant professor of ESL at Tokyo International University of America, Salem, Oregon, in the United States. She teaches listening and speaking, grammar, advanced English, applied English for content courses, and TOEIC preparation classes.

Lora Yasen is an associate professor of ESL at Tokyo International University. She teaches reading and writing, advanced English, applied English for content courses, and business English classes.

APPENDIX A: STUDENT INSTRUCTIONS FOR DEFINITIONS TASKS

For Listening/Speaking Class

1. With a partner, ask two Japanese people and two Americans for their definitions of the word *sustainability*. Be sure to write your definitions

as quotations. Ask the speaker if it is OK for you to use their name and definition in your poster presentation.

2. Share the definitions with your group and together choose two favorites that you could include on your poster.

3. Type the definitions in software such as Microsoft Publisher Quick Publications (Microsoft Office, 2003). Use a large font so it will be easy to read on your poster from a distance.

For Reading/Writing Class

1. Look up the definition of sustainability in an English–English dictionary. Copy the definition exactly using quotations and a reference.

2. Find three definitions for sustainability on the Internet. (Wikipedia is a good place to begin.) Copy the definitions exactly using quotations and a reference.

3. In groups, choose one definition and write a paraphrase of it together. Be sure to give a reference.

4. Consider all of the definitions and write a definition of sustainability in your own words.

5. Share all of your definitions with your group and together choose several that you could include on your poster.

6. Type the definitions in software such as Microsoft Publisher Quick Publications (Microsoft Office, 2003). Use a large font so it will be easy to read on your poster from a distance. You may include a colorful border around your definition also.

APPENDIX B: EVALUATING INTERNET SOURCES

Directions: Make a check if the following information is given or can be decided about the Web site.	☑
Author information: (Reliable sources usually provide more author information.)	
Name	
Job title/education/experience	
Organization name	
Address/telephone number	
E-mail address	

Web site type: (URL address can indicate Web site source and purpose.)	
Educational: .edu	
Commercial: .com	
Government: .gov	
Personal: ~ name	
Other	
Web site purpose: (Some Web sites include more opinions than facts.)	
Educational	
Informational	
Commercial	
Persuasive	
Personal	
Entertainment	
References and dates: (Reliable sources usually provide more information.)	
Links to other Web sites	
List of references	
Date published/copyright date	
Last date updated	
Quality of information: (Reliable sources usually provide more examples, evidence, and unbiased viewpoints.)	
Analysis, explanation, or discussion of information	
Facts, statistics, graphs, tables, reviews, or reports	
Quotes, paraphrase, or summary from expert sources	
Objective viewpoint (no bias)	
Subjective viewpoint (opinions or biased information)	
My evaluation:	
This is a credible Web site.	
This is not a credible Web site.	

APPENDIX C: INTERVIEWING AN EXPERT ON ENVIRONMENTAL SUSTAINABILITY

Read the interview between a student and an expert on alternative fuel sources and answer the questions below.

Student: Can you tell me about the different kinds of fuels being used in Oregon?

Expert: There are many different fuels used in Oregon, from fossil fuels to hydropower to wind power. Would you like to know about all of them?

Student: Let me be more specific. I am interested in alternative energy sources, those that do not cause global warming. Could you talk about those?

Expert: Sure. First, hydropower is very important in Oregon. We have many dams on rivers to generate electricity.

Student: Pardon me, but could you explain the word, "dam"? I don't understand what that is.

Expert: Of course. A dam is a structure that is built across a river to stop the flow of water. Water is let through a small opening which makes the force of the flow stronger. This force runs turbines which make electricity. Is that clear?

Student: Yes, thank you. How much of Oregon's electricity comes from hydropower?

Expert: About 38%, but we also send lots of power to California.

Student: Are there other types of fuels?

Expert: I'm sorry? Do you mean other alternative energy sources?

Student: Yes, other sources of energy.

Expert: Yes, Oregon uses energy that comes from the sun, solar power and energy that comes from the wind, wind power.

Student: Thank you.

Language Questions:

1. What phrase does the student use to show he will narrow down the question? What other phrases could he or she have used?

2. What words does the student use to ask for clarification or to interrupt? What other words could he or she have used?

3. Circle the phrases used to check for understanding.

4. What does the expert say to paraphrase the question and make it more specific?

5. What words are used to make the questions polite?

APPENDIX D: INTERVIEW A COMMUNITY EXPERT

Follow these steps to complete this assignment:

1. Prepare your interview questions. Include questions from each group member. Explain what type of answer you expect for each question. For example, is the answer a statistic? Give a first draft of your questions with answer types to your instructor for feedback.

2. Practice interviewing several partners in class. Be ready to explain the questions in more detail or paraphrase them. You should also be able to provide sample answers. Take brief notes and report back to your group some of the responses you noted.

3. Practice interviewing your instructor. Take notes on the answers. Write down only key words and main ideas—do not try to write down the answers word for word; this is not a dictation exercise.

4. Use a phrase of clarification or repetition if you do not understand an answer.

5. Did you notice any difficulties with your questions and answers? If so, change the questions and check them with your instructor.

6. Interview the expert assigned by your instructor. One student should ask a question while others take notes. Note taking is an important skill and practice will help in your university classes next semester. Take turns asking the questions and taking notes.

CHAPTER 14

This Class Is a Disaster: Public Information, Natural Disasters, and the ESL Classroom in the United States

Christopher Miles and Bill Powell

Whether they come in the form of earthquakes, hurricanes, tornadoes, or floods, we can count on confusion and disorder as naturally occurring human factors in the aftermath of a natural disaster. In the United States, the confusion is often magnified for nonnative-English-speaking communities, which continue to be an increasing segment of the U.S. population. Immigration rates have increased steadily over the past 20 years for both documented and undocumented individuals, and this increase has created new and complex issues in some regions of the country. These increases have occurred so quickly that many states have made little to no changes in infrastructure to accommodate needs. For example, in the 4 years preceding Hurricane Katrina, "the most destructive and costly natural disaster in U.S. history" (FEMA, 2006), Camaroda (2005) estimated that Mississippi saw a 148.7% increase in immigrants, the highest in the country. The Mississippi Gulf Coast in particular, which bore the brunt of Katrina in August 2005, was caught off guard in effectively preparing its nonnative speakers of English (Peng, 2005) for the hurricane. With communications networks down, most immigrants in the affected area relied on word of mouth and rumor to get basic survival supplies during the aftermath of the storm (Miles, 2006). Although there was an effort to disseminate information before and after the storm, the organization of materials coupled with embedded cultural assumptions made accessibility and comprehension truly problematic for many.

This chapter focuses on the pedagogical implications of the language of disasters. Specifically, we outline activities that are designed for high-beginning to intermediate-level adult English as a second language (ESL) learners. These activities may be implemented in adult education programs such as ESL classes in churches, community service centers, or outreach programs in schools for parents of immigrant children. We present naturally occurring disaster preparation and recovery language based on authentic data in the ESL classroom. Via task-based instruction (TBI), we explore different simulations of disasters through role plays and other classroom activities. Additionally, we address the teaching of pertinent vocabulary and language structures as they naturally occur.

CONTEXT

In the aftermath of Hurricane Katrina, we analyzed how information did—and did not—flow both before and after the devastating storm, with meeting non-native English speakers' needs as our focus. Specifically, the affected immigrant population in Mississippi was from a variety of Spanish-speaking Latin American countries including Mexico, Guatemala, Honduras, and Nicaragua. Additionally, there is a large Vietnamese community located on the Gulf Coast that was particularly devastated.

What we found in studying state preparedness material on the Web was that disaster preparation materials were written in a technical, bureaucratic style that could certainly challenge language skills. Part of the complexity of such texts stems from the vocabulary of storm preparation and recovery, which includes a number of relatively infrequent terms and variants to more common meanings, further complicating communications. Some common vocabulary we noted that would prove potentially problematic included the following terms:

- **Storm and weather:** prediction, forecast, hurricane, warning or watch, tornado, issued, likely, severe, conditions, category, hits, landfall, major, strengthen

- **Disaster:** evacuate, supplies, curfew, disinfect, thawed, spoiled, restore, debris, shelter, damage, breaker, power lines, nonperishable, emergency, necessity, outage, precautions, relief

- **Bureaucratese:** contraflow, converge, vehicle, order, official, declare, mandatory, warn, management, notify, comment, federal, burn ban

- **Generic:** area, region, cancel or postpone, distribute, items, materials, resident, traffic, hazardous, repair, district, operations, personnel, roof, service, resume, fuel, available drop-off, pick-up, vital, expect

We also found a tendency in the organization of both pre- and post-storm print information for key information to be somewhat buried in the publication, often spread throughout the pages of a newspaper and then sometimes further embedded within articles themselves. Individuals with developing English literacy skills and unfamiliar with the organization of information in newspapers would likely encounter difficulties in ferreting out important information. Furthermore, information was often presented with the assumption of knowledge of the local area; for example, announcements on pick-up sites for essential supplies identified the site, such as a church, but the location of that church would not be included. The information available through radio and television stations was similarly presented and likewise posed potential comprehension problems for immigrant community members. As one individual put it in the aftermath of the storm, "It really hurts not to know English" (Radalet, 2005, p. 4a).

CURRICULUM, TASKS, MATERIALS

A Task-Based Approach to Teaching Disaster Preparedness

Using the abundance of authentic text available on disasters, TBI is an effective mechanism for dealing with the language and informational challenges illustrated by the circumstances before and after Hurricane Katrina. Over the past decade, research in task-based language instruction has been defined and categorized for a variety of teaching and learning contexts (Ellis, 2003; Leaver & Willis, 2004; Littlewood, 2004; Nunan, 2004; Pica, 2005), including traditional language classrooms and specialized classes in non-academic settings. TBI is diverse in that there is an element of utilitarianism embedded within its structure (real-world orientation), which allows activities to be tailored to fit a variety of learning contexts and curricula. Theoretically, TBI emphasizes the importance of the link between form (including structure and lexis) and meaning. Authentic materials lend themselves to the development of experiential learning tasks that replicate real-world contexts and mirror daily life. It is our belief that in the event of a disaster, the use of authentic materials is paramount. Being familiar with real public information before and after a disaster occurs creates a schema of its organization and a familiarity with both the lexical and structural aspects of that information, which is the first step in preparation itself.

All of the suggestions for activities in the next section subscribe to Leaver & Willis' summation (2004) of a typical task cycle that consists of "a *pretask* phase, where teachers set up relevant topic schemata, *the task itself*, where learners focus on meaning, and a *posttask phase*, drafting, finalizing, and presenting the outcome or finished product to others" (p. 37). We suggest the activities be conceived of as a group of lessons with each phase occupying a single class lesson of about 50 minutes. In this way, Day 1 would consist of pretask activities, Day 2 would consist of the task itself, and Day 3 could encompass the posttask phase, though these tasks could be expanded or compressed to adapt to local learning contexts. Ellis (2003) suggests opportunities to focus on form and lexicon in all phases of a task. The activities draw on a variety of authentic sources of public information, including Web sites, newspapers, and pamphlets. As they are produced by public sources that exist in all 50 U.S. states, their corresponding nonprofit, state, and federal offices are easily accessible and often offer copious materials online. The sources of information are organized as either static or dynamic and occur either before or after a disaster. Static information is reliable information that is not expected to change very much in the event of a disaster. Dynamic information is subject to variation and to the dynamics of changing situations. Table 1 provides an overview of sources of information on disasters.

Potential Tasks for Language Instruction

The following are possible tasks for adult ESL classes incorporating authentic materials on disaster preparedness before, during, and after a disaster survival:

- Using copies of newspaper articles and recordings of TV and radio broadcasts after a disaster, learners focus on extracting vital information, thereby learning how information is organized within a news source. The language of disaster and recovery is highlighted for attention.

- The real language of disasters is presented in the news as the source of what Ur (1981) has called "survival games" (p. 70), wherein learners decide

Table 1. Sources of Static Versus Dynamic Information

	Static Information	Dynamic Information
Pre-disaster	• government or nonprofit disaster preparation materials, that is, pamphlets, mail outs, Web sites with disaster preparation (e.g., FEMA.gov) • newspaper articles and television/radio segments with information on safety tips, home preparation, shelters, evacuation routes, storm supplies, etc.	• live television/radio news and newspaper articles updating the situation, school and government office closings, supply availability, evacuation route and traffic updates, shelter availability, etc.
Disaster	• limited broadcast capabilities providing general safety tips • fixed auditory signals (tornado sirens) or beeping radio signals	• limited dynamic sources depending on availability of radio/television broadcast capacity, power, etc.
Post-disaster	• government or nonprofit preparation materials, (e.g., pamphlets, mail outs). • live television/radio news and newspaper articles on safety tips, water purification techniques, chain saw operation, general public health information, cleanup tips, insurance claims, etc.	• live television/radio news and newspaper articles updating situations, essential survival supplies (e.g., water, food, medicine, ice, gasoline, generators), pick-up points, school closings, open businesses, utility restoration, boil water notices, curfew announcements, etc.

among themselves how to respond to a desperate situation. Simulations and role plays that generate awareness of both the language of disaster and local disaster relief resources is included in such classroom activities.

- A thematic unit on disaster draws on materials from the Red Cross. Though developed mainly for K–8 use, the agency's *Masters of Disaster* series (http://www.redcross.org/disaster/masters/) can easily be adapted for ESL learners at all levels. Similarly, general information on disaster preparation available through the Red Cross and on its Web site (n.d.) (see http://www.redcross.org/preparedness/cdc_english/home.asp) can serve as authentic text for class reading and discussion.

- A sourcebook on a specific disaster, such as Hurricane Katrina, or on disasters in general can be created and maintained for use across a language program curriculum (Powell & Ponder, 2001). A variety of sources from a range of media can be compiled and continuously updated in order to supply an array of resources on specific topics. For example, a sourcebook on a natural disaster would include not only news sources but also samples of oral histories from people who experienced the event (Howard, 2007), documentaries, and the inevitable novels and movies set within the context of the disaster. A centralized sourcebook of authentic data would contain many examples of both static and dynamic information that would provide source materials for lesson design and implementation. Furthermore, materials and the tasks drawing on the materials can be adapted to accommodate a variety of linguistic competencies and skill levels.

Disaster Preparation Guide: Student-Centered Tasks

The following unit of instruction focuses on disaster preparedness. Drawing on printed and online materials available through newspapers, relief agencies, and local, state, and federal governments, students prepare their own disaster preparation guide, one that succinctly and in accessible language includes critical information on preparing for and recovering from a disaster within the local context. The linguistic complexity of the document is tailored to the proficiency level of the learners; for example, less proficient learners can create a document using more visuals, while more proficient learners can prepare a more narrative or descriptive guide. Ellis (2003) suggests the following task performance options, which must be tailored for any given teaching context:

- Decide how much time to give students at each stage in the task cycle.

- Decide whether to allow students to use exact output data (brochure) during the activity, and if yes, to what extent.

- Introduce an element of surprise.

The following sample task cycle is based on the state of Mississippi's Emergency Management District Brochure (see Figure 1), which is mailed out to all residents of Forrest County at the beginning of hurricane season in June. Students at the intermediate level were envisioned for this task sequence, but modifications could be made to accommodate students at lower levels.

How Can We Be Better Prepared for Disasters?

Purpose

The purpose of this Hazard Preparedness Brochure is to provide Forrest County residents with the best information on how each household can be prepared for any hazard that could affect our County. Forrest County can be impacted by any of the disasters listed below and some tips are provided for those that occur most frequently:

- Dam Failure
- Drought
- Earthquake
- Flood and Flash Flood
- Hail
- Hazardous/Radiological/Nuclear Incidents
- Hurricanes, Tropical Storms, and High Winds
- Power Failure
- Terrorism
- Thunderstorm and Lightning
- Tornado and Funnel Clouds
- Transportation Incident
- Urban and Wildfires
- Winter Storms

Hurricanes, Tropical Storms & High Winds

- Develop a plan for you and your family at home, work, and school.
- Have a NOAA Weather Radio with a warning alarm tone and battery back up to receive warnings. NOAA will issue a hurricane watch 36 hours before a hurricane's arrival to an area, and a hurricane warning 24 hours before the arrival.
- Sterilize stockpiled empty milk jugs and plastic soda bottles and fill with water and store in your freezer. If your home loses power, these ice blocks can be placed in your cooler. They will stay frozen longer than bagged ice cubes.

Thunderstorm & Lightning

- Go indoors if, after seeing lightning, you cannot count to 30 before hearing thunder. Stay indoors for 30 minutes after hearing the last clap of thunder.
- If you can hear thunder you are close enough to be struck by lightning.

Flood & Flash Flood

- Stay away from floodwaters. The water may be contaminated by oil, gasoline, or raw sewage. The water may also be electrically charged from underground or downed power lines.
- Moving water can be easy to misjudge. In fact, as little as 6" can sweep you off your feet. Just 12" can move most cars off the road. This includes heavy SUVs, which can be more buoyant because of their size. Always keep a hammer in your car. If your car becomes submerged, you'll be able to break a window so that you can exit the vehicle.

Tornado & Funnel Clouds

- Do not try to outrun a tornado in your car. Instead, leave it immediately for safe shelter in low lying land such as a ditch.

Hail

- When hailing, never go outdoors. If in your vehicle, do not get out. Try to pull over under a garage or a highway overpass. Stay away from car windows. If possible, get down on the floor with face down on seats with back to the windows. Put small children under you and cover their face.

Communication

Limit telephone usage. Designate an out of town contact person to report your status, then allow other friends and relatives to seek information through that person. Use text messaging instead of calls. Input I.C.E. (In Case of Emergency) number into your cell phone for an emergency contact.

Emergency Preparedness Kits

- First aid kit
- Flashlight
- Radio and/or TV (battery operated)
- Tool kit
- Fire extinguisher
- Jumper cables
- Blankets/sleeping bags
- Toiletries
- Water
- Non-perishable foods
- Non-electric can opener
- Essential medication
- Appropriate clothing
- Pet supplies
- Games/books
- Local map
- Emergency phone charger

Documents

Some of the documents suggested here will serve as ready resources during a storm or disaster. Most of the others are records that could be difficult or impossible to replace. Collect and organize these items using a three-ring notebook with protector pages to lessen the possibility of documents getting wet. Keep a copy of these documents, along with other emergency supplies. Make a second copy to send to a trusted friend or relative in another state, in the event you are not able to return to your community. Store originals in a safe deposit box, or other secure and dry location.

- Bank account records
- Birth and marriage certificates
- Car titles and registrations
- Credit cards (both sides)
- Divorce decree
- Driver's license or other photo identification
- Health insurance information/cards
- Homeowner's papers (mortgage, deed, title insurance, lease)
- Tax returns and related records
- Will, power of attorney
- Loan documents
- Medical records
- Military records
- Passport, green card
- Pay stubs
- Photo of each family member
- Photo of pet
- Proof of residence (electric bill, mail)
- Retirement account records
- Social Security cards
- Home inventory list
- Insurance policies (home, auto, life)

Information Resources

State Departments:

- Mississippi Department of Transportation – 601.359.7017 or www.GoMDOT.com
- Mississippi Emergency Management Agency – 1.800.222.MEMA or www.msema.com
- Mississippi Highway Safety Patrol – 1.800.843.5352 (if in state), 601.987.1530 (if outside of state)
- Mississippi Division of Tourism – 1.866.SEE.MISS (1.866.733.6477)
- Department of Wildlife, Fisheries and Parks – 1.800.GO.PARKS (1.800.46.72757)
- Louisiana Department of Transportation – 225.379.1232
- Alabama Department of Transportation – 334.242.6358
- Tennessee Department of Transportation – 615.741.2848

Media

Local Radio Stations: FM Radio Coverage area: Jackson, 91.3 – Meridian, 88.1 – Biloxi, 90.3 and Pine Belt Radio Station: FM 95.9, Mississippi Public Broadcasting Station: Biloxi WMAH 90.3

Local Television Stations: WDAM-TV 7 (NBC, Hattiesburg) – WLOX-13 (ABC, Pascagoula) WXXV-25 (FOX, Gulfport) – WHLT-22 (CBS, Hattiesburg) Weather Channel (Comcast-8), (Direct TV –362) and (Dish Network- 214)

Figure 1. Mississippi's Emergency Management District Brochure (reprinted with permission)

Pretask

Students are introduced to the topic of disasters and disaster preparation in general and for their specific locale. Some sample pretask activities include the following:

1. Brainstorming and creating lists of events considered disasters, for example, hurricanes, tornadoes, earthquakes, and terrorist attacks.

2. Discussing what students know about disaster potentials in the local area.

3. Discussing questions like: Have you ever been in a disaster? Can you describe what happened? If you know a disaster is coming, where do you go and what do you do? What are the names of meeting points near your home?

4. Skimming the brochure to analyze organization. Sample questions include: What are the titles of the text? What information is where? What is each section describing?

5. Reading the brochure and going over unfamiliar vocabulary. We predict the following terms from the Emergency Management District Brochure might be problematic yet useful: *dam, failure, funnel, incident, drought, hazardous, charged, downed lines, outrun, shelter, overpass, sterilize, designate, jumper cables, toiletries, NOAA Weather, radio, nonperishable, hail,* and *supplies.*

6. Reading the brochure with a focus on the structures of necessity and advice. Note with your learners both imperatives and modal verbs. By raising students' awareness of these language structures, students will be better prepared to participate in the role play and simulation.

For homework, we have students find out (if any) disasters their friends and relatives have experienced. We also ask them to come up with their own definitions of terms in the vocabulary list or prepare questions on language structures.

During Task

During this phase, students are asked to develop two tasks in groups: (a) plan and create a disaster preparedness kit, and (b) perform a role play or simulation activity informing family members and others in the neighborhood of a pending hurricane. Students at this stage are encouraged to be creative and introduce an element of surprise. If you live in an area that does not have hurricanes, the simulation task can be a role play of potential local emergencies, or what to do during a disaster that may be unforeseen, such as an earthquake.

1. Disaster Preparedness Kit

As an information gap activity, each student is given a note card with a list of items that are mentioned in the Mississippi Emergency Management District Brochure as necessary components of an emergency preparedness kit. None of the students receives a complete list; instead, they have to go around and compare lists to find items they do not have and work toward creating a complete list. As a reading activity, students can check their lists with the list in the brochure. The following are four sample lists, each to be placed on a notecard:

appropriate clothing	toiletries	radio and/or TV	tool kit
jumper cables	blankets	pet supplies	flashlight
local map	first aid kit	water	medication
games and books	fire extinguisher	phone charger	can opener
nonperishable foods	can opener	appropriate clothing	local map
tool kit	flashlight	can opener	blankets
first aid kit	jumper cables	first aid kit	first aid kit

As a follow-up discussion, have students discuss how many of these items they have on hand at home.

2. Disaster Simulation or Role Play

Students are asked to role play informing their family members, friends, and others in the neighborhood of a pending hurricane. Students work together in groups and develop a dialogue. Preparations may also begin as homework, which promotes immigrant parents in sharing this vital information with their children. When partnered with schools, adult ESL disaster preparation can enable parents, children, and communities to learn vital information together.

Student instructions for a dialogue or simulation:

Option A: You are watching TV and news comes on informing you that a hurricane is approaching. You must inform your family and make preparations.

Option B: You are driving in your car with a friend during bad weather. In the distance, you spot a tornado. Create a dialogue with your friends about what actions you should take to ensure your safety.

Option C: You are shopping in a mall with some friends when suddenly an earthquake strikes. What do you and your friends do? Create a dialogue with your friends indicating what to do.

Posttask

Students perform their dialogues by first providing the context to their audience. After role playing, students summarize the outcome of the task, and the teacher reviews learner language use, with a particular focus on errors. Refocusing on form can raise language awareness in learners, thus promoting language acquisition. The teacher should consider the language generated by the students during the task to determine learner need and posttask lessons.

REFLECTIONS

The preceding suggestions for activities provide ample opportunities for nonnative speakers of English to acquire the skills necessary to effectively function and survive in the event of a natural disaster. The activities serve to create a linguistic schema based on authentic materials. Although the primary focus of the activities is tailored for adult learners, very often in the case of immigrants with families it is the children themselves who become the disseminators of the information as they are taught in the public school system. Information of this type and the skills associated with comprehending it can have a ripple effect throughout a community as the children report to their parents and parents speak with other parents. Again, community-school connections work to foster learning.

The dissemination of materials and their accessibility to the immigrant communities is always a challenge. In addition, factors such as literacy level and lack of resources become very relevant when dealing with populations of people with limited first language literacy or computer skills and access. Although intensive English programs (IEP) can incorporate the language of disaster into pedagogical units, most academic settings exist inside a preestablished network of individuals who are less vulnerable to being completely cut off. Thus, this curriculum is particularly well suited for more grassroots types of organizations catering to immigrant communities via ESL classes at churches and civic centers or in places of business, which sometimes offer language support classes.

Still, disaster-related materials and awareness-raising can be used in a variety of instructional settings and educational levels. For example, the inclusion of first aid training in the ESL or English as a foreign language classroom demonstrates the potential of sustained content and TBI to enhance learning. Whereas younger learners might respond well to first aid and the Red Cross' *Masters of Disaster* series (n.d.), learners in pre-university IEP work might extend their study into more analytical dimensions, with readings on controversies surrounding past disasters and the role of governments during such events. Teachers as material developers need only to adapt tasks and materials to their learners and the learning and social context.

A task-based approach to using the language of disaster in the classroom opens up many avenues for creative lesson plan design and affords a number of opportunities to study public information and its organization before being confronted with a chaotic situation. The information presented in this chapter may help some nonnative English speakers better comprehend the information from public sources and ensure their safety and the safety of their families and communities.

Christopher Miles is an assistant professor of Spanish at the University of Southern Mississippi in the United States, where he teaches both Spanish and TESOL courses. His research interests include language and identity and online teaching and learning contexts.

Bill Powell is an associate professor of TESOL and French at the University of Southern Mississippi, where he teaches courses in second language acquisition and teaching. His research interests focus on curriculum and program development. He also has taught EFL in Cameroon and ESL in the United States.

Authentic Purpose, Authentic Medium: Technology in Language Learning

The Times They Are A-Changin': Strategies for Exploiting Authentic Materials in the Language Classroom

Alex Gilmore

There's a battle outside
And it is ragin'.
It'll soon shake your windows
And rattle your walls
For the times they are a-changin'.
—Bob Dylan, 1964

For many teachers, authentic texts have great appeal as source material for the English language classroom. Like Bob Dylan's lyrics above, they stem from an author's desire to communicate ideas or emotions and, as a result, often have the power to affect students at a deeper level than contrived texts, whose primary function is often to display lexico-grammatical features of language. Gilmore (2007a) and Woodward (1996) see a growing sense of dissatisfaction with current language teaching practices: a battle between proponents of contrivance and authenticity is raging in the academic journals, and the walls and windows of our classrooms are shaking with the expectation of change. It appears that we are on the verge of a paradigm shift, but the fundamental question facing us is what, exactly, we should shift to. One possibility is a syllabus structured around communicative competence models (see Figure 1), aiming to exploit the wealth of authentic materials now readily available to teachers worldwide through media such as the Internet, television, and DVDs.

This chapter outlines reasons for reducing the role of textbooks in the

Communicative competence is generally seen as consisting of five components:

1. **Linguistic competence** refers to a speaker's lexical, morphological, orthographical, syntactical, and phonological knowledge of the language and only deals with the literal meaning (or *locutionary force*) of utterances. This is the type of knowledge that has traditionally been the focus in English to speakers of other languages (ESOL) classrooms, but in the current model of communicative competence it takes on a lesser role, seen as only one aspect of language proficiency.

2. **Pragmalinguistic competence** refers to a speaker's ability to understand or convey communicative intent appropriately in a given context based on knowledge of phrases typically used by native speakers in those situations. This kind of competence describes a speaker's ability to interpret the *illocutionary force* of utterances, for example, understanding that "Can you open the door?" is an informal request rather than a question.

3. **Sociopragmatic competence** refers to a speaker's knowledge of what is socially or culturally appropriate in a particular speech community, including an understanding of politeness or social conventions, or nonverbal behavior. An example is knowing that in Japan business cards should be exchanged at the beginning of an initial meeting, handed to the recipient with both hands and a slight bow.

4. **Strategic competence** refers to a speaker's ability to exploit verbal or nonverbal communication strategies when communication problems arise, compensating for deficiencies in other competences. These include four common types:
   a. *avoidance or reduction strategies* such as topic avoidance or message abandonment to try to keep conversation to areas where the speaker feels in control
   b. *compensatory strategies* such as circumlocution or mime when a word is not known
   c. *stalling strategies* such as using hesitation devices or repetition to hold a turn in conversation while a message is formulated
   d. *interactional strategies* such as asking for repetition or clarification or other linguistic resources to maintain conversation

5. **Discourse competence** refers to a speaker's ability to produce unified, cohesive, and coherent spoken or written discourse of different genres. In writing, this might include the use anaphoric reference in a text. In speaking, it would include developing a conversation naturally by taking up a subtopic from preceding talk or the use of different generic structures such as narratives, gossip, or jokes.

Figure 1. Components of Communicative Competence (based on Canale, 1983; Canale & Swain, 1980; Celce-Murcia, Dörnyei, & Thurrell, 1995; Leech, 1983)

curriculum or sometimes even abandoning them altogether. This is not meant to suggest that there is never a place for textbooks—good quality publications may meet the needs or interests of a particular group of students and save the teacher a lot of time. Furthermore, many modern textbooks already incorporate authentic material in some form so that the distinction between *authentic* and *contrived* is becoming ever more blurred. However, learners often find teacher-prepared authentic materials more motivating, and the richer input they provide allows a focus on a greater variety of discourse features. Strategies for selecting appropriate authentic materials for the language classroom and for exploiting them effectively through task design are suggested and an example is presented to illustrate how this can work in practice.

CONTEXT

The materials and approaches discussed here evolved from classroom-based research carried out in the Japanese university system (Gilmore, 2007b). Japanese university students often have good receptive knowledge of English grammar or vocabulary (linguistic competence), particularly of more formal registers, and they tend to perform well on paper tests. But they rarely have the ability to personalize and activate this knowledge in actual communicative activities. Much class time is therefore devoted to improving learners' listening and speaking skills in less formal contexts, more appropriate for conversation with friends, as well as developing their confidence to repair talk when communication breakdown occurs. Readers will have to consider which components of the communicative competence model need developing in their own learners and select materials and tasks that best meet those goals.

CURRICULUM, TASKS, MATERIALS

What Is Authenticity?

Authenticity means different things to different people. Each definition has implications for syllabus design and classroom practice, so it is important to be clear about exactly what kind of authenticity we are interested in before selecting materials and developing tasks. Figure 2 gives a brief overview of different perspectives on authenticity and their implications for classroom practice.

In this chapter, I focus on exploiting authentic spoken text in the classroom and define authenticity in the same way as Morrow (1977) as "a stretch of real language, produced by a real speaker or writer for a real audience and designed to convey a real message of some sort" (p. 13). In particular, I exploit extracts from films and TV programs in language teaching, which, although lacking some of the characteristics of spontaneous spoken discourse, are much easier to access and are often far more entertaining than the humdrum conversations of everyday life.

Why Not Use Textbooks?

It would be unrealistic to suggest that authentic materials replace textbooks in all teaching contexts: many teachers lack the time, and others the experience, to create their own syllabi from scratch, and a well-written textbook may serve as an excellent foundation for a course. Nevertheless, there are many reasons for a greater use of authentic materials in the classroom. Authentic materials are increasingly easy to access worldwide through the Internet and on alternate media. Search engines allow us to locate texts or images efficiently, and these can

Authenticity As...	Assumptions & Implications
The language produced by native speakers for native speakers in a particular language community	Native speaker (NS) English is regarded as superior to nonnative speakers English—learners should try to mimic NSS and prepare themselves for communication in an English-speaking community.
The language produced by a real speaker or writer for a real audience, conveying a real message	Authentic language is any communication of a real message—textbooks and materials using contrived language are inferior because their intent is often only to display language forms.
The qualities in a text as perceived by the reader or listener and not inherent in the text itself	Any text is authentic if learners perceive it as such—the original purpose of the text is less important than the learner's "authentic" response. Authentic and contrived texts are of equal worth for the classroom.
The interaction between students and teachers as a "personal process of engagement"	Authenticity reflects the learning that takes place within the classroom through student-teacher interaction rather than the materials used.
The types of task chosen	Classroom tasks exploit materials in the same ways as their original intent (e.g., physically carrying out instructions from a "how-to" manual).
The social situation of the classroom	The social nature of the classroom is authentic in itself—the focus is on exploiting this environment to develop meaningful relationships.
Assessment	Tests should accurately assess learners' competence to perform real-world tasks.
Culture, and the ability to behave, think like, or understand the target language group to be recognized and validated by it	ESOL classrooms focus on different behaviors, values, and ways of seeing the world as well as language itself.

Figure 2. Different Perspectives on Authenticity With Teaching Implications (see Gilmore, 2007a, 2007b)

be readily copied and pasted into Microsoft Word documents. Video material on sites such as YouTube (http://www.youtube.com/) or the BBC's Video Nation (http://www.bbc.co.uk/videonation/) are conveniently categorized into themes and provide learners exposure to a wide variety of accents, solidly contextualized through the visual medium. Online encyclopedias, such as Wikipedia (http://en.wikipedia.org/wiki/Main_Page), are excellent sources for student projects, essays, or presentations. Music, movies, and podcasts can be downloaded through providers such as iTunes, and the lyrics (http://www.getlyrical.com/) or scripts (http://www.script-o-rama.com/) are also often available. Online corpora such as the British National Corpus (http://www.natcorp.ox.ac.uk/) or the COBUILD Concordance and Collocations Sampler (http://www.collins.co.uk/

Corpus/CorpusSearch.aspx) allow learners to examine real concordance lines, extracted from word banks comprising millions of words. English language movies are widely available through television networks and video rental stores—DVDs are particularly useful because they provide easy searching through chapters and the option of subtitles in English or the students' mother tongue.

Internationally produced textbooks often fail to address local needs: When teachers select materials, they have greater control over the syllabus and are more likely to meet learners' interests and needs. Textbooks also are often extremely dull: sometimes because they have been contrived to display particular language features rather than to entertain, other times because the content has been kept deliberately bland and sanitized in order not to offend differing sensibilities in the worldwide market (Wajnryb, 1996). Authentic materials, in contrast, are frequently more motivating for both teachers and their students because they can be crafted to meet local needs and interests and are not subject to the constraints placed on textbook writers. According to Schumann (1997), three important components of our "stimulus appraisal system" (which determines to what extent we engage with input) are novelty, pleasantness, and goal/need significance. Authentic materials have the potential to be evaluated positively on these criteria and can lead to sustained deep learning.

Textbook materials frequently fail to develop a range of learners' communicative competencies because they are often organized around a graded, structural syllabus, with lexico-grammatical features sequenced according to perceived difficulty. Although this "generates clear and tangible goals, precise syllabi, and a comfortingly itemizable basis for the evaluation of effectiveness" (Skehan, 1998, p. 94), syllabuses like this are not supported by language acquisition research and tend to develop learners' linguistic competence at the expense of other communicative competence components (Nunan, 1996; Skehan, 1996).

Selecting Authentic Materials for the Language Classroom

Despite the many advantages of authentic materials over textbooks, exploiting them successfully is no easy matter and requires teachers to have thorough language awareness and a clear sense of their learners' interests and needs. Below are general guidelines teachers will find useful for selecting authentic materials.

Choose Interesting Texts

Learning another language is hard work, and students will have little compulsion to engage with texts that do not catch their imaginations. Because classroom time is limited, creating interest encourages students to explore materials in more depth. For example, by showing learners key scenes from movies and then making the complete versions available for self-access, we can encourage them to devote more time to language learning outside of the class.

Identify and Meet Learners' Needs

The knowledge and skills students acquire in the classroom are directly related to the kind of input they receive along with the associated tasks. Learners who only read newspaper articles are likely to become proficient at reading about current affairs, although they may, for example, remain incapable of making a hotel reservation on the telephone. Viewing the curriculum in terms of the kinds of communicative competencies and skills needed provides teachers with a systematic approach, ensuring that learners receive the knowledge and skills to operate successfully in a target speech community. A needs analysis (e.g., Ellis & Sinclair, 1989, p. 10) is therefore a good place to begin planning a course.

Provide Learners With a Variety of Topics and Tasks

Because the individuals who make up any class will have different needs and interests, and will be at different stages of language development, a variety of topics and tasks is the best way to ensure that all of their needs are satisfied to some extent. Schumann's (1997) stimulus appraisal theory suggests that variety is an important factor in maintaining interest.

Select Texts of Appropriate Difficulty

Many different factors combine to influence a text's difficulty—some of these are characteristics of the texts themselves, whereas others depend on the learning context in which they are used. Gilmore (2007a) identifies such factors as

- text length

- lexical density

- proportion of low- vs. high-frequency vocabulary

- grammatical or syntactical complexity

- text genre (static genres, such as descriptions, are easier than dynamic ones, such as narratives, or abstract ones, such as political debates)

- number of elements (characters or events) in a text and how easily they can be distinguished from one another

- quantity of presumed background knowledge or idiomatic language

- speech rates

- type and variety of accents

- visual support offered (video and still images, realia, or transcripts)

Select Audio-Visual Texts

Audio-visual materials taken from Web-based sources or DVDs should be given priority over the more traditional (audio-only or text-only) materials typically used in language classrooms. Visual elements provide learners with an enormous amount of additional pragmatic information on the context, the speakers' ages and social positions, and the relationships between different participants (Brown & Yule, 1983). Contextual details dictate the kind of speech and nonverbal communication speakers employ and can be used to sensitize learners to language variation in English (pragmalinguistics) as well as the behavioral norms in the target speech community (sociopragmatics). Being able to watch the speakers as they talk also supports learners' listening comprehension because, as Brown and Yule remind us, the "extra articulatory effort" (p. 86), reflected in mouth movements, facial expressions, and gestures provides valuable information on which words are key content words.

Select Stand-Alone Texts

With spoken texts, post-listening activities in the classroom often involve intensive language work on various aspects of the discourse frozen in the transcripts. This means that relatively short video extracts, of up to around 10 minutes for intermediate or advanced learners, are most suitable, and these should be accessible to students without excessive introduction or contextualization in the lead-in stages. In other words, scenes that rely too much on earlier events in the plot should be avoided unless the teacher can quickly summarize them. Heavily edited extracts, with frequent cuts, also should be avoided because the rapid changes in speaker and context are likely to increase comprehension difficulties.

Maximize Accessibility in Transcripts

In order to facilitate the intensive language work suggested for post-listening stages, and to encourage learners to become conversational analysts, transcriptions should be made available to students. These can often be located online or extracted from DVDs using optical character recognition (OCR) software such as SubRip (http://zuggy.wz.cz/dvd.php). Decisions have to be made in terms of how much detail to include in the written representation of speech. A "thick description" (Geertz, 1973) could include phonological, turn taking, or nonverbal communication features as well as the actual words spoken. However, too much information can be off-putting for learners, so it is usually better to keep transcriptions simple on pedagogical grounds, unless there is some particular reason to include more detail. Besides, many of these details students will notice themselves and may even be asked to mark on their own transcripts, adding back the missing detail while reading the transcripts. Transcription lines can be numbered for ease of reference and double-spaced to give students space for note taking on discourse or other features of interest.

Select Materials That Stand the Test of Time

Finding and preparing authentic materials that fulfill all of the above criteria can be a time-consuming process, so it is essential to select texts that can be reused over many years with different classes. Instructors can build up a materials bank with different teachers sharing their transcripts. Careful categorization of the files, detailing the topic, context, extract length, and key discourse features, can be helpful to teachers for easy access. The transcripts also can be used to build up a corpus, using software such as Wordsmith Tools (http://www.lexically.net/wordsmith/). Such corpus linguistic tools allow teachers to quickly identify word frequencies in the materials bank as well as texts where particular discourse features occur.

Developing Tasks for Authentic Materials

Of course, selection of appropriate texts is only the first step in the process of exploiting authentic materials in the classroom. Tasks then need to be created to suit the level and needs of the learners. Below are some suggestions for effective task design.

Ensure Success

It is possible to adapt authentic materials to different proficiency levels by varying the *task* rather than the *text*. Mariani (1997) describes classroom activities in terms of the level of challenge and support they provide. Support can come from a variety of sources: the teacher, other students, reference materials, or through careful task design. Different combinations of these two factors result in different learning consequences as represented in Figure 3.

Effective learning is most likely to occur when materials and tasks provide both high levels of challenge and support. Even when texts are too difficult for learners, there is no reason why they should feel unmotivated by them as long as the tasks are achievable and students acquire new knowledge in the process. Indeed,

Figure 3. Variation in Instructional Challenge and Support (see Gilmore, 2007a, p. 112; adapted from Mariani, 1997)

it might be beneficial for learners to become tolerant of only partial comprehension because even native speakers experience this at times—textbooks, which tend to expect 100% comprehension, run the risk of overprotecting students from the uncertainties of the real world.

Include Pre-, While-, and Post-Listening Tasks

Pre-listening tasks are typically designed to raise learners' interest in topics, clarify difficult vocabulary, and provide any necessary cultural background knowledge to facilitate comprehension. These kinds of activities help students develop schemas and scripts for the scenes they are about to watch, which can support, or scaffold, learning (Bruner, 1983). One option at the pre-listening stage is to ask learners to first write and role-play their own versions of scenarios occurring on the film clip before they see the original versions. This not only aids in comprehension but also encourages students to notice the gap between their own interlanguage and the NS discourse, enhancing the acquisition of intake.

While-listening tasks focus on meaning first before shifting to form, to avoid overloading learners' language processing systems. While-listening tasks typically begin with gist questions followed by more detailed comprehension questions, to encourage effective processing strategies.

Post-listening tasks are designed to revisit the material in a new way. This can involve a wide variety of tasks such as recycling vocabulary, focusing on target discourse features, or getting students to use target language in speaking or writing activities. By looking at the same material again from a new perspective, we increase the efficiency of the learning process because valuable time may be lost when we have to constantly set up or contextualize new input.

Let the Text Suggest the Task

After working closely on a spoken text to produce an accurate transcript, appropriate tasks often suggest themselves to the teacher or materials writer. Oral narratives, for example, highlight typical features of narrative structure such as shifts to the historic present to dramatize events. Songs highlight features of rhythm (stress-timing) or rhyme (phonology) in English. Lyrics, like those from Dylan's famous song, tend to stick in our minds as fixed phrases, which can be deconstructed for vocabulary and collocation analysis and acquisition.

Vary Task Design to Encourage Accuracy, Fluency, and Complexity

Skehan (1998) illustrates how task design can affect the accuracy, complexity, or fluency of learners' output. By increasing the time allowed for preparation, for example, we can encourage greater complexity, whereas decreasing preparation time can encourage greater fluency. Teachers should therefore consider their learners' needs and design activities accordingly. Japanese university students, for example, typically have very poor fluency as a result of excessive emphasis on accuracy at junior and high school. Therefore, I often design tasks so that they have little time to plan their output (for example, in role-play activities) in order to encourage them to develop greater fluency.

Syllabus Design With Authentic Materials

Text-driven (Mishan, 2005), "principled communicative" (Celce-Murcia, Dörnyei, & Thurrell, 1997) approaches rely on teachers and learners selecting materials and designing tasks for themselves, rather than relying on textbooks to meet all their needs. The syllabus for the course is therefore arrived at retrospectively, shaped by whatever materials are chosen for inclusion by the participants in the classroom events. Although this runs the risk of producing a syllabus that seems rather haphazard or chaotic, we can systematize it by preparing a checklist of items to be covered (perhaps organized around key components of communicative competence in Figure 1) and filling in any gaps as the course proceeds.

Sample Task Series

The following sample materials taken from the movie *Secrets & Lies* (Leigh, 1996) illustrate how the guidelines given above shaped the choice of texts and tasks. In this scene, Hortense, a young Black woman who was adopted as a child, visits a social worker, Jenny, to begin the process of tracking down her real mother. The scene was selected because it met a number of the criteria for text and task selection.

Selection Criteria

The scene depicts events in the plot leading to one of the narrative peaks in which Hortense discovers her real mother is actually White. The narrative peak creates interest in the events and encourages students to engage with the materials. As with much authentic discourse, meaning is often left implicit, and in this scene, learners have to infer meaning for themselves, also creating interest. The scene stands alone and is comprehensible when extracted from the movie, requiring little in the way of contextualizing in the lead-in stages.

The text illustrates many features of authentic, unscripted spoken discourse. In particular, this scene shows authentic listener responses in interpersonal discourse, important for Japanese learners who tend to be exposed to predominantly transactional, rather than interactional, language. The scene also shows how speakers employ ellipsis when there is a degree of shared information, also useful because many Japanese learners tend to be overly explicit.

The visual elements of the scene provide learners with useful sociopragmatic information about Britain. In this scene, Jenny, a government employee, takes a very informal approach to the interview, sitting next to Hortense rather than behind her desk, and eating chocolates as they chat. She also comments on the dilapidated state of her office in a way that might be considered improper in Japan.

The scene provides learners with an appropriate combination of challenge and support—the challenge is to deduce the topic of the conversation from the predominantly implicit language, but this is supported by the visual input and the comprehension questions, which lead students toward a deeper understanding.

This film has the additional advantage that it can be reused over many years without appearing excessively dated.

Task Development

The tasks accompanying multiple viewings of the scene display the typical pre-, while-, and post-listening stages recommended for exploiting authentic material (see the Appendix for a sample using *Secrets & Lies*). In the pre-listening stages, some of the lower frequency vocabulary, less likely to be unfamiliar, is introduced, and students' interest is encouraged by focusing on the movie's title. In the while-listening stages, students are first asked to complete a gist listening task to try to reach a general understanding before answering more detailed comprehension questions, encouraging listening for specific information. In the post-listening stages, students are able to read the transcript to clarify any parts of the scene that still remain unclear after the listening tasks. The focus then shifts to specific discourse features highlighted by the text (in this case, "listener responses" and ellipsis). Finally, the tasks involve students developing their speaking skills and fluency with role-play activities based on Hortense's meeting with her real mother and debates on the issues of adoption and freedom of information.

REFLECTIONS

The guidelines for selection and exploitation of authentic materials described here are meant to be sufficiently general to be applied to a wide variety of learning contexts. Many teachers, of course, will not have the freedom to design their own syllabus and will be required by their institutions to use particular textbooks. It is hoped, however, that they might be able to supplement with authentic materials, by establishing thematic links, in order to develop a wider range of communicative competencies in their learners.

Developing materials from authentic sources can be an extremely time-consuming process, so strategies for reducing teacher workloads, such as producing a shared "materials bank," need to be established institutionally. By working collaboratively, teachers can get valuable feedback on the success of their materials from others and hone their design skills further. Despite the investment of time and energy involved, I believe that it is well worth the effort: both teachers and learners will be more committed to texts that they have chosen themselves to work on, and this is likely to lead to higher levels of sustained learning. In addition, because it is the participants in classroom events who decide the course content, it is far more likely to meet specific language needs. As the title of this chapter suggests, the times are, indeed, changing and teachers need to seek new approaches and strategies to prepare their students for the challenges that await them in the environments of another culture's speech communities.

———————

Alex Gilmore is a visiting lecturer in applied linguistics at Kyoto University, Japan, where he teaches English for academic purposes. He is also a teacher trainer for the Cambridge certificate in English language teaching to adults (CELTA) course. Research interests include discourse analysis, materials development, and classroom research. He has taught English in Spain, Britain, Mexico, Saudi Arabia, and Japan.

APPENDIX: STUDENT MATERIALS USING *SECRETS & LIES*

A. The following expressions connected with *Secrets & Lies* are used in a film by the British writer and director Mike Leigh. What do they mean?

- to keep a secret
- a closely guarded secret
- a little white lie
- to lie through your teeth
- to have a loose tongue

Ask your partner some questions using these expressions, for example: "Can you keep a secret?"

B. Before you watch, match the following words from the scene to their definitions:

• prison cell	• to go somewhere for a short time
• moaning on	• official rules which are unpopular
• red tape	• to look at something
• have a shufti	• a small room to keep criminals locked up
• an optometrist	• complaining
• to put something off	• what you believe will happen
• to pop in/back	• to think something
• irreplaceable	• the problem
• environment	• physical conditions around you
• expectations	• an eye specialist
• under the impression	• impossible to replace
• the snag	• to change something to a later date

C. In this scene, Hortense visits Jenny Ford. Watch and try to find out what they are talking about. Who do you think Jenny Ford is?

D. Watch the scene again and answer the questions below.

1. What time of day is it?

2. What does Jenny keep putting off? How can Hortense help her?

3. Does Hortense live with anyone else?

4. When did Hortense's mother die?

5. Did Hortense have a happy childhood?

6. Who is Hortense looking for?

7. What does Jenny give to Hortense?

8. Why do you think Jenny leaves the room?

E. Jenny Ford is a very sympathetic listener and uses a lot of "listener responses" when she talks to Hortense. Read the script below and try to write appropriate responses in the spaces. Listen again and check your answers.

1 Jenny:	Hortense, hello *Jenny Ford. *Nice to meet you. Come this way.	
2 Hortense:	Oh hi	
3 Jenny:	How are you? *All right?	
4 Hortense:	*Fine thank you.	
5 Jenny:	_____ Sorry about this prison cell, we've been moaning on about it for years but there you go. Have a seat, make yourself at home. Now, before we go any further, have you got any ID? Passport? Driving license?	
6 Hortense:	Yeah	
7 Jenny:	*Have to get used to all this red tape. Would you like a Rolo?	
8 Hortense:	No thank you.	
9 Jenny:	*You sure?	
10 Hortense:	Yeah. There you go (hands over her ID).	
11 Jenny:	Hm, *have a shufti. That's great Hortense thanks.	
12 Hortense:	Thank you.	
13 Jenny:	*You on your lunch break?	
14 Hortense:	Yeah, *an extended one.	
15 Jenny:	Have you had any lunch?	
16 Hortense:	No, not yet.	
17 Jenny:	No, me neither. So what do you do?	
18 Hortense:	I'm an optometrist.	
19 Jenny:	_____ _____ that's one of those things you keep putting off and putting off isn't it? And I've got to the stage now with the Guardian crossword where I'm, I'm going like this so I think the time has come* don't you? I'll have to pop in, you can give me a test. Where do you live?	

20 Hortense: *Kilburn.

21 Jenny: _____ _____ *In a flat?

22 Hortense: Yes.

23 Jenny: Do you share*?

24 Hortense: No, I live on my own.

25 Jenny: _____ I lived on my own for about six years before I was married. It's all right* isn't it?

26 Hortense: Yeah.

27 Jenny: Right Hortense. Let's talk a little bit about you shall we? Now obviously you've been giving a great deal of thought to things and you've come to a decision which is good. But for me, the question is "Why now?"

28 Hortense: I just feel that it's the right time* that's all.

29 Jenny: _____ _____ *You thinking about getting married?

30 Hortense: No.

31 Jenny: D'you have children?

32 Hortense: No.

33 Jenny: *You thinking about having children?

34 Hortense: No.

35 Jenny: _____Are you sharing this with your parents? Do they know that you're here today and how do they feel about it?

36 Hortense: They're both dead actually... (the conversation continues).

(Reprinted with the kind permission of Mike Leigh)

E. In spoken English, we often leave out words when the meaning can be understood without them. This is called *ellipsis*. Look at the transcript above and decide what words are missing when you see an asterisk (*). For example:

Hello, *Jenny Ford   =   Hello, *my name is* Jenny Ford.

F. Hortense finds out that her real mother, Cynthia, is White but decides to contact her anyway. What do you think happens when they meet? What will they say to each other? How will they behave? Write a script and act it out with your partner. Don't forget to use listener responses and ellipsis where appropriate!

G. If you were adopted, would you look for your "birth mother"? Why or why not? In Britain, children now have the right to find out who their real parents are. Do you agree with this law? How is adoption managed in Japan? What rights do birth parents and adopted children have?

CHAPTER 16

Lights, Camera, Action: Scripts for Language Learning

Gregory Strong

With so much student interest in pop culture, language teachers are bringing more television programs and films to their classrooms than ever before. Whether videos, DVDs, or accessed from the Internet, the speech is authentic, containing "the real cadences of the target language," and such characteristics as quick speech, contractions, dropped consonants, and fragmentary phrasing (Field, 1998, p. 114). Like many teachers, in the past we used these materials to teach listening, often transcribing conversations or finding scripts to help us develop better classroom tasks. But we soon discovered that we could use scenes and speeches from these scripts for extended language practice. Extended use of such media allows students to rehearse and perform in English, sometimes using them as a springboard for creating their own films and documentaries.

Unlike the large body of research supporting the use of video materials for language learning, there have been few reports on using scripts. Wessels (1991) describes the enthusiasm with which her class collaborated on a play, noting there was no shortage of ideas. Heath (1996) claims that literature and playmaking create "natural repetition, reflection on language and how it works, and attention to audience response on the part of learners" (p. 776). Pollock (2005) notes the motivation among her graduate teaching assistants using scripts from television programs and movie scenes to improve oral communication skills. Most undergraduate business students at Rikkyo University in a new English for academic purposes (EAP) class focusing on script reading and performance found the approach effective and highly motivating (College of Business, 2007). Of the 140 students responding to a questionnaire, 96% of the males and 69% of the females strongly agreed or agreed that it was a good way to explore American business English and culture. "Students consistently indicated that performing with and for their classmates helped them to develop confidence in speaking English," and many noted a new awareness of "speed, rhythm, intonation, volume, and body language when speaking English" (p. 102).

CONTEXT

In the English department at Aoyama Gakuin University in Tokyo, Japan, we also seek to build students' confidence with English in natural contexts. We offer elective content courses in film and literature to 650 Japanese second-year university students in their final year of a 2-year language skills program. Each class is small, with a maximum of 25 students whose language skills range from lower to upper intermediate. Prior to their sophomore year, students have had 6 years of English language training in middle and high schools and 1 year of freshman English courses emphasizing reading, writing, listening, and speaking skills. But most students lack confidence in their ability to understand English used in authentic interactive contexts, and few of the students have ever read a script aloud before.

CURRICULUM, TASKS, MATERIALS

Script reading is not like rehearsing for a play. Instead of interpreting characters, students watch video sequences and model their performances on that of professional actors. The scripts form the basis of staged readings in which students rehearse to try to speak as naturally as possible while taking on the persona of the screen actor.

We follow Willis' (1996) framework for teaching tasks, employing pretask activities, a performance cycle, and posttask activities. The materials for the tasks range from short, easy oral readings using scripts such as movie trailers and commercials, to longer, more challenging readings with scripts such as movie scenes. Language and content learning occurs during all three phases. In the pretask phase for different script types, the teacher helps students access their knowledge of a commercial product, a movie, or news story, and introduces basic terminology for each script.

In introducing the movie trailer to the students during the pretask phase, for example, the teacher explains such basic dramatic terms as character, conflict, situation, climax, and resolution of the conflict, terms also relevant to movie scenes and to some commercials. The teacher can reinforce these themes by showing examples. News scripts and documentaries offer insights into broadcast journalism, whereas scenes from films, plays, or television programs provide an opportunity to further examine elements of fiction such as character, conflict, climax, and resolution. With news, the teacher can describe the process of news-gathering and help students identify key elements of a news broadcast, such as, Who or what is the story about? Where does it take place? When did or will the event occur? How did it happen? Various news broadcast elements, such as interviews, features, or in-depth news stories, also can be highlighted. To help students understand speeches, the teacher can explain the historical, social, and political context of the speech, or students can conduct their own research online. Teachers and students can discuss the goals of the speech and techniques the speaker used to persuade his or her audience. Students also can be asked to chart the emotional range of the speech. No matter which type of script is used in class, groups of students collaborate on vocabulary work, decoding key words and phrases and drawing on their own knowledge and experience.

In the performance cycle of the task, students plan performances, choose characters, rehearse, and provide each other with feedback. During this cycle, students must view the video sequences again to compare performances. Finally, they perform the script before the class. Willis and Willis (1996) and Willis and Edwards (2005) argue that this performance before peers pushes language learners toward greater fluency and accuracy than would simple practice with partners. After each performance, during the posttask phase, students evaluate each other's efforts, and the teacher provides a more formal assessment. The teacher also may introduce various extension activities to recycle the vocabulary and phrases that the students have learned or focus on form, demonstrating both strengths and weaknesses in a performance.

Types of Scripts

Several types of scripts can be used in script-reading tasks, as illustrated in Table 1.

Because movie trailers are so short, an entire task cycle can be completed in a single class. The Web site English Trailers (www.english-trailers.com) has links to 85 film trailers, transcripts, cloze versions of them, and questions. The Internet Movie Database (www.imdb.com) has production information on most contemporary English language movies and links to their trailers. Student tasks could include altering lines for comic effect (see Appendix for a complete list of Internet resources).

Commercial Scripts

Commercials make for good short scripts as well as provide for fascinating cultural study. Only older commercials are available on video or DVD; however, a selection of both older and newer commercials also can be viewed on YouTube (www.youtube.com). Students can learn about rhetorical devices such as the persuasive language of an emotional appeal, for example, from a commercial of a new car streaking down an open road with the narrator's voice declaiming its ease, freedom, and power. After performing commercial scripts, students can create their own products, devising attractive names and performing their own commercials for them. As with movie trailers, parody is an easy and highly motivating approach.

Table 1. Task Phases for Script Readings With Potential Instructions to Students

Movie Trailers and Commercials	News Broadcasts	Speeches	TV and Film
Pretask Phase 1. activating pretask knowledge of the product, subject, or situation 2. identifying characters and situation 3. viewing and discussion of the video sequence with the teacher			
What questions does the trailer pose? Compare several types of commercial appeals.	Listen for key facts in a broadcast and reading the script to confirm them. Differentiate between types of news broadcasts.	Find key words and phrases in a speech. Determine the rhetorical devices used and the persuasive goal.	Determine the conflict, climax, and resolution.
Task Performance 1. choice of characters or roles 2. rehearsal with peer feedback to achieve a fluent reading 3. additional viewing of the video sequence 4. teacher monitoring of group and individual progress 5. student performance for the class			
Memorize script roles.	Try to achieve an authoritative tone of voice.	Try persuasive tones and body language.	Try to convey character.
Posttask Phase 1. peer assessment 2. teacher assessment 3. extension activities and recycling language			
Create new lines for the trailers. Create commercials in similar styles.	Predict outcomes for the news items, then write follow-up stories.	Use the same language and rhetorical devices to make a speech from the opposing viewpoint.	Create another scene with the same characters, or make a different ending to the earlier scene.

News Announcing

The major English language news organizations offer various forms of video streaming, some with broadcast transcripts and program DVDs for sale. The CBC public affairs program, The Fifth Estate (www.cbc.ca/fifth), posts key documents from news broadcasts for study. A recent documentary reported on a missing person's case, and the CBC Web site included family photographs, a timeline of events, the missing person's poster, and a police report. CNN International (http://edition.cnn.com) offers a variety of news on business, entertainment, living, technology, travel, and interviews with Larry King with "student transcripts." As with real news announcers, students playing the role of an announcer do not memorize a script but become familiar enough with it to read it fluently and accurately, make some eye contact with their audience, and convey a news announcer's authoritative tone.

Famous Speeches

Speech transcripts can expose advanced students to more rhetorical devices and potential lessons about culture and history. Speeches, or portions of them, can be performed as monologues after rehearsal with a partner who offers feedback. American Rhetoric (www.americanrhetoric.com) provides movie transcripts and the texts of 100 top political speeches in the United States, including Barack Obama's 2004 keynote address to the Democratic Presidential Convention. One particularly good example of rhetoric and culture in this collection is the stirring and frequently quoted Martin Luther King "I Have a Dream" speech, delivered August 23, 1963, describing the aspirations of African-Americans. Practicing such famous speeches empowers students to convey emotion and meaning through their own renditions.

Scenes from TV and Movies

TV and movie scenes can be found to fit most themes or courses. For example, in the Rikkyo University study cited earlier, scenes from business-themed movies were incorporated into a global business course (College of Business, 2007). In the first semester, students learned vocabulary and contributed comments to a blog on two other business-themed movies, and they watched and critiqued scenes being rehearsed by their classmates. In the second semester, they created and developed their own scenes using similar characters and conflicts and employing the vocabulary they had learned. TV and film scripts are readily available, and we have made extensive use of these at Aoyama Gakuin University. A large collection of such scripts can be downloaded from Drew's Script-o-rama (www .script-o-rama.com) or purchased from The Script Shack (www.scriptshack.com; see Appendix).

Creative Projects Using Scripts

Various creative projects, from storyboarding to photo strips and scriptwriting, can be based on these different script types. Students can perform live in class or use dialogue to create poster presentations of drawings and dialogue or computer-generated comic strips using photos and dialogue.

Storyboards

Film directors and crews extensively employ storyboards showing the action, dialogue, and setting in a film to plan their shoots efficiently. Underneath each drawing in a storyboard are commentary, dialogue, and production notes. Storyboards help in analyzing how plot, conflict, and camera angles contribute to a film. Artist Josh Sheppard's Web site (www.thestoryboardartist.com) showcases storyboards for different genres of film. The department of education's Web site at the University of Hawaii (www2.hawaii.edu) offers a complete 28-panel storyboard for an instructional video on parking a car. The site also includes a downloadable storyboard with blank lines for students to note visuals, audio, transitions, and tracking time. Showing these materials in class can help explain the usefulness of storyboards.

The Photo Strip

In another script-based task, students create a scene for a TV show, the backstory to an existing film (the story that occurred before the movie starts), or prepare a different ending to an existing story or film. Most new laptops have built-in cameras, or Webcams are relatively inexpensive to purchase. Shooting snapshots and altering them with special effects such as distorted images, negatives, sepia tones, or high contrast shots is easy for students to do. Comic Life (http://plasq .com) comes bundled with Mac Powerbooks, and it also can be downloaded as a 1-month free trial for both Mac and PC platforms or purchased as an inexpensive download. This software enables users to caption photographs with cartoon-style printing and include dialogue and character thoughts in speech balloons. Our students used Comic Life as part of a field trip to see an amateur theatre production of Bernard Pomerance's 1979 play, *The Elephant Man*, portraying a man whose hideous deformities lead to his nickname. Students created scenes from the play's backstory, his early life. Figure 1 shows how one student group imagined the Elephant Man's birth (this comic was slightly modified for content and form for presentation here).

Scene Writing

Scene writing is a difficult task requiring a good grasp of dialogue, conflict, and situation. TV and film scripts also have a particular format in terms of scene description, directions to the actors, and dialogue. Students can view authentic scripts in class as models for script and scene writing, and they can use a downloadable scriptwriting template available from the BBC Writers' Room (www.bbc .co.uk/writersroom; see Appendix).

The easiest scene writing project is to have students finish a scene from part of a movie shown in class. For some years, we have been using the scene from *Kramer vs. Kramer* (Fischoff, 1979) in which Joanna Kramer leaves her husband, Ted, and their son, Billy. The movie's theme of relationship breakdown, divorce, the father's struggle to become a better parent, and the courtroom battle over child custody is of great interest to our students in terms of language and culture. We play the scene just to the point at which Ted begs Joanna to stay, leaving it open-ended as to whether or not he can convince her to stay with him and their son. Then we ask pairs of students to finish the scene by deciding whether or not

Figure 1. Back Story Comic for The Elephant Man

Ted convinces Joanna to stay. The students write the ending to the scene and perform it before the rest of the class.

Scene writing provides opportunities for collaborative writing and can be facilitated by updating the ready-made situations, characters, and conflicts in fairy tales and folk tales, particularly ones well known to students. Burke and O'Sullivan (2002) suggest changing the gender roles in these stories to enable students to critically examine how fairy tales, especially the Walt Disney versions, promulgate views of youth and beauty as the most important female traits.

To Record or Not To Record?

One goal for scenes is class performance, but students practice a great deal of language rehearsing, and recordings can enable later playback of these sessions in class. Recording is best done when knowledgeable students film and edit performances. However, any recording will take much more class time and increase the technical demands on students unless studio or classroom space and homework can be devoted to the project. If done outside of class, students may have trouble meeting even if class time has been devoted to scripting.

Teachers need to consider whether or not to record, and then choose the appropriate medium. For example, an audio recording of a scene requires minimal equipment and training. Furthermore, in an audio recording, students can read from their scripts rather than try to memorize their parts. Sound effects can be added to enhance the imagination of both listener and producers. A higher tech solution is using microphones with digital portable recording devices and a computer for downloading and mixing sound effects, such as those available from the Freesound Project (www. freesound.org). Filmmaking, though much more challenging, provides students with a unique opportunity to explore their ideas and gain an appreciation for the complexity of film production. Gromik (2006) contends that "collaboration on a complex, authentic task such as a video project stimulates language intake and consolidates retention because students share their knowledge of the language and focus on problem solving for authentic purposes" (p. 122).

Student Filmmaking: Commercials, Scenes, and Mini-Documentaries

There are a number of basic requirements for digitally filming scenes in class. To begin with, teachers need to evaluate their equipment, including access to digital cameras, school computer labs, and software. Students need to be introduced to basic camera shots such as close-up, medium, and long shots and high and low camera angles. Free online tutorials on filmmaking and editing can be accessed on iMovie Tutorial (www.apple.com/support/imovie) and Windows XP (see Appendix).

Gromik (2006) outlines a series of film projects for beginner to advanced students, illustrating how language and content can be developed using film props and settings. Beginners can film a guided tour of the city. Students at the intermediate level can create a game show, a documentary, or write and film a dramatic scene. Advanced students can engage in eco-activism projects, longer documentaries, and instructional and fund-raising videos. There are a growing number of online resources, too. Michael Moore (2008) includes teachers' guides for *Fahrenheit 9/11* and *Bowling for Columbine*, two of his controversial films, and he includes simple instructions for students to create their own documentaries. The British Columbia Ministry of Education (see Appendix) offers teachers the online curriculum guide for a fine arts course in film and drama with very useful learning outcomes, resources, suggested projects, and student assessment scales.

An easy project is producing a commercial. Students choose a product, brainstorm a name for it, select the words and images that might best reach an audience, write and storyboard the commercial, then film and edit it. Class discussion afterward focuses on: (a) how each commercial tried to get the audience's attention with language, visuals, and rhetorical persuasion; (b) how the characters and the product or service appeared in the commercial; and (c) how likely other students might be to purchase the product.

The student project for our film communication course is done in small groups. The groups write, storyboard, and film a scene in the genre of comedy, love story, horror, or thriller. Early in the course, students choose a genre and develop characters, setting, a conflict, and a climax for their scene. Throughout the project, time is given in class for students to plan and discuss and for the teacher to work with groups to help them to refine their ideas. The teacher provides an orientation to filming (such as use of a tripod) and editing using software available in our computerized language laboratory. The teacher also outlines a simplified process for creating a film, broken down into preproduction, production, and postproduction and tries to keep students on that schedule (see Figure 2).

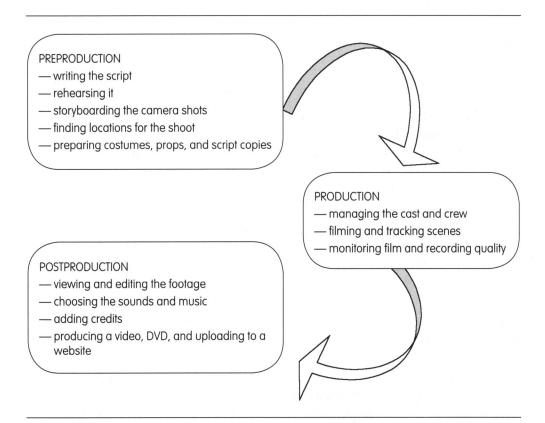

PREPRODUCTION
— writing the script
— rehearsing it
— storyboarding the camera shots
— finding locations for the shoot
— preparing costumes, props, and script copies

PRODUCTION
— managing the cast and crew
— filming and tracking scenes
— monitoring film and recording quality

POSTPRODUCTION
— viewing and editing the footage
— choosing the sounds and music
— adding credits
— producing a video, DVD, and uploading to a website

Figure 2. The Student Filmmaking Process

Samples of student projects can be found online on the Apple Student Gallery (http://edcommunity.apple.com/gallery) or at Campus Movie Fest (www.campusmoviefest.com), which organizes an annual contest and also sells DVD compilations of the best student films. Student awareness of the variety and quality of other student films helps in integrating the project into a course.

The short student-made documentaries featured in several courses in our language program are approached using a similar production schedule. However, students must establish certain key facts in their documentaries: describing their issue, where it takes place, and who is involved. Other aspects of documentary filmmaking should be presented in class including verbally introducing interviewees or captioning them on the screen, both techniques often used in TV documentaries. They also need some familiarity with on-camera announcers and the use of voiceovers. Moore (see Appendix) suggests groups of five to six students brainstorming hot topics, developing a list of potential interviewees, storyboarding the documentary and sequencing the interviews, and then filming them. Moore's Web site also includes exercises in interviewing using clips of celebrity interviewees. Students may present their films and documentaries in class, and if they burn DVD copies of their work, these can be shown in any venue, such as a campus art show, school festival, or open campus event. Student films and documentaries can also reach a larger audience on YouTube.

REFLECTIONS

If introduced in a supportive environment, the use of scripts offers varied, highly motivating language tasks for English language classes at different levels of ability. Naturally, students need a supportive environment. Negotiate with them as to when laughter is appropriate and how to encourage one another through applause. Vocal exercises and jazz chants can sensitize students to English intonation, prosody, rhythm, and stress, supplementing the tasks and activities described here. Performing scripts works best if introduced early in a course and done regularly. Offering students choices, even limited ones, in the selection of speeches, film, and TV scenes will help engage their interest. Encouraging the students to rehearse scenes several times until everyone is satisfied with their performance provides valuable language practice. As students become more familiar with the characteristics of a movie trailer, a commercial, a film script, or a news broadcast, they can develop their own scripts and model their performance. Of course, teachers should aim for balance in linguistic varieties, such as British and Australian English, for example, to make students aware of the contrasts between pronunciation, vocabulary, and interaction styles.

At the same time, the technology and tasks need to be selected appropriately: Recording should not be viewed as an end in itself. The exception might be with larger classes in which it might be hard to organize rehearsals or performances. With large classes, it might be better to do a scene as a term project in which students rehearse over a period of weeks, meeting both in and outside of class. Alternately, filming a scene with a stationary video camera and doing minor editing through immediately reviewing and reshooting scenes would minimize, perhaps even eliminate, the need for an extensive and time-consuming editing process. Teachers who intend to try filmmaking with students would be well advised to try smaller projects with their classes first, such as scripting and storyboarding, then gradually move into larger, more ambitious projects.

TV and film scripts not only offer the potential to develop students' speaking and writing abilities, but they also can provide the cultural and historical background for many areas of studies. For a general language course, news items and film scenes can be directly linked to course themes and tied to students' interests and abilities. Ultimately, script-based tasks serve an important function in our classrooms. They help us to better educate our students and ourselves about the possibilities and limitations of media in our lives.

Gregory Strong is an English professor and coordinates the Integrated English Program at Aoyama Gakuin University, Tokyo, Japan. He has also worked in China and Canada as a curriculum writer, teacher educator, and tester. He has published widely, in education, travel, and literature, and other volumes in TESOL's Classroom Practice *series.*

APPENDIX: INTERNET RESOURCES

American Rhetoric
   http://www.americanrhetoric.com

Apple Student Gallery
   http://edcommunity.apple.com/gallery/student/

BBC Writers Room, Scriptsmart
   http://www.bbc.co.uk/writersroom/scriptsmart

British Columbia Ministry of Education, Fine Arts, Drama 11 and 12: Filmmaking and Television, Curriculum Support Materials, Integrated Resource Packages
   http://www.bced.gov.bc.ca/irp/film1112/filpref.htm

Campus Movie Fest
   http://www.campusmoviefest.com/

CBC Fifth Estate
   http://www.cbc.ca/fifth/

CNN International, Transcripts
   http://edition.cnn.com/TRANSCRIPTS/

Comic Life
  http://plasq.com/downloads/

English Trailers
  http://www.english-trailers.com/index.php

Drew's Script-o-rama
  http://www.script-o-rama.com/

Freesound Project
  http://www.freesound.org

iMovie Tutorial
  http://www.apple.com/support/imovie/tutorial/index.html

Internet Movie Database
  http://www.imdb.com/title/tt0381061/trailers

Moore, M.
  http://www.fahrenheit911.com/library/book/index.php

The Script Shack
  http://www.scriptshack.com/shop/enter.html?lmd=39263.025301

Sheppard, J.
  http://www.thestoryboardartist.com/Site/Home.html

University of Hawaii, Department of Education, Storyboard Template
  http://www2.hawaii.edu/~ricky/etec/sboardtemplate.html

Windows XP, Creating and Sharing Great Movies
  http://www.microsoft.com/windowsxp/using/moviemaker/create/default.mspx

CHAPTER 17

Authentic Video as Passport to Cultural Participation and Understanding

Christopher Stillwell

Any teacher who has used video[1] material in the classroom and paused a scene in the middle can attest to the gripping power of storytelling, for sighs of disappointment from students wanting to watch more is the common response. Perhaps this power to engage is the best reason for authentic video use. How often do students react in the same way to the interruption of other classroom activities? Although the surface benefits to authentic video for language learning may be fairly obvious, the advantages can extend far beyond such things as vocabulary development and listening practice. For learners of English as a foreign language (EFL), this material can provide a sort of surrogate experience to fill in for the natural lack of opportunities to experience the target culture directly. And although English as a second language (ESL) learners may enjoy a far richer environment in terms of experiencing the language in a variety of contexts, the meaningful use of video can play an equally important part in the development of learners' awareness and ability to participate in that culture. For ESL learners, day-to-day interactions bring countless occasions in which ordinary communication breakdowns bring the threat of embarrassment and loss of face, potentially making their cultural experience excruciatingly stressful. Authentic video can offer both ESL and EFL learners an alternative, providing safe opportunities to encounter language and culture in preparation for adventures in the real world.

The power of video to interest learners in their language study is considerable. Owen, Silet, and Brown (1998) state that material of this nature has the potential to be the "most powerful educator in America" (p. 33). This chapter outlines

---

[1] The term *video* is used in the very general sense of filmed media, including user-friendly DVD formats that allow for easy access to virtually any part of a program (with or without subtitles) with just a few presses on the remote control.

the benefits of using video for language learning, for both classroom instruction and independent learning. Authentic video is here viewed as any content that exists primarily for the enjoyment of native speakers—to a certain extent, it is content that could be said to embody and even create the target language culture. Although video material is frequently scripted and therefore arguably less authentic than naturally occurring communication between native speakers, it is authentic insofar as it has not been expressly produced for language teaching.

CONTEXT

Learners and teachers are often eager to make use of authentic video material as an entertaining way of independently developing language skills and experiencing language and culture as it occurs in ordinary life. My work with video in language teaching began at Cambridge Schools, an intensive English program in New York City where adult ESL learners expressed the simple goal of "being able to understand and enjoy movies in English." Although these learners had studied English for several years before coming to the United States, they were frustrated as they went to cinemas, watched television series, or bought DVDs, for these forays into American culture often made the gaps in their language abilities painfully clear. Further development of this approach took place in workshops at Teachers College Columbia University, which aimed to help second language teachers find ways of empowering their students to use authentic video to learn English independently. This work continued at Kanda University of International Studies in Chiba, Japan, where students make use of a self-access learning center that offers training in independent learning with workshops and study modules on learning English through movies, among many other things. Although my work has involved primarily adult learners, the practices discussed in this chapter could apply to learners of any age.

CURRICULUM, TASKS, MATERIALS

Authentic Material vs. Textbooks

Although there may be many pedagogically sound reasons for organizing a curriculum around the tidy units of study found in language textbooks, relying on the modified and simplified language of such texts alone leaves something missing. In the case of listening, Garrett (1991) notes that differences between tightly controlled pedagogical audio and natural spoken language typically lead to a difficult transition for classroom language learners. In order to provide a closer approximation of real-life listening experience, authentic passages should be incorporated to expose learners to the randomness of naturally occurring everyday English while providing practice at making sense of it.

Another concern about standard English language pedagogical material is that although it tends to be full of useful linguistic examples, we cannot say that it typically provides learners with direct *experience* of the target language culture. In a sense, this gulf between textbook English and authentic language parallels the distinction between reading a synopsis versus reading the real thing, or indeed between hearing a description of a sports event, witnessing it firsthand, and even directly participating. Experience with authentic material like television programs and movies that are a part of the target language speakers' world helps turn language learners into consumers of and participants in the culture, and it can do so with relatively little risk of the frustration and embarrassment that can come from real-life interactions with native speakers. As a result, learners may even feel empowered to explore a world of conversational possibilities outside the classroom as feelings of cultural distance diminish and they discover that they now share something in common with native speakers.

Perhaps the simplest and best argument in favor of using authentic video material in the classroom is that direct exposure to the target culture is also likely to sustain motivation for language learning, not only because of the greater sense of accomplishment that comes from understanding material made for native speakers, but also because such material is expressly designed to maintain the viewer's interest. For the learners in New York and Japan, this quality led to an increase in independent study, as students got hooked on particular movie genres or television series.

Selecting Authentic Video for Classroom and Independent Use

The first step in using movies and television for language learning is to make wise choices in the selection of material. Some questions to consider:

Will the material be sufficiently interesting to maintain interest over repeated viewings?

Losing interest in material is usually not an issue. Learners are often eager to get a second chance (or indeed a third or even a fourth chance) to understand material, especially if viewings are well managed and class discussion reveals additional clues to unlocking meanings. Still, it is important for teachers to choose video that is engaging so as to provide learners with experiences that they will be eager to repeat outside the classroom.

Will the material expose learners to useful vocabulary and pronunciation, or will it generate a lot of questions and confusion about areas of language that are not worthwhile?

All authentic material is not equal in complexity and usefulness. A swashbuckling Johnny Depp movie may be a popular choice at first, but if it has a lot of uncommon vocabulary and unusual accents, it could ultimately prove frustrating. Of course, virtually any material that learners find motivating is to some extent justifiable, but movies with characters, environments, and situations that are similar to those that learners might actually encounter are of greater value and generate greater interest for repeated viewings.

Will the material help learners acquire knowledge that is transferable to other language tasks?

For classes focusing on academic vocabulary, it may be beneficial to look at programs related to science and the news. Popular TV series may be more appropriate for conversation-oriented classes, with the added advantage that once learners have sufficient exposure, they will likely find it easier to comprehend subsequent episodes, for oft-repeated instances of vocabulary, speech patterns, and pronunciation will become more familiar. Knowledge of the characters' personalities and tendencies makes the action more comprehensible, creating conditions for target language patterns to be internalized.

Does the material lend itself to support from other media?

Perhaps the first question is whether any contextual information is necessary prior to viewing. As listeners, we generally have contextual knowledge about the speaker, awareness of the reasons for the talk, and understanding of its connection to our own purposes (Ur, 1996). We may have already read a news account before hearing of a news event on TV or radio, and we may already have read the novel, know some of the actors, or have read a review prior to viewing a movie. Context provides a framework on which to build understanding.

Background information can be provided through the integration of additional authentic media. For instance, TV news can be supported by newspapers, with an added benefit that because newspapers vary in complexity and readability, teachers can choose a newspaper to match the learners' level. With movies, comprehension can be significantly enhanced by reading the related novel or short story, or through the analysis of reviews, synopses, or background information easily found on the Internet (see Appendix for Internet resources). The teacher can ask students to make predictions about a program based on snippets of the supporting material, or students in groups may be assigned particular resources to locate and make themselves authorities on, after which they will be mixed into new groups in jigsaw fashion to consolidate and share discoveries. Movie reviews can also provide authentic practice with prereading strategies, such as reading the first and last paragraphs, skimming for gist, and sampling by reading only the first sentence of each paragraph, allowing the learner to become acquainted with the text (and, by extension, the film) without being exposed to too many spoilers.

Teaching and Learning Language Through the Use of Authentic Video

A common concern among language educators regarding the use of authentic video is that its difficulty will prove overwhelming to learners. This concern is a legitimate one, because nonnative listeners face a number of frustrations not found in first-language listening, particularly as they try to understand what they hear despite the speed, reduction, and connectedness of natural speech (Hinkel, 2006). It can be difficult for native-speaking teachers to appreciate the challenges inherent in second language listening: Native speakers can simultaneously listen to a message in conversation and craft their response to it, but second language listeners require more processing time to decode aural input (Meskill, 1996).

Second language listeners may be unable to fully perceive the input because they have fewer resources available to focus on higher order processes like making inferences and predictions (Schmidt, 2001). These cognitive challenges can quickly lead to exhaustion, but skilled classroom use of video material can assist learners in managing frustration without compromising the rich quality of the language input. Ideally, this exploration should be conducted in such a way as to model techniques that are transferable to independent learning, such as breaking the action into segments of reasonable size, asking the right kinds of questions, allowing for repeated viewings of scenes, and making judicious use of subtitles and transcripts.

Breaking the Action Into Segments

The first step in not overwhelming learners is to limit the length of clips so that the material can be sufficiently processed through multiple viewings. In deciding precisely where to break up video clips, a range of issues must be considered, such as the depth of recollection expected of the students—if only understanding of the gist is required, a longer clip may be suitable, particularly if the visuals provide a great deal of support. It is equally important to make sure that the clip is not so dense as to be overwhelming. Making expectations clear to students in advance as to exactly what sort of information they will be expected to process and on what level will reduce frustration. Once a scene has been paused and analyzed, repeated viewings can reinforce lessons learned as well as the discovery of new items of interest.

Another concern is that pausing the video at awkward moments may disrupt the flow of the narrative, annoying the viewers. It is a good idea to be mindful of the rhythms films and television programs have and to "go with the flow" whenever possible, so that the learners/viewers are naturally inclined to turn their attention from the video to their language work. Otherwise, the goals of the teacher and students become misaligned, with the teacher intruding on students whose primary concern is to satisfy their own needs for narrative closure. Changes of time and place provide obvious points in video to take a break from the action. Entrances and exits of major characters also provide obvious breaking points. The teacher can pause the video in mid-action in order to draw attention to points that would probably be forgotten by the end of the scene, but it is probably best to allow the students to view the scene in its entirety first and then return to the moment of interest.

Asking the Right Kinds of Questions

Teachers who rely heavily on questions about details may intensify students' frustration by creating the impression that it is necessary to understand every word. In reality, native speakers rarely catch every word they hear, but they use inference and other strategies to fill in gaps. Students should be encouraged to do the same. A tolerance for ambiguity can be fostered by favoring broader questions and welcoming multiple interpretations. Furthermore, there will be times when scenes will be impenetrable even to native speakers. Teachers can model an ideal approach to such material, demonstrating their own comfort with ambiguity and providing encouragement to students by admitting when aspects of the material are challenging for native speakers too.

Use of Subtitles and Other Textual Support

Turning English subtitles on creates additional opportunities for noticing while making the material more comprehensible, but users must be clear about goals. Although these readily available transcripts of authentic speech can be a valuable linguistic resource, their usefulness for developing listening skills is debatable because they render attentive listening unnecessary. Skilled classroom use of subtitles should model effective choices that do not interfere with listening skill development. Teachers should present subtitles by urging restraint, reserving their use for checking comprehension late in the repeated viewing cycle of reflection, discussion, and additional viewings. In classrooms with a shared first language, the comparison of subtitles in the students' native language with the original audio can be a rich source of discovery and debate about translation choices made—an authentic bilingual viewing practice. English subtitles may also be used as part of previewing preparation, with students watching scenes first with sub-titles on and sound off to discover key vocabulary.

Transcripts found on the Internet, published screenplays, or even novelizations can be used for classroom activities that prepare learners for viewing tasks and promote discoveries of authentic spoken language (see list of Internet Resources for Movie Integration in the Appendix). For instance, unscrambling transcripts of movie dialogue in which the lines are out of sequence can allow students to become familiar with movie content while discovering common cohesive cues in scripted discourse. This can be particularly effective with dialogues in which utterances are closely connected.

Discovering Language in Transcripts

Additional work with transcripts prior to viewing a scene can allow for new insights on nonlinguistic ways of communicating meaning, both in film and in everyday life. Transcripts from popular sitcoms can provide rich material for analysis, particularly in situations where comedy is derived from various sorts of communication breakdowns. Learners may first be provided with a transcript like the one below[2] and asked to make predictions individually about what is taking place.

A *Hey Bob, howyadoin?*

B *Hello.*

A *Long time no see!*

B *Yes.*

A *Boy, it sure is nice to see you. The last time we talked, when was that? At the Christmas party?*

B *Maybe.*

A *It has been too long, that's for sure.*

B *Alright.*

A *Well, I'll let you go. Hope to see you again soon!*

B *Goodbye.*

At first glance, students might not pick up on anything odd in the transcript, for on the surface it appears that the two participants have a fairly normal, if slightly banal, conversation. Once the students have come up with individual interpretations, they share their ideas with partners and perform the dialogue aloud to make additional discoveries. In this particular case, the dialogue may reveal that partner B does not actually say very much, and that B's language is more formal than A's. Students may be invited to speculate on the cause for any irregularities. The scene from the video can then be viewed, and the class can further discuss what is really going on and how additional cues like body language, intonation, and stress play a role in communicating meaning. In this particular case, the video may confirm that partner B is not interested in engaging in conversation as the action in the scene may show how A's warmth and engagement is not being reciprocated by B. Once a consensus has been reached on what is happening, students can revisit the transcript to look for additional clues in the language that support their interpretation.

---

[2] This generic dialogue was invented for the purposes this chapter and is meant to represent the sort of simple conversation found in many sitcoms, where communication breakdowns are used for comic effect. For actual classroom use, the teacher should use a real video transcript.

REFLECTIONS

The practice of using authentic video in the classroom is not without its challenges. Because this material is not designed for second or foreign language learners, language forms may appear chaotic, especially in comparison with the tight constraints of textbook presentations. However, the messiness of authentic language is a virtue, for unlike the tightly controlled scripts of pedagogical audio, authentic material provides learners with an experience representative of the challenges faced by all users of English in the real world—understanding language even when there are ambiguities.

As teachers become familiar with the material through their preparations for class, it may be easy to lose sight of the fact that the story is the most salient aspect for first-time viewers. A teacher may notice an interesting bit of connected speech, or a telling choice of verb tense in the dialogue, but first-time viewers will be focused on big picture issues of the video. Instead of beginning post-viewing discussion of a scene with questions about particular language points, students should first be given a chance to share their overall reactions, as well as their opinions of what it all means and how it will affect future events. Once such discussion has run its course and the learners' natural desire to understand the story has been satisfied, attention can more easily be trained on useful vocabulary, grammar, pronunciation, and prosodic features in the scene.

Christopher Stillwell has worked with authentic video as an ESL/EFL language learning tool for fourteen years in such varied contexts as intensive English programs in Spain and New York, international conferences and Teachers College Columbia University workshops, and self-access learner training at Kanda University of International Studies in Chiba, Japan.

APPENDIX: INTERNET RESOURCES FOR MOVIE INTEGRATION

The Internet Movie Database is the authority on film. It includes cast lists, memorable quotes, reviews, and links to other Web sites.

http://www.imdb.com

Script-o-rama offers hundreds of movie scripts and transcripts.

http://www.script-o-rama.com

Rotten Tomatoes offers snippets of movie reviews as well as links to the original full texts.

http://www.rottentomatoes.com

The English Learner Movie Guides provides ELL support and activities for a number of movies available on video.

http://www.eslnotes.com

English Trailers has movie trailers with accompanying cloze activities, discussion questions and more, all designed for English learners.

http://www.english-trailers.com

Sharing the Food and Fun Through Restaurant Review Blogs: An Integrated-Skills Project Approach

Timothy R. Healy

This chapter presents a fun integrated-skills project centered on publishing a student blog. Learners collaborate to visit, analyze, discuss, and then write reviews of local restaurants, such as the following samples from my students:

> The food is tasty. You can try the garlic grilled shrimp with brown rice or the best fried fish you will ever try. However, this is not a place to go to for lunch when you are in hurry because the service is slow.

> The atmosphere is delightful and original. It's a big place and the illumination is soft. The colors are well matched and invite you to stay longer. The music is not loud and lets you hear your friends.

> Javiera Olivares Iriarte, Rocio Olivares Iriarte, & Alali Sultan
> (Reprinted with permission.)

Students publish their reviews—including photographs they take—on a blog for an authentic audience. The project is best suited to intermediate or high-intermediate reading and writing courses where exposition and argument in the well developed essay are taught or refined. The project motivates students to do their best work and promotes learning because it is authentic, integrative, and collaborative. Publishing on a blog platform is also easy; neither the instructor nor the students need any Web-publishing skills or experience.

CONTEXT

Integrating blog reviews into language instruction promotes speaking, listening, reading, and writing. Learners build oral/aural language skills and autonomy by dining together in groups or pairs at a restaurant, interacting with service personnel, and negotiating and justifying their opinions about the experience in subsequent discussions in preparation for writing reviews. The writing process includes four main steps:

1. generating and organizing ideas

2. writing the first draft

3. editing, revising, and formatting in subsequent drafts

4. publishing on the blog

Students first write individually and then collaboratively with their dining partners. In the group composition process, students critically read their dining partners' texts and collaborate on a joint piece of writing. By conducting peer reviews across groups, they also read and compare the experiences of other students dining at different restaurants. Reading is integrated in a number of ways. In preparation for writing the review, students analyze authentic reviews to become familiar with form and content. Other reading tasks include researching restaurants, rereading drafts, and conducting peer reviews of drafts.

The project integrates an array of teaching and learning settings and configurations. It includes class work, field work, and homework, and learners work individually, in small groups, and as a class. Because the project gets students out into the local community, it has proven very motivating in our intensive English program.

Publishing restaurant reviews gives students the opportunity to use their English skills authentically. The number of restaurants and cafes in our communities makes plain that people in the United States enjoy dining out. Similarly, the huge number of restaurant reviews available online shows that a great many of us also enjoy writing about our experience after we eat. Yelp (http://www.yelp.com), a Web site that promotes itself as "the fun and easy way to find, review, and talk about what's great—and not so great—in your area," features thousands of reviews of restaurants in over 100 U.S. cities, written by amateurs. In eating out and then writing about the experience, students do what multitudes of other people do every day. People generally read restaurant reviews to help them choose where to eat. Students also can choose, even within instructor-imposed limits, where to eat. In taking responsibility for their choice of restaurant, they have a greater stake in the outcome. Thus empowered, they are motivated to do their best (Karchmer-Klein, 2007).

Instructors can motivate students to participate by designing activities that seem fun and easy. Enjoyment and ease exert a pull on second language learners just as they do on native-language writers. And like native-language writers, when English language learners have the goal of posting online, they can see a real purpose and mode to communicate with an audience outside the classroom. Such communication can motivate learners because they see their work as content to be put into type form and published for an audience (Bicknell, 1999). Using the tools of today's technology to publish may be a motivator in and of itself. The majority of international students in my classes consistently report that they do most of their reading and writing online. In the course of this project, students use word processing, e-mail, and browser technology, which encourages them to write because it meets their conceptions of reading and writing in the digital age.

CURRICULUM, TASKS, MATERIALS

Restaurant Reviews as Integrated Skills

To initiate a restaurant review project, teachers can activate students' background knowledge by asking them to describe their favorite restaurants. The instructor, or an able student, can list key vocabulary words on the board. Students can then analyze the list in pairs, adding more words and categorizing them into main topics and supporting details. Usually students come up with the four main topics of *food*, *service*, *atmosphere*, and *location*, with corresponding details such as *delicious*, *speed*, *dark*, and *convenient*. By honing in on vocabulary specific to restaurants and dining out, schematic background knowledge is brought to the fore.

Good reviewers need to define the form and function of a restaurant review. By reading short reviews as homework or in class, groups or pairs can identify which main topics the author emphasizes. Students can compile a list of vocabulary from the text for each main topic, or add to the lists prepared above. As a tip, teachers can find short reviews online and in local and weekly newspapers. Groups can read the short review previously read by another group and original readers can report their observations on main topics and vocabulary.

Students build autonomy by researching restaurants for the project. Students can ask people outside of class for suggestions, such as other students (Bauer-Ramazani, 2008), friends, or roommates. In class, they can work in groups to choose a location collaboratively by comparing notes on recommendations and discussing options. Students can then justify their decisions by writing, perhaps collaboratively, why they want to review the restaurant they chose.

Once students have decided on a restaurant, they can perform their field research by dining at the restaurant and taking notes, photos, and maybe collecting a sample menu, a packet of matches, or a business card. Students should be reminded to take notes, perhaps on a handout with the main topics the class had decided on. As a tip, be sure to review the location, local tipping customs, and staff expectations with students before they go. Role playing in class may provide additional support, especially to intermediate level students.

When following up in class, make sure that students have tools at their disposal for analyzing their experiences. Have them use their notes as a springboard in class to review the experience, noting opinions and further ideas and details with their own and other groups. In preparation for writing the review, groups choose which main topics to focus on. Groups that dined together can collaborate on an outline for the review with a working thesis statement that mentions the main topics. As homework, students should prepare a first draft.

In class, students read each other's drafts and compare ideas. For group review, have students focus on thesis statements, topic sentences, and supporting ideas. Students can give each other tips on organizational issues such as the use of coherence devices. As a twist, students can reverse outline a peer's text as they read. Reverse outlining demands critical thinking, and it also produces a written record of ideas that serves as a visual reference for subsequent discussion with authors. Further, the requirement to write a document to parallel their peer's text helps students overcome a reluctance to criticize another's work, or even to read critically.

At this stage, the instructor may want to read each student's draft and provide comments or confer with students individually. For homework, students can write a second draft. A third draft can be prepared collaboratively by reading and discussing second drafts with the dining partners. Because the third draft is the product of a group composition process, it combines the strengths of each member's second draft. The teacher should read and provide comments for revision, but before the instructor makes any editing suggestions, students should review their draft—or that of another group—with the goal of finding, identifying, and fixing mistakes of vocabulary, punctuation, and grammar. Because they have already revised these drafts, students read their texts at this stage for the express purpose of finding mistakes, of which there are two especially important types: those which concern the content of the class lessons, and those which each individual student has found to be their most frequent and persistent.

For support and guidance, students can refer to a checklist of editing symbols that includes explanations and suggestions for correcting. The more they have used such a list in editing their previous work, the more effective it can be. The instructor can also lead students in the use of editing strategies such as rereading a text multiple times from beginning to end and each time checking only one grammar or mechanics point (e.g., subject-verb agreement, verb tense, prepositions, and punctuation). By comparing what they find and explaining mistakes and corrections to a partner or the group, students receive confirmation of their interpretations or alternative meanings. In addition to allowing instructors to highlight and guide students in correcting their own mistakes, editing symbols can help students become more self-aware as writers. The instructor can require students to tally the mistakes they make by symbol (type) in order to create a list that, over time, reveals to students their most intransigent writing problems. Identifying these problems can lead students to study specific grammar points they have not mastered and search for these patterns while rereading their own writing in the editing stage.

After students have edited the review, the instructor can read the texts and find language issues that can serve as opportunities for instruction. For example, the instructor can pull out some grammar points or editing suggestions in order to create mini-lessons designed for the whole class.

Collaboration

At the heart of this project are learners working together. As they go out of the classroom and into restaurants and cafes, they do so in the safety of a group. And, as a group activity, dining out requires them to negotiate a series of choices. Time, place, and what to order are subjects of debate. Learners who speak different languages need English to negotiate these choices. In addition to conversing with each other, students must interact with the restaurant staff. By observing other diners and ordering by themselves, students develop appropriate social skills, and the successful meal can open the door to further confidence in dining out—and using English.

Writing collaborative reviews demands the authentic sharing of opinions. Although most reviews are posted online by a single person, many reflect the opinions of the author's dining mates. By writing collaboratively and expressing and justifying opinions about their dining experience, learners engage in real conversation, even in the classroom.

Blog Preparations: Word-Processing, Photo Editing, and E-mailing

Students can word-process the final group draft, upload and edit photos, and e-mail everything to the instructor (working in groups on one computer so the skills are illustrated to all—collaborative interactions in English are encouraged). Channeling all documents through the instructor maintains control over blog postings. The following tips are essential for successful blogging:

- We know our institution's policy and rules regarding posting student work online. Usually, students or their guardians are required to sign a waiver to allow posting of pictures and texts.

- For ease of receipt and posting, we choose a standard size for photos. Students must edit their photos to this size before they send them.

- To respect the privacy of others, we explain to our students that photos they take of people must also be accompanied by a signed waiver. If they do not have such documentation, we as blog editors do not post them.

Blogs can be created easily, and many are available free online and offer a variety of templates into which the teacher can plug student content. At www.blogger.com teachers can "Create a blog in 3 easy steps": create an account, name your blog, and choose a template.

Ease of Blog Publishing

It has always been easy to share restaurant recommendations, either positive or negative, with friends in casual conversation, but now it is nearly as easy to post these observations online for anyone with a browser to read. Using a widely available hosting site with a simple interface, you can literally create a blog in minutes, which is probably why the number of blogs has exploded the last few years. In addition to not needing software or Web-building skills, instructors do not need a computer lab. Because a lab can be useful in allowing students to compose together and work on the creation and design of the blog, it is not necessary to have computer access as a class to complete this project. Students can word-process, edit photos, and e-mail their work from any suitably equipped computer or not use a computer at all.

For instructors who are publishing online for the first time, this project is an opportunity to learn to design and use a blog by actually doing it. And because creating a blog is so easy, instructors can offer learners multiple opportunities to publish a variety of written products (Richardson, 2006). The restaurant review project uses a blog principally as a "publishing platform" (Braun, 2007). However, once the original texts are published, the online reading and writing discussions can begin, either as an interactive class writing activity or as a response to unsolicited reader postings.

Potential Challenges

There are challenges instructors may face in leading this project. If dining out costs too much for some students, the instructor can institute procedures or spending limits. Students can be asked to anonymously submit any amount of money under a limit, which can then be pooled and distributed equally to each group. Limits can be set on how much students can spend and in what types of restaurants they can eat. We can look to our institutions for support, too.

Financial challenges can actually be beneficial. Paying attention to money can help learners define their audience and more wisely use available resources, like online restaurant guides or tourist guides. When money is an issue, value becomes important, and cost and value are real considerations for diners. To ask students to take them into account is to acknowledge a common reality. A focus on value can lead students to visit those places where people having little income—such as students—tend to eat, and make their reviews useful to an authentic audience. In the event the financial challenge is too great, students can visit establishments during off-hours and order beverages only, while reviewing the menu and taking note of the atmosphere. Or, they can review free public attractions, such as parks or malls.

Another possible challenge is if learners do not have access to computers and, therefore, cannot produce or e-mail an electronic final draft. In this case, instructors can word-process the final drafts if the pieces are relatively short and the class is relatively small. Because the texts are group projects, there are fewer in number, making any typing task more manageable. Blogs are certainly cheap and easily accessible examples of student learning. As such, they can be cost-effective and powerful marketing tools if, for instance, featured on an institution's Web site for potential students to read. Teachers working in educational settings that lack adequate technologies can present such arguments to administrators in seeking such resources.

REFLECTIONS

The project has been successful as a language and digital literacy learning tool. Many student restaurant reviews have been published and read, and have elicited responses. My students report enjoying the task, and I saw them making progress in various skills while having fun. Additionally, students tried restaurants they read about and continued to visit their favorites. In other words, they have lived as locals do (to view sample class blogs, see *Seattle Area Restaurant Reviews* at http://acerestaurantreviews.blogspot.com/).

The project empowers students to enter the authentic world of publishing where their voices can be heard on a topic that people care to read and discuss. It unites students in a group with common goals and gives them the opportunity to share their work with distant family and friends. Once launched, the restaurant review project blogs became a tool of inclusion, informing and orientating new students to the school's community. Other review projects to serve the local community also can be easily prepared, focusing on such area attractions as movie theaters, malls, theaters and museums, and parks and recreational facilities. The blogging possibilities are limitless!

Timothy R. Healy teaches ESL and academic literary skills at the American Cultural Exchange English Language Institute at Seattle Pacific University in Seattle, Washington, in the United States. He has also taught at Bellevue Community College in Bellevue, Washington, where he co-developed the ESL class whose students write the literacy newspaper, Northwest News.

CHAPTER 19

Using Wikis for Collaborative Writing and Intercultural Learning

Geoffrey P. J. Lawrence, Terry Compton, Clayton Young, and Hazel Owen

In recent years, opportunities for authentic English language and cultural inter-action have dramatically increased due to rapidly evolving information and com-munication technologies (ICTs). From e-mail exchanges, computer conferencing, blogs, and more recently wikis, a variety of user-friendly interactive environments have emerged that enable students to communicate directly with other learners and native English speakers in a range of authentic contexts that cross national boundaries. Such transnational collaboration has the potential to build not only English language communication skills but also the intercultural awareness and curiosity increasingly required in our modern, interconnected world.

Research into the effectiveness of computer-mediated language learning has revealed increases in student-centered discourse, motivation, interaction, and improved language acquisition, as well as opportunities for more egalitarian participation (Blake, 2000; Emde, Schneider, & Kotter, 2001; Lawrence, 2000; Mabrito, 1991, 1992; Schultz, 2000; Sullivan & Pratt, 1996; Warschauer, 1997, 2004). Asynchronous computer-mediated writing environments, where com-munication does not take place in "real time" but has an interval of time before a response is received (e.g., e-mail writing), can offer a self-paced, reflective com-municative medium where students can review, edit, and reflect on their writing (Cummins, 2000; Lawrence, 2000; Owen, 2005; Warschauer, 2004). Such learning environments can allow students to share more details about themselves, thereby enhancing classroom culture. Classroom-based research additionally indi-cates that when ICTs are applied within an appropriate learning framework, they can create conditions conducive to collaborative learning, sustaining interactions that lead to higher order learning.

The Distinctive Nature of Wiki-Based Writing

Wikis are a Web-based communication tool that is collaborative and community-based and therefore well suited to a social constructivist teaching approach. As a recent evolution in computer-mediated communication, wikis provide shared, co-editable writing environments that have the potential to provide a rich forum for authentic language interaction, writing production, and learning community development. Wikis are expandable, flexible Web sites that can easily be established and then manipulated by students and teachers to create new Web pages with text and photos as well as links for collaboration, discussion, and interaction. Wikis are distinctive in that students can edit, delete, and add to each other's work, whereas blogs and most other current forms of computer-mediated communication (CMC) are not co-editable. In a blog, e-mail, or computer conference, once a writer adds their posting, other members can only see the posting, they cannot change it. In wikis, everyone has equal "rights" and can add text, images, and links and can edit all other contributors' postings. As a result, wikis provide an opportunity to use a completely collaborative mode of writing that can be motivational and challenging.

This chapter outlines an intercultural wiki-based writing project involving English language students from two distinct geographical, institutional, and cultural environments, with varying English as a second language (ESL) abilities. In this 5-week project, ESL students in an intensive university English language program in Toronto, Canada were grouped with English as a foreign language (EFL) students at a postsecondary college in Dubai, United Arab Emirates (UAE), to work on a collaborative wiki project. They were asked to work together using a wiki to write a collaborative research essay examining the life of a famous person of mutual interest. By detailing the background, specific curriculum, tasks, and materials for student interaction, as well as the lessons learned, we hope to provide guidelines on how to effectively use wikis in an ESL-EFL environment.

CONTEXT

To assess the potential benefits of collaborative wiki-based writing across cultural and geographical boundaries and examine the impact of blending wiki-based writing into a real-time class, teachers in Canada and the UAE launched a 5-week pilot project. The project goals included the development of academic writing and higher order critical thinking skills through intercultural, collaborative interaction in an authentic student-centered setting. Using both synchronous (simultaneous platforms like "chat") and asynchronous communication, the project was designed to promote peer interaction, feedback, mentoring, and tutoring among students as they developed effective academic writing and research skills.

This collaboration involved two classes of adult English language students in postsecondary preparatory programs in English-speaking institutions. One class was at Dubai Men's College (DMC) in Dubai, UAE, which offers a selection of career-oriented and vocational courses ranging from a certificate to bachelor's level. The other class was housed in one of Canada's largest research institutions, the University of Toronto (UT), located in an urban, multicultural environment. The Dubai class consisted of employed male students studying in the evening section of the institution's foundation program. The students were of a similar age and from common cultural and linguistic backgrounds, and all had laptops and wireless connectivity. Although the majority of students entering this program possess fairly high oral competency, most have a limited vocabulary, exhibit fossilized grammar errors, and show little awareness of formal writing conventions (Owen & Madsen, 2008). Thus their English classes (11–14 hours per week) are intended to address these issues and bring student proficiency levels up to the minimum standards required for entry into the college's career programs. There is also an emphasis on study skills, self-directed learning, and using information sources.

The UT students were from a wide variety of cultural and linguistic backgrounds. Countries of origin included Haiti, Mexico, China, South Korea, Japan, Taiwan, Yemen, and Saudi Arabia. Both male and female, their ages and life experiences varied considerably. The academic preparation program offers three 14-week sessions per year at 20 contact hours per week with computer labs available. Students acquire English language and study skills needed to succeed in university programs in Canada and abroad. Most students are highly motivated, and about 25% have already been conditionally accepted into graduate programs by the university.

There was a noticeable difference in the level of English language and study skills between our two institutions: The DMC students were reading and writing at the low-intermediate level, whereas the UT students were highly motivated to improve and were reading and writing at upper intermediate and low-advanced levels. We predicted that this disparity in abilities would disadvantage the advanced students; however, results from previous studies (Owen, 2003) indicate that participants feel it assists their own understanding when they have to explain or give an example of language structure to a peer. As long as positive group dynamics are fostered, multilevel students experience alternative learning strategies and skills as well as develop positive interdependence. Thus we felt that the wiki-based writing project created opportunities for scaffolding, that is: "produced opportunities whereby a learner, if supported by a more advanced peer or teacher, can bridge the gap between assimilated knowledge or skills, and knowledge or skills yet to be assimilated" (Owen, 2005, p. 197).

CURRICULUM, TASKS, MATERIALS

The wiki forum for the project was developed using a free provider, Peanut Butter Wiki (http://pbwiki.com). We chose the Peanut Butter Wiki environment due to ease of set up, simple user interface, and suitable features. The topic for this collaborative project was to research a famous person. This general topic was chosen as it was largely uncontroversial and accessible for low-level students yet interesting enough to motivate high-level students. To expedite the project, students were not given any opportunity to suggest a topic nor were they asked which famous persons they preferred to see on the short list. The DMC students each chose a famous person from the short list, and the UT students were then instructed to select a partner based on the famous persons that had been selected. Although this approach did expedite the project, in retrospect, it limited student autonomy and their ability to choose a partner. This, as we shall discuss in the reflections section, may have been one factor that limited the development of positive and productive collaboration.

Given that students involved in this project were adults in postsecondary learning environments, the development of critical thinking, research, and academic writing skills was a key goal that could be facilitated through the use of asynchronous communication. Recognizing the delayed and disconnected nature of asynchronous interaction, which can stifle the development of online relationships (Thorne, 2003), we decided to integrate synchronous communication into the project using Microsoft's MSN chat alongside regular face-to-face classroom sessions. The project design attempted to capitalize on the potential benefits of collaborative writing tasks that pool student knowledge about research and writing processes and conventions. The student-centered environment encouraged students to identify and choose the support they needed. We provided clear instructions and objectives along with supportive tools, examples, and suggestions for group and peer cooperation. Because students would be working on tasks in an unfamiliar environment with people they had never met, the need to scaffold interaction and tasks seemed paramount. Teachers also had to guard against doing too much for the students, to avoid leaving them with little reason to collaborate with peers. Finally, because the project's credibility ultimately rested on how relevant it was to students' future academic study, we attempted to relate the project to the wider curriculum in each institutional environment As a result, the wiki project exploited language learning through laptop/wireless environments at DMC, and encouraged the development of online research skills and broader learning outcomes required in both the UT and DMC programs.

In order to design and manage the project, the teachers involved set up additional pages in the wiki for the teachers to discuss project design ideas and post reflections about student work, project concerns, and successes. These pages were crucial to the successful management of the wiki project as they centralized project management and discussion. As a result, e-mail was used minimally, often simply to refer teachers to comments posted in these wiki pages that needed feedback.

As illustrated in Figure 1, which shows all stages of the wiki-based project, we began in Stage 1 by having students orient themselves to the wiki-writing environment by writing, designing, creating, and posting an introduction (including

Stage 1: Wiki Orientation
- discuss "netiquette"
- post online introductions
- post/reply to questions written in response to introduction
- pair off & select topic
- collaborate & research using online fact sheets as a guide
- post written reflections in wiki

Stage 2: Essay Collaboration
- discuss writing conventions
- use fact sheet information to write essay drafts
- give partner/peer feedback
- amalgamate two drafts
- jointly write essay

Stage 3: Peer Interviews
- conduct peer MSN interviews about other students' famous people
- summarize & analyze interview data
- reflect on results

Stage 4: Consolidation
- reflect/discuss what learned experienced
- give an assessed oral presentation/ write assessed noncollaborative essay

Figure 1. Stages of the Collaborative Wiki-Based Writing Project

an image if desired). These sessions were facilitated by teachers at both institutions who encouraged students to take the online tutorial and experiment with the wiki features. Students invested a lot of time developing "appropriate and desirable" online identities, despite the fact that UT students only had limited access to computer labs. Students wanted to present aspects of themselves, including their interests and hobbies, in a positive light, to interest and engage their foreign student partners. Once these identities were posted, students were encouraged to visit other community members' introductions and post questions or comments. These tasks were seen as crucial components in orienting students to the online medium and building a connected learning community.

After this introductory step, students were asked to

1. Pair up based on the mutual choice of a famous person.

2. Create in pairs a wiki Web page for a teacher-created online fact sheet (see Figure 2), which was designed to guide, diversify, and build students' online research skills and awareness of strategies to avoid plagiarism.

3. Collaboratively complete the fact sheet by collecting and collating data about their famous person.

4. Copy and paste the completed fact sheet into a new wiki Web page to facilitate essay writing processes.

5. Share the completed research thus forming a "database" open to all wiki members.

6. Post reflections about their wiki experience to date, offering students a voice in the process and helping guide teachers on additional support required as well as refinements for future wiki-based projects.

Once the fact sheet was completed in the wiki (Stage 2), students began working alone to draft an essay based on the collected data. This online writing was supported by classroom lessons and work with individual students reviewing essay writing structure, paragraph format, spelling, and appropriate grammar. Students then worked with their international partners to peer review their writing. Here again, teachers worked with students to develop effective editing strategies and ensure appropriate and constructive peer feedback. Students proceeded to integrate their essays into one joint essay using the flexible collaborative features of the wiki. These features, which are similar to features in Microsoft Word, allowed students to highlight (bold or italicize) areas in the essay that they wanted to discuss or give feedback on. Students would often write their comments or revisions in brackets beside these highlighted sentences, or they would insert them at the end of the draft essay along with more general feedback. As discussed below, due to the time constraints of this project, students often did not merge their draft papers but instead adopted one version of the essay as their final essay, limit-

Fact Sheet

Name of the famous person you have chosen _____

Date of birth _____

Nationality _____

Home town _____

Marital status _____

Children (names/ages) _____

Occupation _____

Appearance (what this famous person looks like) _____

Character (what this famous person is like) _____

Hobbies _____

Likes and dislikes _____

Education _____

Parents' names? Occupations? _____

Other famous relatives? _____

_____

Figure 2. Famous Person Fact Sheet

ing revisions and collaboration. The draft that was chosen was often the version most thoroughly developed or the version deemed most grammatically correct.

Stage 3 involved a student interview exchange using Microsoft MSN chat whereby students were required to interview three wiki community members to identify student opinions about what characteristics make people famous. This information was collated and reflected on, and findings were uploaded to the wiki.

The final stage, Stage 4, was classroom based and refocused the relevance of the wiki-based writing project to each institution's curriculum. For example, UT students were asked to write a 500-word essay about their famous person, integrating interview data collected through chat, while the students at Dubai were required to prepare and conduct an oral presentation using Microsoft PowerPoint to exhibit their findings. As a final step, both groups of students reflected on and discussed what they had learned and experienced (both positive and negative) by undertaking a collaborative wiki-based writing project.

REFLECTIONS

Interaction within the wiki indicated that students were motivated by the public nature of the wiki to produce a better standard of writing. The following trends were observed:

- Some students (especially those from DMC) produced longer pieces of writing than usual that contained good development of ideas.

- Students became more confident in their own abilities regarding their writing.

- Students realized they did not have a sufficient range of vocabulary, which motivated them to formulate strategies to address this deficit.

As this project was designed as a pilot, the collaborating teachers kept a running log within the wiki forum to document actions, reflections, and discussions of required refinements. Students also provided reflections and feedback through discussions, online interaction, and posted comments. Based on this feedback, our guidelines and recommendations for setting up Wiki-based collaborative writing projects are summarized below.

Establish Early Contact With Another Institution

Use existing contacts, word of mouth, recommendations, or ESL message boards, chat rooms or conferences to seek partners who are willing to collaborate on a wiki-writing project. Once contact is established, begin the task of collaboratively designing the project, including goals, groups, interaction timelines, instructions, and other support needed to implement the project.

Build Community and Promote Collaboration

In this project, both teachers and students expressed a desire to slow down and give the project more time. It is crucial to allocate plenty of time for social interaction that actively encourages participants to build a productive learning community where they feel invested and comfortable with each other. This requirement may entail conducting icebreaking activities in the wiki to encourage students to interact socially, sharing ideas and backgrounds along with common hopes and goals. Such community-building activities have the potential to break down the anonymity of online environments and build a sense of commitment among group members before project deadlines begin. As mentioned above, allowing students to choose partners and topics based on potential friendship, not just shared topic interest, may help promote more autonomy and group bonding.

Although collaboration may appear a simple task, the wiki environment can have unforeseen—sometimes adverse—effects. For example, in our project, students were responsible for writing their own essay draft and then editing their partner's, with the goal of preparing a merged collaborative version. Unfortunately, this design often resulted in one partner using her or his draft as the template for their final version, thereby disengaging the other partner. To help avoid this tendency, an alternative, more inclusive approach would be for students to collaborate on producing a shared essay outline and then dividing up the parts, writing sections, and finally integrating them into a shared finished product. Creating a joint outline is also likely to promote more mutual investment in the writing process, whereas merging the final essay from two "finished" essays can potentially create disagreement and negative interaction, especially when learners are at different proficiency levels, as ours were.

Supply Effective Instructions in a Variety of Formats and Mediums

Instructions in this pilot were developed and uploaded to the wiki ahead of time. Students appeared to be overwhelmed by the number of text-heavy guidelines. Therefore, consider releasing instructions only when relevant, provide a master calendar with links to instructions in varied media, and include a reminder function to inform students of upcoming deadlines and responsibilities. Also, where possible, use video and audio rather than print and still images alone. In order to encourage more comfort with following instructions, it may be beneficial to phase in classroom work and discussions that encourage students to accept more responsibility for their role as self-directed learners.

Establish and Negotiate Roles

Feedback from some students indicated that they were uncomfortable with the amount of self-direction required. We suggest setting mandatory communication deadlines and establishing time limits for guiding the process and ensuring that the workload is evenly shared. As such, it is advisable to discuss and negotiate the roles and expectations of faculty and students as well as deadlines, although it is also important to remain flexible should a task require more attention.

Overtly Teach Online Peer Feedback Skills

Students sometimes found it challenging to accept feedback from peers with whom they were not that well acquainted, particularly when language levels and cultural assumptions were dissimilar. This phenomenon may have been compounded by the lack of nonverbal cues and interpersonal connection, along with the resulting lack of investment with each other as noted above. Unfortunately in our project, little orientation was provided as to the nature of peer editing and how to tactfully offer constructive criticism. As a result, some students felt personally attacked when peers offered feedback and editing changes. To address these issues, discuss peer editing with a focus on giving feedback in an online environment before the editing stage begins. Building consensus through discussion will increase student buy in, and it will emphasize the importance of this aspect of collaborative writing.

Raise Awareness of the Cultural Aspect of Intercultural Collaboration

Feedback from teachers revealed the importance of the social dimension inherent in effective collaboration. Participation in a wiki-based project offers students a glimpse into another social and educational reality, which was recognized by many students as one of the most motivating aspects of the project. However, students may underestimate different expectations and attitudes toward study and ways of learning and interacting. As such, pre-project activities and classroom debriefings need to focus on developing intercultural communication skills, encouraging students to suspend judgment, ask questions, and expand their interpretation of interactions. More reflection by students of their own cultural self, judgments, and interpretations may help suspend such assumptions.

Promote Ownership

Ownership of a wiki-based writing project is achieved in collaborative and supportive environments where initiative and risk-taking are encouraged. All teachers concerned should be directly involved in the design of a project that reflects their educational philosophies and addresses their students' needs. Choices about interface, choice of tools, and resources can be made collaboratively. Ownership can be encouraged through the development of a strong learning community where suggestions and feedback are actively elicited.

Provide Training and Support for Technology Issues

Do not underestimate the impact of varying levels of technical expertise—for both teachers and students. Although this wiki forum was easy to set up and use, technological challenges were evident in the preliminary stages, and there was a marked mismatch in ICT expertise and access by faculty and students in Canada and the UAE. It is important to ensure that all teachers have had some form of training or practice in the wiki forum and associated tools before a project is implemented. It is also essential that all participants have access to compatible technology, the Internet, and all of the required computer applications.

Encourage an Environment Where Mentoring Thrives

We discovered from using the various technologies that faculty sometimes found themselves relying on students as technology mentors. However, it is important to ensure that students do not dominate the wiki purely because they have the necessary skills. Parity of input and output is important for effective team work, and mentoring can be a valuable strategy to ensure collaboration (Owen & Allardice, 2008). Faculty and students can be encouraged to buddy up with suitable partners, thereby providing opportunities for mutual support in an environment that encourages autonomy. If collaborating partners are at different language levels, this is an ideal place to use mentoring strategies to support and empower multilevel groupings.

Concluding Thoughts

Our pilot project highlighted the important reminder that using ICTs in education does not automatically inspire teachers to rethink their approach or students to adopt different methods of learning. As such, the design of collaborative wiki projects needs to be underpinned by a learning theory that emphasizes the social, collaborative aspect of learning and the invaluable function that scaffolding performs in the learning process. In addition, setting up a wiki-based writing project needs careful consideration (see Appendix). In spite of the inherent challenges in integrating such a project into an ESL/EFL program, especially one where international collaborative ties are encouraged, the pedagogical and motivational benefits are considerable.

As students and teachers explore the wiki environment, they will recognize that there are extensive opportunities for collaborative learning and the development of authentic, intercultural communication skills. Wiki-based projects can enhance language learning by giving students access to authentic interaction within dynamic knowledge-building communities. Using an online approach enables students to share project results easily with their peers in the next classroom or around the world. It can also provide students with the experience of working in collaborative team-based environments, developing Web-based research skills, and practicing critical thinking skills—transferable tools for life in the 21st century.

Geoff Lawrence is an ESL/EAL instructor and teacher educator currently completing his PhD in second language education at the Ontario Institute for Studies in Education of the University of Toronto, Canada. His research interests include the development of online and blended learning environments to foster second language learning and intercultural communicative competence.

Terry Compton is an instructor at the English language program at the University of Toronto, Canada, where she has alternately studied and worked since 1978. In addition to teaching academic preparation, Terry is involved with teacher training, curriculum development, and language testing. She particularly enjoys working with internationally educated professionals.

Clayton Young teaches English at Dubai Men's College. He has interests in computer-assisted language learning (CALL), materials development, and language testing. Before coming to Dubai, United Arab Emirates, Clayton worked for 15 years as an ESL instructor in the English language program at the University of Toronto, gaining experience in all areas of ESL instruction.

Hazel Owen is an information and communication technology (ICT) enhanced learning consultant in New Zealand. She has been involved with the implementation of ICT for 9 years, providing training for faculty as well as developing blended and online courses. Her research interests include instructional design and ICT enhanced learning underpinned by sociocultural principles.

APPENDIX: TEACHABLE TIPS FOR SUCCESSFUL WIKI COLLABORATIONS

➢ In wikis, students are often concerned about making changes to another's writing; however, most wikis have a "history" feature, which allows members to retrieve, compare, and bring back older versions of the same Web page (before changes were made).

➢ There are a large number of free online wiki services available. When choosing a wiki, consider potentially useful features: an online tutorial; free/upgradeable versions; Web page templates; privacy options with password protection; ability to upload a range of file types and create hyperlinks; and a history feature that allows for the retrieval, comparison, and reconstitution of all earlier page versions.

➢ When setting up an online community with students who have never met each other, try to integrate both asynchronous and synchronous communication tools. Research shows that students often find the delayed interaction of asynchronous communication frustrating when getting to know other students online (Levy, 2007; Thorne, 2003) and that synchronous communication (e.g., chat, audio or video-conferencing) builds deeper, more immediate connections. Tapping into the iGeneration's enthusiasm for instant messaging is a key to making online learning relevant to younger learners.

➢ Students often demonstrate incredible investment in "creating" and developing an online identity. Exploit this by focusing students on refining their writing and editing skills, writing for an online audience, and creating the desired impression. It is also an ideal time to build intercultural curiosity and awareness. Ask students to share their impressions of individual online identities.

➢ Set up a page for reflections and thoughts for both students and teachers to post suggestions and concerns on the wiki writing process. These reflections will offer participants a sense of ownership over the process and will help guide improvements in teaching and learning.

➤ Start with a small scale, manageable project (possibly in-house before approaching international collaborators), allowing you and your students to try out the wiki medium and learn from experience. This will help guide you through the challenges of a larger-scale, collaborative project.

➤ Try an icebreaker activity to help students interact and become familiar with the wiki by setting up a wiki networking or café page. Here you can encourage writing-focused interaction by using activities such as a chain story, allowing students to have fun writing creatively and connect with each other while exploring the wiki medium. Alternatively, ask students to identify their interests in their personal profiles. The teacher can then set up a wiki page to enable further dialogue between students on their topics of interest.

➤ When working with multicultural groups, integrate intercultural awareness of others and of the self and intercultural communication activities into class learning.

CHAPTER 20

Developing Specialized Discourse Resources for International Teaching Assistants Using a Multimedia Wiki

Barbara Gourlay, David Kanig, Joan Lusk, and Stewart Mader

International teaching assistants (ITAs) often have difficulty mastering the pronunciation of discipline-specific terminology they need to succeed in the classroom. Even with strong everyday and general academic English, ITAs often slip into incomprehensible speech when using specialized terms, many of which are unusual polysyllabic words with difficult articulations and stress patterns. Proper production and use of this terminology is essential because undergraduates in classrooms taught by ITAs first learn the discourse of the discipline from them.

This collaborative project was developed at Brown University by a development team consisting of an English as a second language (ESL) specialist, a chemist, an audio technologist, and an instructional technologist. The self-study materials we developed for chemistry model the pronunciation of words and expressions to help ITAs clearly pronounce the chemical terminology necessary for teaching and learning. The materials, which are accessed through a multimedia wiki, have helped ITAs in chemistry improve their articulation of key terminology and communicate more successfully with undergraduates, graduate students, and faculty in their department.

CONTEXT

Existing materials designed to help nonnative speakers improve their pronunciation focus on everyday English or general terms common in academic discourse.

Materials designed to help ITAs develop speaking skills for teaching in a U.S. university, such as introducing a syllabus or explaining a concept, rarely address the specialized terminology necessary for successful communication in the disciplines. As a result, a large gap exists between what is taught in language classes designed to improve the spoken language of ITAs and their actual performance in the academic disciplines. To increase their facility in this critical skill, ITAs need easy access to materials that model the production and use of the specialized terms, as well as opportunities to practice producing the terms and engaging in meaningful interactions using the terminology.

In addition to general instructional goals, ITA preparation requires discipline-specific materials from a wide variety of academic disciplines. One common approach is to ask ITAs to bring examples of technical vocabulary to class to use as source material for classroom activities (Celce-Murcia, Brinton, & Goodwin, 1996), focusing on the terminology they actually use and allowing them to take an active role in their language development. However, ITAs also need to learn to produce the terminology clearly, accurately, and spontaneously in more contextualized and meaningful interactions. To effectively guide and support learning the authentic discourse of the specific disciplines, instructors of ITA courses need to collaborate with specialists in other content areas (Petro, 2006).

Instruction in Brown University's English for International Teaching Assistants Program addresses a great variety of ITA needs. Students in the program come from all disciplines (sciences, mathematics, social sciences, and humanities) and have varying levels of spoken English proficiency (basic to advanced). They generally have little prior experience at U.S. institutions of higher education. For efficiency's sake, courses in our program must provide ITAs the foundational linguistic and cultural information they need for teaching in the United States and also help them work independently to master discipline-specific discourse. Thus there is a clear need for resources tailored to self-study.

Because the chemistry department at Brown had a large number of ITAs and a faculty member interested in collaborating to create materials, we began our development work there. The ITAs from chemistry already knew a great deal of chemistry and had demonstrated good reading and writing skills in English, including technical English. However, they had not had much opportunity to use English technical and chemical vocabulary in face-to-face interactions. Chemistry ITAs needed to hear how teachers and students used spoken language in the discipline, including how technical words were articulated, ideas phrased, and information emphasized. Our materials provide typical models, exercises, and activities for these chemistry ITAs.

The specialized discourse resources discussed here are the result of an ongoing collaborative project that began in 2001 and has evolved with ideas from multiple perspectives: ITAs, an ESL specialist, a chemist, an audio technologist, and an instructional technologist. The project had very humble beginnings: a simple request from ITAs who reported that their inability to accurately produce specialized terminology limited communication with their undergraduates. Every stage of this project has been guided by needs that arose as we made improvements to the materials. ITAs provided many of the terms. The ESL specialist identified linguistic issues that were problematic for the ITAs, and our content-area specialist provided extensive textual resources that authentically captured chemistry discourse. With the help of an audio technologist, we created recordings to supplement our resource materials and to promote learner autonomy. The instructional technologist introduced the wiki as a Web-based delivery system, which has allowed us to expand the amount and type of information available and has the advantage of making the materials accessible 24 hours a day to an unlimited number of users, both on and off campus.

CURRICULUM, TASKS, MATERIALS

Specialized Discourse Resources for Chemistry: Delivery Method

We organized our materials for key terms in chemistry (textual resources, audio files, and visual images) through a wiki (see the Appendix for a list of Internet resources). Other delivery formats (e.g., print materials, audiocassettes, and CDs) were available; however, we chose a Web-based delivery system to facilitate distribution. A wiki seemed the most promising means to deliver the content because it is easy to update and conveniently accessible both by students and content developers. A wiki can provide large amounts of material to a large number of users and also can make ancillary materials available to more focused audiences, such as a section designed for our chemistry ITAs that models how to express certain mathematically-based expressions. Offering the materials on the Web provides nonlinear access and flexibility, permitting users to work with the terms or activities that interest them most at their own pace. The wiki also has granularity, meaning that ITAs can more easily locate and work with small units of information. With the Web-based delivery of materials, access is easy through any computer with an Internet connection. Audio files are compressed without compromising audio quality, and they are so brief that a broadband connection is not essential for good performance.

Digital audio recordings accompany textual resources for each key term. ITAs have the option to listen to a female speaker (our chemist) or a male speaker (our audio technologist) so they can hear variations in native speaker speech. In addition to modeling speech patterns, the recorded speakers have different degrees of familiarity with the material, reflecting the speaking patterns of a novice (e.g., as a native-speaking learner) and an expert (the teacher). A visual image accompanies each term and is incorporated into the supplemental activities, providing opportunities for description, discussion, or explanation. With the integrated materials (text, audio, and visuals images), ITAs can move beyond repeating and imitating the modeled language to more meaningful types of communicative exchanges through our online exercises.

For each key term, ITAs are provided three pages of information: the home-page for each term, a page with related word forms, and a page with contextualized exercises and related expressions. To access these pages, ITAs can select the term they want from an alphabetized list, or they can select a term based on its syllable structure and stress patterns (e.g., three-syllable words with primary stress on the first syllable). Figure 1 shows the different pathways for finding and selecting a term and also for linking to the ancillary materials.

Key Terms

The materials are organized around key terms frequently used in introductory-level chemistry courses that are often problematic for ITAs to produce and, as a result, difficult for their undergraduate students to understand. ITAs from chemistry first identified terms for which pronunciation was either difficult or had been the source of communication breakdown, such as *amine, ion, insoluble, orbital, oxygen,* and *positive charge.* From a database of over 500 ITA-identified terms, we selected 71 for expansion and use in this project, with additional terms serving as support. For example, ITAs in chemistry reported that *oxidation-reduction* was difficult to articulate. While not selected as one of the 71 key terms, *oxidation-*

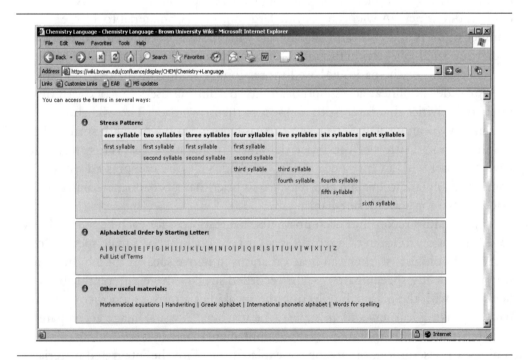

Figure 1. Options for Selecting a Term from the Chemistry Language Wiki

reduction was incorporated into the statement supporting the key term *electro-chemical*: *Every oxidation-reduction reaction involves the transfer of electrons, but in an electrochemical cell those electrons are transferred via a circuit.* In this way, we provided practice materials for far more than the 71 selected key terms.

We estimate that if ITAs worked for 10–15 minutes per term each day, they could complete the materials for all 71 terms over the course of a semester. Currently, as a Web-based resource, ITAs can access information in the chemistry language wiki in any order. In general, we encourage them to select the term for the day based on what seems particularly relevant to their syllabus or is of interest to them. Once they have selected a term, they are presented with a homepage for the key term, and from there they can access the other two pages of supplemental information.

For each term, we begin with information about its syllable structure and primary stress pattern, reinforcing an important linguistic feature of English taught in ITA preparation courses: word stress. Nonnative speakers of English often struggle to gain control of English stress patterns, and recent research has emphasized the importance of nonnative speaker control of English stress for intelligible speech (Field, 2005; Hahn, 2004; Murphy & Kandil, 2004). The materials also address other linguistic issues through broader discourse of the contextualized sentences for each term to develop overall fluency (rate of speech, pausing, grouping, phrasing, linking, and blending) and intonation patterns for statements and questions.

Key Term Homepage

The homepage for each term includes information about syllable structure and stress patterns and has contextualized examples written by a chemist illustrating how a given term may be used in a chemistry lecture or laboratory classroom. Figure 2 shows the homepage of the key word *catalyst* with information about its syllable structure and stress pattern and samples of ways the term may be used in a statement of fact, an instructor's question, and a student's question. A non-technical example is included when appropriate. Each key term's homepage also includes a image associated with the term and the embedded audio files, which ITAs can replay as many times as desired.

Statements

Statements provide ITAs with examples of definitions or descriptions common to chemistry. ITAs practice clear production of the terms in isolation and in full sentences. They practice phrasing information using appropriate emphasis and intonation as modeled by native-speaker samples. For additional practice, ITAs are encouraged to change the statements into yes/no questions or wh-questions. For example, with information from the statement provided in the example for *catalyst*, ITAs can create questions, such as, How does a catalyst speed up a chemical reaction? or, Does a catalyst undergo a net change?

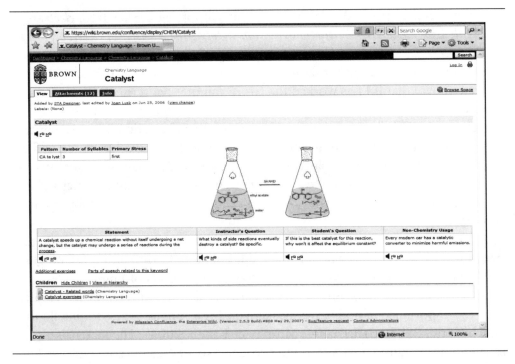

Figure 2. Homepage for Catalyst

Instructor Questions

Instructor questions model ways in which faculty may ask ITAs questions in their graduate classes, providing support for ITA listening comprehension development and active participation in their courses. Instructor questions also model ways in which ITAs might pose questions to their own undergraduate students. Source materials include yes/no questions, wh-questions, and imperatives. As a follow-up activity, ITAs are encouraged to formulate responses to these questions, and they are encouraged to discuss their responses with others in the department

Student Questions

Student questions are included for the chemistry ITAs because as lab teaching assistants, their primary duties are to respond to undergraduate requests for information. These examples reflect both forms and topics of typical undergraduate questions. ITAs are encouraged to formulate responses to these questions, providing another opportunity for the chemistry ITAs to talk about chemistry with others in their department. They can extend their practice by creating questions from a student's perspective for the graduate classes they are taking.

General Usage

Many technical terms in chemistry, such as *measure, iron,* or *catalyst,* often have ordinary English usages. These source materials are included to promote use of the key terms in everyday conversations, as well as to alert ITAs that a possible source of miscommunication with undergraduates may stem from the multiple interpretations, both general and technical.

Supporting Web Pages

When ITAs are ready to move on to additional materials, they click on the appropriate link at the bottom of the homepage: *Additional Exercises* or *Parts of Speech Related to the Key Word.* Although they can select which page they will work on next, ITAs are encouraged to begin with the related word forms first. On the *Parts of Speech* page, ITAs see a simple table (text with no embedded audio) showing the various related words and word forms, with stress patterns marked (see Figure 3). The rationale for including this information is that a sophisticated speaker in this context needs to have the verbal dexterity to use different parts of speech. Therefore, when learning a new term or expression, ITAs need to be able to recast terms, expressing the information in alternative grammatical forms. For example, if a chemistry ITA accurately uses the verb form *reverse the reaction,* then the ITA should be able to accurately describe the process as a *reversible reaction.*

If ITAs need or want to hear the word forms spoken, they are encouraged to ask a native speaker in the discipline to say the words for them, providing one activity in which they can move beyond the materials to consult with an expert. In this way, ITAs expand the number of speakers they hear and do not depend exclusively on the recorded speakers we provide through the wiki. For convenience, the *Parts of Speech* page also has a link to a Web-based dictionary, which includes pronunciation information.

Information and activities on the *Additional Exercises* page (see Figure 4) are designed to prompt ITAs to incorporate the term into meaningful expressions spontaneously, focusing on talking about chemistry from a teaching and learning perspective. Here, ITAs work with three types of information: (a) the visual image associated with the term, (b) instructions to explain information to undergraduates, and (c) additional useful words that would likely be part of a response. Our chemistry specialist created and recorded these materials to help ITAs expand their speaking practice in meaningful ways.

Noun	Verb	Participle Forms	Adjective	Adverb
CA ta lyst	CA ta lyze	CA ta lyzed	ca ta LY tic	ca ta LY ti cal ly
ca TA ly sis		CA ta ly zing		

Figure 3. Related Words for Catalyst

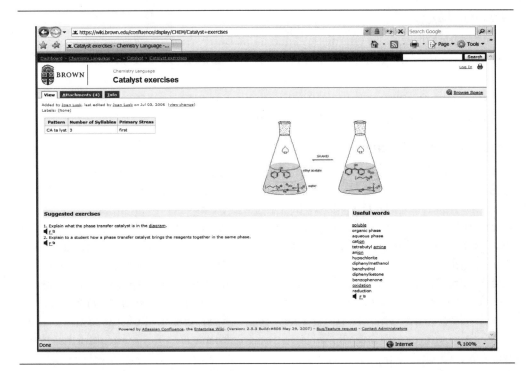

Figure 4. Additional Exercises for Catalyst

REFLECTIONS

Feedback from chemistry ITAs who have used the materials to supplement their work in their language classes has been very favorable and indicates we are meeting many needs ITAs have when developing their communication skills as teachers and learners. These ITAs are engaged with the materials because they enjoy working with resources that are meaningful and directly connected with their professional lives. ITAs from other disciplines also have found the materials to be useful because they use some of the same terminology that the chemistry ITAs do. Some of the materials meet these more general needs by demonstrating how student questions are initiated, fostering the development of classroom listening and observational skills. The most frequent requests we hear from ITAs are to add more key terms in chemistry and develop similar self-access resources for other fields.

The self-study format of our wiki-based materials and activities is appealing because ITAs are able to select the materials they want to work with and replay the audio as they develop their listening comprehension skills and practice production. The specialized discourse resources for chemistry were designed to be free-standing and self-explanatory, providing chemistry ITAs the opportunity to explore and experiment independently with language that they use in their professional interactions. We regularly encourage chemistry ITAs in our ITA classes to work with the materials, and ITAs who use them can obtain feedback on their linguistic development from the instructors in their ITA classes and content-area feedback from members of their department.

Using a wiki for ITAs to access discipline-specific resources provides great versatility for student use, and it allows some monitoring of student use—at least in a general way—by looking at page hits. This feature, in addition to a recently added blog feature allowing users to send us suggestions, will provide useful feedback and information as we determine the next phase of development for this project. One current limitation of the materials is that we have not yet established ways for students to record themselves, listen to their own work, and share their work with their instructors, but we hope to incorporate such mechanisms in the future.

Barbara Gourlay coordinates and teaches in the English for International Teaching Assistants Program at Brown University in the United States, and has directed the program since its inception in 1992. She has taught ESL to undergraduate and graduate students since 1983. Her research interests include intercultural communication and technology in language teaching and learning.

David Kanig, manager of technical services at Brown University's Language Resource Center, is a programmer and media designer. He has designed and taught ESL courses for refugees and has an extensive background in languages (Russian, Chinese, and Spanish). He also has acted on stage and radio.

Joan Lusk, associate professor emerita of chemistry at Brown University, has always been interested in languages. She became aware of the needs of international graduate students as a faculty member teaching and supervising teaching assistants, as an associate dean, and from having studied internationally herself, albeit merely in England.

Stewart Mader is the founder of Future Changes. He is a wiki consultant, public speaker, and author of the books Wikipatterns *(2007, Wiley Publishing) and* Using Wiki in Education *(2005, Lulu Inc.). He teaches people at Fortune 500 companies, universities, nonprofits, and small businesses how to improve productivity and collaboration using wikis.*

APPENDIX: INTERNET RESOURCES FOR WIKIS

Atlassian (Contributor)
http://www.atlassian.com

Future Changes
http://www.ikiw.org

Wikipatterns.com
http://www.wikipatterns.com

Using Wiki in Education
http://www.wikiineducation.com

I Tube . . . Do YouTube? Virtual Portfolios for Reflective Learning and Peer Review

Kathleen Snyder-Parampil and Joel Hensley

This lesson sequence illustrates how a popular culture digital tool, YouTube, can be utilized as a "private" video-sharing site where students and classmates can view their own authentic videos. YouTube (http://www.youtube.com) provides a space for students to develop virtual portfolios of their videotaped oral presentations, allowing learners to monitor the development of their own oral skills as the course progresses. In addition, classmates and teachers can access the videos to learn presentation skills and strategies from each other in informal viewings.

CONTEXT

The following lesson sequence was developed for use in the intensive English language program at Eastern Michigan University (EMU). According to online course descriptions, ESL (English as a second language) Academic Communication "is designed for nonnative speakers of English to improve their oral communication skills for participation in graduate-level classes in their degree program. Students read authentic texts and develop skills and strategies for oral presentations and critical response" (EMU, n.d.). Students in the course are typically from diverse language backgrounds and cultures, are generally in the 18–25 age range, and are in the course to improve their academic speaking abilities. These students are concurrently taking graduate-level courses in a variety of academic subject areas, including business, engineering, computer science, and nursing. They generally are comfortable navigating the Internet and most had already visited YouTube on their own.

So what is YouTube? It is a video-sharing site created in 2005 that allows users to upload video clips, which range from music videos to movie clips to home-made video and animation shorts. Unregistered users can watch the videos for free, but users must register for access to upload video content and to be invited as a "friend" to a private group. Comment boxes below videos allow anyone to post a written response to any video, providing a rich tool for textual interactions.

Because privacy is an issue, teachers should be aware that YouTube allows for private groups to be created with up to 25 members, and only invited group members can view postings within the group. Classes also can be broken down and several smaller groups created. Sample instructions to students on setting up private viewers are provided in Figure 1, or for more information on setting videos to private, try YouTube's user-friendly help center.

The instructor can manage the videotaping and video uploading, so students need no further computer knowledge. In my class, we videotape students using a digital video camera and then rip the individual videos for uploading. For example, we can take 30 minutes of video and separate out individual 5-minute video clips to rip for uploading. This can be done with software called Easy DVD Rip, which can is available at www.download.com. YouTube officially accepts uploaded videos in the following formats: WMV, AVI, MOV, MPEG, and MP4. (Most digital video cameras use one or more of these formats. It is important to record in the correct format or to use software to change the original recording to the correct format.) Once students have their own YouTube account, they can view their videos as well as those of their designated classmates. No one outside of the group can see the videos.

One YouTube feature that lends itself to class management is the teacher's ability to create groups and designate students to a specific group (see Figure 2).

Once the technicalities are taken care of, the convenience of YouTube becomes immediately apparent. Students can not only watch any video at any time (provided they have an Internet connection), but they can also post com-

---

Setting Up a YouTube Account for Private Viewing

1. Everyone in class who will watch the videos online must sign up for an account at http://www.YouTube.com.

2. Anyone who is to have access to the uploaded videos must make their username "friends" with the username of the poster. Becoming friends can be initiated by sending an invitation to the desired username. Teachers provide learners with lists of usernames for members of their partner group so that students can designate who can watch their video as friends.

3. Any student video uploaded to YouTube must have its broadcast options changed to "private."

Figure 1. Student-Controlled Friends' Groups on YouTube

Creating Private Viewer Groups in YouTube

For additional privacy, a group was created where only approved members are able to see the videos that have been uploaded.

1. A YouTube username is required by the moderator, or in this case the teacher. The moderator logs on and clicks "Create a Group" under My Account.

2. The moderator must "invite" group members to join by sending an invitation.

3. Upon receiving the invitation to join the group, students must (while logged in) navigate to that group's page within YouTube and click "become a member."

Figure 2. Moderator-Controlled Viewing Groups on YouTube

ments on individual videos, thus providing avenues for immediate feedback and interaction. For viewing, we recommend at least a broadband connection. If students do not have a computer at home, many university or city libraries offer free computer use with reasonably fast connections. If need be, there are options for limiting or even disabling comments for both individual videos and groups available on the options menu while logged onto YouTube.

CURRICULUM, TASKS, MATERIALS

As early as 1980, Meloni and Thompson reported in *TESOL Quarterly* that oral presentations were valuable for the intermediate ESL classroom. The idea of students giving an oral report is not new, but what this YouTube-inspired lesson does is make the presentation more accessible, more immediate, and more authentic through video. Students see their growth and their peers' growth during the course as multiple video clips are posted to YouTube throughout the semester. Sometimes it is difficult to note what we are doing wrong but easy to pick out mistakes in others. Conversely, in some cultures finding fault does not come easily, so teaching students how to make constructive comments is valuable, and posting written comments on the class videos themselves has proven to have positive effects on students' oral production. It is important that students understand the difference between criticism and constructive feedback though, and the teacher's constructive comments can serve as a model for providing meaningful feedback to peers.

ESL Academic Communication begins with an informal pretest of speaking abilities in which students are videotaped introducing themselves to the class. It is important in a course such as this for students to feel comfortable making mistakes in a supportive environment; knowing one another from the beginning is useful in creating the right atmosphere. The initial informal presentation is about 1–3 minutes long, and the resulting video is then posted on YouTube in a group established specifically for the class. Students are asked to review their own video and also are assigned one peer to evaluate. Students post their comments to the peer directly on YouTube. Usually at this preliminary stage of presenting in front of the class, students are nervous and often stare at the floor. The topic is well known as students are talking about themselves, but the information is often random and does not flow. It is important for students to have this baseline measure of where they are in terms of public speaking. Through this process, students realize the benefit of the course and have a baseline to gauge their improvement throughout the course.

Early on, teachers should introduce the basic format for presentations, including an opening, the development of an argument, a conclusion, and appropriate visuals. The second presentation allows students to apply and practice these skills. The topic is informing the class about something relevant to their area of study. This presentation requires a formal presentation of about 5–8 minutes, and the resulting video is again posted on YouTube. The presentations are evaluated using the rubric presented in the Appendix, which reflects skills taught during this course.

During this presentation, students usually demonstrate improvement in organization, but they still lack skills needed to be successful public speakers. Teachers should address appropriate body language, eye contact, voice modulation, and other techniques, and students then complete a third presentation on a different topic of their choice for another 6–8 minutes. In addition, note-taking skills should be taught, and students should be asked to "take notes" from one peer's video. An advantage of YouTube is that students can watch videos multiple times before giving the feedback to the peer. They can simply log on to YouTube and watch the peer video as many times as necessary, pausing as necessary and making notes. From these, peers write comments in the comment space provided underneath the video on YouTube (see Figure 3).

The final assignment combines everything students have learned throughout the semester about academic communication. Students have ample opportunity to reflect on their own presentations as well as those of their peers, and the focused feedback provided by peers and the teacher highlights students' strengths and weaknesses and areas that need work. The ability to look at their previous videos and incorporate feedback comments, both enabled by YouTube, makes it easier for students to prepare for their final presentations. If they have any questions about how they organized a section of a presentation or the appropriateness of their eye contact or other nonverbal signals, they have immediate access to the video. The time length for the final video is 8–10 minutes, and it also is posted on YouTube. At this stage, most students pull together everything they have learned during the course and prepare and present a cohesive and professional talk.

After students have completed their final presentation, students are asked to write a final reflection to be turned in, not posted online. Students are asked to look at all of their videos as a portfolio and compare previous videos to their final

Figure 3. YouTube Window With Comment Function (lower left; reproduced with permission)

presentation, noting improvements they have made and areas for further growth. Hopefully, they can see the visual progression from staring at the floor to making appropriate eye contact with the audience. They can also note organizational improvements in how they present information fluently, or how they use visual support. Often it is difficult to see growth within the course of one semester, but the visual reminder of the YouTube portfolio reflects individual growth.

REFLECTIONS

Some students are reluctant to be videotaped, citing cultural reasons. Generally all students agree, but an alternative can be provided. Students who do not wish to be videotaped would still have to give their oral presentations and another student in class would have to provide written feedback in real time. Student who do not want to be videotaped have to rely on memory to reflect on their own presentations as there is no taped record.

As for the comments on videos, most students post insightful and appropriate feedback most of the time. The moderator of the group has the ability to remove any comments that are inappropriate. Because students are learning how to take notes as part of this course, the comments are often written in note form. Complete sentences are not necessary, and in fact, as comment space is limited in YouTube, students must focus their thoughts. This is a great reinforcement of the note-taking skills they are learning in class.

If students do not have access to the Internet, presentations can still be video-taped and CDs prepared for individual students. This allows learners to reflect on their own presentations, but does not allow for peer review as readily. In fact, this approach was much more time consuming.

YouTube technology can be applied to learners with different language abilities and levels or adapted so students present in teams or pairs. Students can produce commercials for products they develop, practice having informal conversations in pairs, or practice asking for directions—all videotaped and posted to YouTube. Whatever the skill, teachers can incorporate a visual element and tape the performance so students have a permanent record of where they have been and how much they have grown. Students can share videos with future employers or friends outside of class, but because the group is private and not accessible by the public, students would need to select videos they want posted for a wider audience.

The ability to bring in peer review and to combine listening, speaking, writing, and research is valuable. No doubt YouTube as a motivational tool has its appeal, but this is not the only rationale for its use in language education. It is the ability to share videos easily with other members of the class and to review past presentations with ease that is of value to students and teachers. YouTube can enable a virtual portfolio of student work throughout the course and provide a great measure of their growth.

Kathleen Snyder-Parampil has taught high school history for several years and holds a master's degree in TESOL from Eastern Michigan University in the United States. Her interests include sociolinguistics and culture in language teaching. She works at the Koby Language Center in Ann Arbor, Michigan and Siena Heights University in Adrian, Michigan, teaching elementary through university-level students.

Joel Hensley received his bachelor's and master's degrees from Eastern Michigan University in English linguistics/Japanese language and TESOL, respectively. He is interested in the adaptation of cooperative learning in EFL. Currently, he is a full-time English instructor at the University of Nagasaki Siebold campus in Japan.

APPENDIX: PRESENTATION RUBRIC

YouTube Presentation Feedback for ESL Academic Communication

5 means the student demonstrates excellent work, 3 means average work, and 1 means the student needs considerable work in this area.

Opening

Generated interest	1	2	3	4	5
Established rapport	1	2	3	4	5
Previewed the structure of the presentation	1	2	3	4	5

Development

Developed the topic logically	1	2	3	4	5
Stated main points clearly	1	2	3	4	5
Supported themes effectively	1	2	3	4	5
Made smooth transitions	1	2	3	4	5

Closing

Returned to opening remarks	1	2	3	4	5
Restated the main argument	1	2	3	4	5
Included a call to action	1	2	3	4	5
Included a clear conclusion	1	2	3	4	5
Closed smoothly and appropriately	1	2	3	4	5

Visuals

Emphasized appropriate points	1	2	3	4	5
Designed and executed well	1	2	3	4	5
Created a strong impact	1	2	3	4	5

Other comments:

CHAPTER 22

Medical Doctors Using Authentic Webcast Lectures to Learn Lexical Phrases

Susan Olmstead-Wang

Because international physicians and medical scientists are increasingly called upon to give conference presentations in English (Hwang, 2005), they need effective strategies to make the transition from presenting in their first languages to doing so in English. Sophisticated and motivated but pressed for time, medical professionals benefit from authentic professional development materials and convenient delivery modes.

Using real scientific Webcast presentations in the language classroom maximizes physicians' access to authentic material (Kimball, 1998). Easy to locate, medical presentations from international conferences provide authentic examples of professional language and can be replayed for review at will. In addition, physician presenters using English as an international language provide good language models for others to develop their presentation skills.

Of the many applications for Webcast learning, this chapter focuses on lexical phrases as keys to understanding discourse structure in lectures and technical presentations. Lexical phrases function as macro-organizers to frame discourse, facilitate lecture comprehension (Nattinger & DeCarrico, 1992; Rilling, 1996), and enhance presentation. Focusing on lexical phrases alerts learners to strategies by which skilled speakers move logically from point to point in ordinary discourse or from slide to slide in the specialized discourse of science (Dudley-Evans & St. John, 1998). Because physicians already know the medical information structure of introduction-methods-results-discussion (IMRD; Swales & Feak, 2004), language teachers can engage this framework and extend it by teaching lexical phrases as discourse signals indicating the direction and flow of texts (Davis, 2005).

CONTEXT

This chapter describes Webcast-based language lessons at a medical university in Taiwan, which recently decided to convert from teaching in Mandarin to English in the postgraduate medical department. Kaohsiung Medical University's (KMU's) Center for Faculty Development (CFD) established a series of workshops, lectures, and practice sessions to facilitate this challenging transition and improve faculty English speaking skills. Although giving "scientific presentations in any language is an acquired ability" (Walters & Walters, 2002, p. 86), it is particularly difficult for international medical scientists. However, by gaining "mastery of its established genres" (Rowley-Jolivet & Carter-Thomas, 2005, p. 1), medical scientists can extend their speaking skills efficiently. Because Chinese scientists recognize and use IMRD in their reading and writing, we chose to link that existing knowledge to their speaking skills and extend their awareness of key lexical phrases as strategically placed rhetorical markers.

The CFD has provided workshops, lectures, and presentation practices in a lecture hall equipped with Internet connection and projection facilities. As with other lecture-based workshops in English for specific purposes (ESP) for international physicians, times were arranged around physicians' busy schedules and lunch was served (Eggly, 2002). The CFD took attendance and participants were awarded continuing medical education credits. More than 200 physicians and professors from seven departments attended lectures or participated in the speaker training practice.

In the lesson presented here, we sought to operationalize Chinese medical scientists' existing knowledge of medical information structure and their ability to signal that structure through English lexical phrases. The language lesson, conducted entirely in English as a model, consisted of the following:

1. a lecture on discourse analysis, information structure, and lexical phrases commonly used in medical presentations

2. viewings of a Webcast of a real scientific conference presentation

3. work with a transcript that highlighted lexical phrases

4. question and answer time

5. an exit questionnaire

Some of the lecture attendees took the opportunity to deliver prepared conference presentations in a practice session held later.

CURRICULUM, MATERIALS, TASKS

To bring together appropriate materials for the Chinese scientists, this project drew from research on lexical phrases, authentic materials, and the Internet.

Although some of these elements have been combined to inform native English speakers in medicine (Roberts & Sarangi, 2003), or international medical graduates using English in clinical practice (Dudley-Evans & St. John, 1998; Eggly, 2002), few studies have combined these elements to address the needs of speakers of other languages using English for medical purposes in international academic settings.

Discourse Analysis

Discourse analysis includes noting the function of discourse markers to build coherence, indicate direction, increase accuracy and clarity, and signal conclusions. Variously called transition words, linking words, discourse anchors, or lexical bundles (Biber, Conrad, & Cortes, 2004) and lexical phrases or macro-markers (DeCarrico & Nattinger, 1988; Nattinger & DeCarrico, 1992), these features signal coherence and indicate direction, especially for those aware of genre expectations (Johns & Dudley-Evans, 1991, p. 299). This chapter uses *lexical phrases* as defined by Nattinger and DeCarrico (1992): "prefabricated . . . form/function composites" that help learners increase comprehension and develop pragmatic competence (p. 11). Lexical phrases, functioning as global macro-organizers, include topic markers, topic shifters, and summarizers. They enhance "'top-down' processing by initiating the hearer's or reader's expectations and predictions about the discourse, expectations and predictions which are then confirmed and supported by the use of successive discourse signals" (p. 103). Especially important for lecture formats, lexical phrases and global macro-organizers mark the change from interactional discourse (greetings and introductions) at the beginning of a lecture to the transactional discourse (conveying the research information), which comprises scientific lectures.

Conventional use of transition words and linking phrases helps increase message clarity and helps the audience follow the information structure (Davis, 2005; Walters & Walters, 2002). Although noting some distinctions between written and spoken form use of "internal transitional devices," Davis (2005) emphasizes the speaker's responsibility to direct the audience from point to point through "strategic junctures" in slide show presentations (p. 183). Casella (2001) stresses the importance of clear purpose statements and transition words to help the audience "follow and trust" speaker sequencing of information (p. 168). Specifically in reference to scientific presentations, Swales and Feak (2004) suggest that the order of presentation for a scientific speech parallels the IMRD structure expected in a scientific manuscript (p. 215). Typically, the introduction shows general to specific movement and outlines the paper rationale. The methods section provides detail on methods, materials, or subjects under study. Findings are reported in the results section, and the discussion portion generalizes from the findings. In each part, section and subsection headings and macro-organizers help readers or listeners recognize a common information framework. Within sections, sentence connectors may be used in different ways (Swales & Feak, 2004). Knowing the expected order marked by discourse organizers can help international medical scientists accurately engage their existing schema of medical genre conventions.

Classifying kinds of transition words may help lecturers or audience members identify and prioritize key chunks of information. Biber, Conrad, and Cortes (2004) set out a functional taxonomy for how lexical bundles express stance and reference and organize university-level discourse. For the medical university workshop, we identified categories of discourse organizers found in Webcast slide shows, including some derived from IMRD structure and some from other lexical phrase marker schema (e.g., given and known information, implications, conclusion, summary, and closing). We helped workshop attendees understand category functions, identify specific members of a category, and locate these in Webcasts.

Authentic Materials

With improved technology in the language classroom, teachers have been able to use Internet video segments as part of course content. Dhonau and McAlpine (2002) used clips "to produce samples of how to use comprehensible input effectively, to model language production, and to use authentic materials in context" (p. 633). For the KMU workshops, we located current, free Webcasts on medical Web sites, sorted them for clear samples of lexical phrase use, and created typed transcript handouts highlighting those phrases. University IT personnel helped project the Webcast during the lectures and then posted a link on the project Web site so that participants could benefit from repeated viewings.

Internet Access

As Kimball (1998) observes, "discipline specific language learning, such as training in medical English, is situated within the long-established ESP practice of delivering what learners need to succeed in their professional careers" (p. 411). Media for such delivery now includes the Internet, whose accessibility, adaptability, and convenience allow adult learner agency in choosing linguistic structures or narrowly targeted materials. Discipline-specific material is particularly attractive because those modeling professional behaviors are "near-peers" (p. 416). Webcasts combine computer technology and authentic materials from real conferences in which the presentation style and science content material is authentic. Learners move from comprehending to being able to use key lexical phrases at appropriate transition points in giving a lecture.

Teaching

To fully engage learners' existing knowledge of medical information presentation, the workshop focused on explicit, situated teaching of lexical phrases and noticing skills. Teaching professional speaking skills to native-English-speaking medical personnel can be enhanced by moving beyond "trial and error" methods to explicitly teaching "rhetorical models . . . and by making explicit the tacit rules of presentation" (Haber & Lingard, 2001, p. 308). For nonnative speakers of English whose knowledge of the rules of presentation may not be so tacit, it is even more important to explicitly teach presentation strategies. When presenting medical conference posters, medical scientists practicing English in real, task-based environments with science material were able to expand their "lexical selection," repertoire, and self-monitoring by noticing second language (L2) features in interlocutor speech (Lynch & Maclean, 2001, p. 148). Similarly, KMU workshops offered access to real science presentations, explicit attention to the strategic usefulness of lexical phrases, and situated speaking practice with feedback.

The lesson plan included a slide show lecture, two viewings of the Webcast with a detailed transcript handout, question and answer time, and speaking practice sessions with feedback. The lecture presentation introduced five key concepts:

1. studying global lexical phrase macro-organizers

2. engaging discourse analysis as a skill for understanding all sorts of text

3. observing genre expectations specific to medical science fields

4. noticing the match between slide changes and transitional comments

5. practicing appropriate sequences

A transcript highlighting key lexical phrases and associated slide changes was given to the learners during the second Webcast viewing (see Appendix). The featured presenter used a short, formulaic interactional beginning, a transactional main section matched to sophisticated technical slides, and a brief closing. The introduction indicated a relatively close distance to the audience by using personal pronouns ("It's my pleasure," "to share with you") and used contractions ("it's") as in conversational or interactional discourse. In the transactional portion, the speaker conveyed dense technical information by signaling key points with macro-organizers and by relating his comments closely to his technical slides. Cognitively complex and fast moving, the presentation employed global macro-organizers as topic markers, topic shifters, and summarizers. Topic markers included "As you all know." Topic shifters included "By way of background," "As far as," and "I'll turn to X," Summarizers include "So [with a falling tone], if we look at," "In conclusion," "Overall, one patient," and "Maintenance seems to be associated with . . . ." The short formulaic ending ("Thank you very much") may be somewhat interactional, or merely closure for the transactional portion. KMU English language learners first identified the focal lexical phrases in the Webcast then studied their various functions. To enhance this, the facilitator presented a Microsoft PowerPoint slide show on lexical phrases as lecture "road signs"; provided a copy of the slides; and distributed a two-page handout in English with Chinese links, helpful footnotes and Web addresses, and the key lexical phrases associated

with an authentic Webcast lecture (see Appendix). To expand their own repertoire of effective lexical phrases, they planned to gradually add appropriate phrases
to their own lectures.

In the practice sessions, medical scientists presented in English, some for the
very first time. Speakers saw immediate replay of their videotaped speeches and
received feedback from the facilitator and from peers in the audience. Because the
speeches were digitally recorded, speakers have the opportunity to review their
own performances on the CFD website. Although specific student progress was
difficult to measure, exit questionnaires reported strong positive responses.

REFLECTIONS

In spite of the relatively high initial teacher preparation time for transcripts, this
narrow angle approach is worth the investment. When transcripts are readily
available for authentic Webcasts, less preparation time is required for very effective results. For example, at the graduate school of advanced international studies
at which I teach, advanced listening/speaking classes view taped segments of real
televised political talk shows. Complete transcripts for this authentic content are
available online, allowing advanced learners timely access to good support material and focused, relevant lessons. When authentic Webcast materials are used
to their full potential, students have many opportunities to use focal phrases in
context, to receive feedback and explanation in class, and to review at home.

One potential challenge with using real Webcasts is in locating appropriate,
relevant video segments. ESP language teachers may wish to pair up with other
experts to locate and select the best Webcasts. Another potential challenge with
this technique is that teachers may complacently "plug students in" to a video
segment without exercising the full potential of the authentic material.

Syllabus design for advanced professional students should include clear,
prioritized goals and appropriate authentic material with relevant support. Individual lessons should explicitly state learning goals and the means by which the
facilitator plans to achieve them. In this study, a carefully crafted handout given
at the beginning of the session stated that "L2 physicians who use English for
Medical Purposes (EMP) will (1) Understand how genres, information structures,
lexical phrases, discourse markers aid oral medical presentations and (2) Identify
and produce focal structures appropriately." Participants recognized the value of
the authentic Webcast material from a real medical conference and made gains in
learning the focal structures through coordinated support materials including a
Microsoft PowerPoint lecture and transcript as preview, followed by practice and
review of the key structures.

Students are motivated by targeted, high-level lessons that address their
functional language needs and by learning how to engage in discourse analysis.
Roberts and Sarangi (2003) contend that teaching medical scientists how to
do some metacognitive assessment of their own discourse will help them learn

faster and will help to bridge a gap "positivistic, quantitative studies in the 'hard' sciences and discourse-based studies" (p. 341). Teachers of advanced speaking students can link the benefits of Webcasts focused on lexical phrases as a part of such a strategy.

ACKNOWLEDGMENTS

Thanks to Y. H. Yang, PhD, KMU, for creating the questionnaires, collecting the data, and conducting statistical analyses.

Susan Olmstead-Wang researches Mandarin-English code-switching and discourse organization in advanced second language writing. She has taught medical English at the Kaohsiung Medical University and humanities writing at the Johns Hopkins School of Advanced International Studies. She is currently an assistant professor at the University of Birmingham, Alabama in the United States.

APPENDIX: LEXICAL PHRASES ASSOCIATED WITH THEIR FUNCTIONS AND SLIDE CHANGES

(**indicates a slide change)

** Introductions

Mr. Chairman, ladies and gentlemen, on behalf of (drug sponsor) and my co-authors, I . . .

It's my pleasure to share this data with you . . .

As you all know, (definition) is . . .

Given, Known Information

You've seen at this meeting it's been able to . . .

and in papers you've seen that it's been able to . . .

**As a way of background, I'm going to review . . .

Methods

. . . which was defined as . . .

Findings

The summary of the efficacy results . . .

** And this is just to show . . .

You can see that . . .

So, if we look at the end . . .

**Secondary efficacy . . .

**By way of graphics, on the far left . . .

And then . . . and

**As far as concomitant medications . . .

You can see the baseline . . .

And I just want to point out that . . .

So, . . . at the beginning . . .

**As far as results . . .

So here's 87 patients . . .

This shows long-term remission

**Implications

This shows . . .

So now we're talking about 79 patients . . .

And you can see that the majority . . .

**So as far as the long-term summary, the majority . . .

**I'll turn to safety now in this patient population . . .

And you can read down . . .

**As far as the most frequently reported adverse events . . .

If you look at . . .

Again, there's no new signals . . .

**Of interest to the clinician . . . these are the serious adverse events . . .

As far as the safety and immunogenicity, the most common AE . . .

With respect to immunogenicity . . .

**Conclusions

In conclusion, nearly 575 of patients . . .

Overall, one patient . . .

Maintenance seems to be associated with the overall rate of immunogenicity

**Closing

Thank you very much.

References

Althen, G. (1991). Teaching culture to international graduate students. In J. Nyquist, R. Abbott, D. Wulff, & J. Sprague (Eds.), *Preparing the professoriate of tomorrow to teach: Selected readings in TA training*. Dubuque, IA: Kendall Hunt.

American Red Cross. (n.d.). *Masters of disaster*. Washington, DC: Author. Retrieved January 30, 2008, from http://www.redcross.org/disaster/masters/introMOD.html

American Red Cross and the Centers for Disease Control and Prevention. (n.d.). *Preparedness today: What you need to do*. Washington, DC: Author. Retrieved January 30, 2008, from http://www.redcross.org/preparedness/cdc_english/home.asp

Arasaki, M. (Ed.). (2000). *Profile of Okinawa*. Tokyo: Techno.

Asher, J. J. (2003). *Learning another language through actions* (6th ed.). Los Gatos, CA: Sky Oaks Productions.

Bafile, C. (2003). *Reader's Theater: A reason to read aloud*. Retrieved September 16, 2007, from http://www.educationworld.com/a_curr/profdev/profdev082.shtml

Bauer-Ramazani, C. (2008). An integrated skills CALL unit: Student Web projects. *Topics Online Magazine for Learners of English*. Retrieved September 7, 2008, from http://www.topics-mag.com/teachers/christine-b-r-page.htm

Bhagat, R. S. (1999). Getting started and getting ahead: Career dynamics of immigrants. *Human Resources Management Journal, 9*(3), 349–365.

Biber, D., Conrad, S., & Cortes, V. (2004). If you look at . . . : Lexical bundles in university teaching and textbooks. *Applied Linguistics, 25*(3), 371–405.

Bicknell, J. (1999). Promoting writing and computer literacy skills through student-authored Web pages. *TESOL Journal, 8*(2), 20–25.

Blake, R. (2000). Computer-mediated communication: A window on L2 Spanish interlanguage. *Language Learning & Technology, 4*(1), 120–136.

239

Blumenfeld, P., Soloway, E., Marx, R., Krajcik, J., Guzdial, M., & Palincsar, A. (1991). Motivating project-based learning: Sustaining the doing, supporting the learning. *Educational Psychologist, 26*(3 & 4), 369–398.

Braun, L. W. (2007). *Teens, technology, and literacy; or why bad grammar isn't so bad.* Westport, CT: Libraries Unlimited.

Breen, M. (1987). Learner contributions to task design. In C. Candlin & D. Murphy (Eds.), *Language learning tasks* (pp. 23–46). Englewood Cliffs, NJ: Prentice-Hall.

Brown, A. L., & Campione, J. C. (1996). Psychological theory and the design of innovative learning environments. In L. Schauble & R. Glaser (Eds.), *Innovation in learning: New environments for education* (pp. 289–325). Hillsdale, NJ: Lawrence Erlbaum.

Brown, G., & Yule, G. (1983). *Teaching the spoken language.* Cambridge: Cambridge University Press.

Brown, H. D. (2001). *Teaching by principles: An interactive approach to language pedagogy.* New York: Addison Wesley Longman.

Brown, J. D. (1995). *The elements of language curriculum: A systematic approach to program development.* Boston: Heinle & Heinle.

Bruner, J. (1983). *Child's talk: Learning to use language.* New York: Norton.

Buck Institute for Education. (n.d.). Project-based planning form. *The standards-focused project based learning handbook.* Retrieved August 17, 2007, from http://www.bie.org/files/BIE_PBLplanningform.pdf

Bundesministerium für Unterricht, Kunst und Kultur (n.d.). *Lebende Fremdsprache* (Erste, Zweite). Vienna: BMUKK. Retrieved June 19, 2007 from http://www.bmukk.gv.at/medienpool/11854/lebendefremdsprache_ost_neu0.pdf

Burke, A., & O'Sullivan, J. (2002). *Stage by stage.* Portsmouth, NH: Heinemann.

Camaroda, S. (2005). Immigrants at mid-decade: A snapshot of America's foreign-born population in 2005. *Backgrounder.* Center for Immigration Studies. Retrieved November 27, 2006, http://www.cis.org/articles/2005/back1405.pdf

Canale, M. (1983). From communicative competence to communicative language pedagogy. In J. Richards & R. Schmidt (Eds.), *Language and communication* (pp. 2–27). London: Longman.

Canale, M., & Swain, M. (1980). Theoretical bases of communicative approaches to second language teaching and testing. *Applied Linguistics, 1,* 1–47.

Carkin, G. (2005). *Ten MORE plays for the ESL/EFL classroom.* Manchester, NH: Carlisle Publications.

Carter, R., McCarthy, M., & O'Keefe, A. (2007). *From corpus to classroom: Language use and language teaching.* Cambridge: Cambridge University Press.

Casella, P. J. (2001). Speaking for success. In Health Care Communication Group (Ed.), *Writing, speaking, & communicating skills for health professionals* (pp. 157–172). New Haven, CT: Yale University Press.

Celce-Murcia, M., Brinton, D. M., & Goodwin, J. M. (1996). *Teaching pronunciation: A reference for teachers of English to speakers of other languages.* New York: Cambridge University Press.

Celce-Murcia, M., Dörnyei, Z., & Thurrell, S. (1995). Communicative competence: A pedagogically motivated model with content specifications. *Issues in Applied Linguistics, 6*(2), 5–35.

Celce-Murcia, M., Dörnyei, Z., & Thurrell, S. (1997). Direct approaches in L2 instruction: A turning point in communicative language teaching? *TESOL Quarterly, 31*(1), 141–152.

Celce-Murcia, M., & Olshtain, E. (2000). *Discourse and context in language teaching.* Cambridge: Cambridge University Press.

Cobb, T. (1999). Applying constructivism: A test for the learner-as-scientist. *Educational Technology and Research Development, 47*(3), 15–31.

College of Business. (2007). *Keieigakubu Gendai GP.* Tokyo, Japan: Rikkyo University.

Condelli, L., Wrigley, H. S., & Yoon, K. (2003). *What works study for adult ESL literacy students.* Washington, DC: U.S. Department of Education.

Council of Europe (2007a). *Language education policy profile: Country report Austria.* Strasbourg, France. Retrieved October 31, 2007 from www.coe.int/t/dg4/linguistic/Source/Austria_CountryReport_Aug07_EN.doc

Council of Europe (2007b). *Common European framework of reference for languages: Learning, teaching, assessment.* Strasbourg, France. Retrieved October 1, 2006, from http://www.coe.int/t/dg4/linguistic/CADRE_EN.asp

Crandall, J. (2007). *Passing the torch: Strategies for innovation.* New York: Council for Advancement of Adult Literacy.

Crandall, J., & Sheppard, J. (2004). *Adult ESL and the community college.* New York: Council for Advancement of Adult Literacy.

Cummins, J. (2000). Academic language learning, transformative pedagogy, and information technology: Towards a critical balance. *TESOL Quarterly, 34*(3), 537–548.

Cummins, J. (2006). Identity texts: The imaginative construction of self through multiliteracies pedagogy. In O. García, T. Skutnabb-Kangas, & M. E. Torres-Gusmán (Eds.), *Imagining multilingual schools: Languages in education and glocalization* (pp. 51–68). Buffalo, NY: Multilingual Matters.

Curran, T. (2000). Brain potentials of recollection and familiarity. *Memory & Cognition, 28*(6), 923–938.

Davis, M. (2005). *Scientific papers and presentations* (Rev. ed.). San Diego, CA: Academic Press.

Davis, P., & Rinvolucri, M. (1988). *Dictation: New methods, new possibilities.* Cambridge: Cambridge University Press.

Day, R. R., & Bamford, J. (1998). *Extensive reading in the second language classroom.* New York: Cambridge University Press.

DeCarrico, J., & Nattinger, J. R. (1988). Lexical phrases for the comprehension of academic lectures. *English for Specific Purposes, 7*, 91–102.

De Maria, F. (2007, August 13). Rendon redefines today's underserved student. *Hispanic Outlook in Higher Education, 17*(22), 18–20.

Dhonau, S., & McAlpine, D. (2002). "Streaming" best practices: Using digital video-teaching segments in the FL/ESL methods course. *Foreign Language Annals, 35*(6), 632–636.

Dray, S. (2003). Sociolinguistic struggles in outdoor texts in a Creole-speaking community: The significance of embedding. In S. Sarangi & T. Van Leeuwen (Eds.), *Applied linguistics and communities of practice* (pp. 39–59). London: British Association for Applied Linguistics.

Dudley-Evans, T., & St. John, M. (1998). *Developments in English for specific purposes.* Cambridge: Cambridge University Press.

Dylan, B. (1964). The times they are a-changin'. On *The times they are a-changin'* [CD]. New York: Sony BMG Music Entertainment.

Eastern Michigan University. (n.d.). *Course descriptions.* Retrieved January 14, 2008, from https://web4.emich.edu:15010/pls/berp/bwckctlg.p_display_courses

Eggly, S. (2002). An ESP program for international medical graduates in residency. In T. Orr (Ed.), *English for specific purposes* (pp. 105–115). Alexandria, VA: TESOL.

Elbaum, S. N. (2005). *Grammar in context* (4th ed.). Boston: Heinle & Heinle.

Elley, W. B. (1991). Acquiring literacy in a second language: The effect of book-based programs. *Language Learning, 41*(3), 375–411.

Ellis, G., & Sinclair, B. (1989). *Learning to learn English.* Cambridge: Cambridge University Press.

Ellis, R. (2003). *Task-based language learning and teaching.* Oxford: Oxford University Press.

Emde, S. V. D., Schneider, J., & Kotter, M. (2001). Technically speaking: Transforming language learning through virtual environments (MOOs). *The Modern Language Journal, 85*(ii), 210–225.

Esch, C. (1998). *Project-based and problem-based: The same or different*. San Mateo, CA: County Office of Education.

Federal Emergency Management Agency. (2006). *Hurricane Katrina, one-year later*. Washington, DC. Retrieved August 14, 2008, from http://www.FEMA.gov/news/newsrelease.FEMA?id=29108

Federmeier, K., & Kutas, M. (1999). A rose by any other name: Long-term memory structure and sentence processing. *Journal of Memory and Language, 41*, 469–495.

Felix, U. (2005). E-learning pedagogy in the third millennium: The need for combining social and cognitive constructivist approaches. *ReCALL, 17*(1), 85–100.

Field, J. (2005). Intelligibility and the listener: The role of lexical stress. *TESOL Quarterly, 39*, 399–424.

Field, J. (1998). Skills and strategies: Towards a new methodology for listening. *ELT Journal, 52*, 110–118.

Finger, A. G. (2000). *The magic of drama*. Ontario, Canada: Full Blast Productions.

Fischoff, R., & Jaffe, S. (Producers), & Benton, R. (Director). (1979). *Kramer vs. Kramer*. [Motion Picture]. United States: Columbia Pictures.

Fisher-Staples, S. (2003). *Shabanu: Daughter of the wind*. New York: Laurel Leaf.

Fried-Booth, D. (2002). *Project work*. Oxford: Oxford University Press.

Frost, R. (1916). The road not taken. In *Mountain interval* (p. 9). New York: Henry Holt.

Frost, R. (1923). Stopping by woods on a snowy evening. In *New Hampshire* (p. 87). New York: Henry Holt.

Gallacher, L. (2004, March 23). *Project work with teenagers*. BBC & British Council. Retrieved August 26, 2006, from http://www.teachingenglish.org.uk/think/articles/project-work-with-teenagers

Garrett, N. (1991). Technology in the service of language learning: Trends and issues. *Modern Language Journal, 75*, 74–101.

Gee, J. P. (2004). *Situated language and learning: A critique of traditional schooling*. New York: Routledge.

Geertz, C. (1973). Thick description: Toward an interpretive theory of culture. In *The interpretation of cultures: Selected essays* (pp. 3–30). New York: Basic Books.

Gilmore, A. (2007a). Authentic materials & authenticity in foreign language learning. *Language Teaching, 40*(2), 97–118.

Gilmore, A. (2007b). *Getting real in the language classroom: Developing Japanese students' communicative competence with authentic materials*. Unpublished doctoral dissertation, Nottingham University, England.

Gourlay, B., Kanig, D., Lusk, J., & Mader, S. (2008). *Chemistry language wiki.* Brown University. Retrieved September 7, 2008, from https://wiki.brown.edu/confluence/display/CHEM/Chemistry+Language

Gradman, H., & Hanania, E. (1991). Language learning background factors and ESL proficiency. *Modern Language Journal, 75*(1), 39–51.

Grellet, F. (1981). *Developing reading skills.* Cambridge: Cambridge University Press.

Griffin, A., & Bock, K. (1998). Constraint, word frequency, and the relationship between lexical processing levels in spoken word production. *Journal of Memory and Language, 38*, 313–338.

Gromik, N. (2006). Meaningful tasks with video in the ESOL classroom. In E. Hanson-Smith & S. Rilling (Eds.), *Learning languages through technology* (pp. 109–123). Alexandria, VA: TESOL.

Guariento, W., & Morley, J. (2001). Text and task authenticity in the EFL classroom. *ELT Journal, 55*(4), 347–353.

Haber, R. J., & Lingard, L. A. (2001). Learning oral presentation skills. *Journal of General Internal Medicine, 16*, 308–314.

Hahn, L. (2004). Primary stress and intelligibility: Research to motivate the teaching of suprasegmentals. *TESOL Quarterly, 38*, 201–224.

Harding, K. (2007). *English for specific purposes.* Oxford: Oxford University Press.

Harford, J. M. (n.d.). *Follow the footsteps.* Retrieved March 4, 2007, from http://www.gse.buffalo.edu/org/writingstrategies/6-12.htm

Healy, T. R. (2007). *Seattle area restaurant reviews.* Retrieved November 11, 2007, from http://acerestaurantreviews.blogspot.com/

Heath, S. B. (1996). Re-creating literature in the ESL classroom. *TESOL Quarterly, 30*(4), 76–9.

Heidish. P. (2006). Creating partnerships: ITA links in a campus side chain. In D. Kaufman & B. Brownworth (Eds.), *Professional development of international teaching assistants* (pp. 165–180). Alexandria, VA: TESOL.

Hinkel, E. (2006). Current perspectives on the teaching of the four skills. *TESOL Quarterly, 40*(1), 109–131.

Hosseini, K. (2003). *The kite runner.* New York: Riverhead Books.

Howard, J. (2007, September 14). Stories from the storm: Folklorists train survivors of Hurricanes Katrina and Rita to harvest research—and even healing—from their experiences. *The Chronicle of Higher Education*, p. A10.

Hughes, K., & Karp, M. (2006). *Strengthening transitions by encouraging career pathways: A look at state policies and practices.* New York: Community College Resource Center.

Hwang, K. (2005). The inferior science and the dominant use of English in knowledge production: A case study of Korean science and technology. *Science Communication, 26*(4), 390–427.

Hyland, K. (2000). *Disciplinary discourses: Social interactions in academic writing.* New York: Longman.

Jenkins, J. (2007). *English as a lingua franca: Attitude and identity.* Oxford: Oxford University Press.

Jenkins, J. (2006). English pronunciation and second language speaker identity. In T. Omoniyi & G. White (Eds.), *The sociolinguistics of identity* (pp. 75–91). London: Continuum.

Johns, A. M., & Dudley-Evans, T. (1991). English for specific purposes: International in scope, specific in purpose. *TESOL Quarterly, 25,* 297–314.

Kao, S. M., & O'Neill, C. (1998). *Words into worlds: Learning a second language through process drama.* Stamford, CT: Ablex.

Karchmer-Klein, R. (2007). Best practices in using the Internet to support writing. In C. A. MacArthur & J. Fitzgerald (Eds.), *Best practices in writing instruction* (pp. 222–241). New York: The Guilford Press.

Kasarda, J. D., & Johnson, J. H. (2006). *The economic impact of Hispanics on the state of North Carolina.* Chapel Hill, NC: Frank Hawkins Kenan Institute of Private Enterprise.

Kaufman, D., & Brownworth, B. (2006). Collaborative paradigms and future directions in international teaching assistant professional development. In D. Kaufman & B. Brownworth (Eds.), *Professional development of international teaching assistants* (pp. 1–13). Alexandria, VA: TESOL.

Kimball, J. (1998). Task-based medical English: Elements for Internet-assisted language learning. *Computer Assisted Language Learning, 11*(4), 411–417.

Kozub, R. (May 16, 2000). Readers' Theater and its effect on oral language fluency. *Reading Online.* Retrieved September 16, 2007, from http://www.readingonline.org/editorial/edit_index.asp?HREF=august2000/rkrt.htm

Krashen, S. (2004). *The power of reading: Insights from the research.* Portsmouth, NH: Heinemann.

Krashen, S., & Terrell, T. (1983). *The natural approach: Language acquisition in the classroom.* Oxford: Pergamon.

Larmimer, R. E., & Schleicher, L. (1999). *New ways in using authentic materials in the language classroom.* Alexandria, VA: TESOL.

Laughlin, M. K., & Latrobe, K. H. (1990). *Readers Theatre for children: Scripts and script development.* Englewood, CO: Teacher Ideas Press.

Lawrence, G. P. J. (2000). *Teacher belief systems towards computer-mediated language learning: College ESL instruction.* Unpublished master's thesis, the Ontario Institute for the Studies of Education of the University of Toronto, Canada.

Leaver, B., & Willis, J. (2004). *Task-based instruction in foreign language education.* Washington, DC: Georgetown University Press.

Leech, G. N. (1983). *Principles of pragmatics.* London: Longman.

Leigh, M. (Writer/Director). (1996). *Secrets and lies* [Motion Picture]. England: Thin Man Films.

Levy, M. (2007). Culture, culture learning and new technologies: Towards a pedagogical framework. *Language Learning & Technology, 11*(2), 104–127.

Lindholm, C. (2008). *Culture and authenticity.* Malden, MA: Blackwell.

Littlewood, W. (2004). The task-based approach: Some questions and suggestions. *ELT Journal, 58*(4), 319–326.

Lozanov, G. (1978). *Suggestology and outlines of suggestopedy.* New York: Gordon and Breach.

Lynch, T., & Maclean, J. (2001). "A case of exercising": Effects of immediate task repetition on learners' performance. In M. Bygate, P. Skehan, & M. Swain (Eds.), *Researching pedagogic tasks: Second language learning, teaching and testing* (pp. 141–162). London: Pearson Education.

Mabrito, M. (1991). Electronic mail as a vehicle for peer response: Conversations of high- and low-apprehensive writers. *Written Communication, 8*(4), 509–532.

Mabrito, M. (1992, December). Computer-mediated communication and high-apprehensive writers: Rethinking the collaborative process. *The Bulletin,* 26–30.

Maley, A., & Duff, A. (2005). *Drama techniques: A resource book of communication activities for language learners* (3rd ed.). Cambridge: Cambridge University Press.

Mariani, L. (1997). Teacher support and teacher challenge in promoting learner autonomy. *Perspectives, 23*(2), 1–10.

Martin, G. (2007). Charlotte's thriving international community. *International Review.* Charlotte, NC: Chamber of Commerce.

McArdle, W., Katch, F., & Katch, V. (2001). *Exercise physiology.* Baltimore: Williams & Wilkins.

Meloni, C., & Thompson, S. (1980). Oral reports in the intermediate ESL classroom [Electronic version]. *TESOL Quarterly, 14,* 503–510.

Meskill, C. (1996). Listening skills development through multimedia. *Journal of Educational Multimedia and Hypermedia, 5*(2), 179–201.

Miles, C. (2006). Vaya tormenta! In the shadows of Katrina. *The Southern Quarterly, 43*(3), 32–39.

Miller, E. R. (2007). Learning English, positioning for power: Adult immigrants in the ESL classroom. In M. Mantero (Ed.), *Identity and second language learning: Culture, inquiry, and dialogic activity in educational contexts* (pp. 119–141). Charlotte, NC: Information Age.

Mishan, F. (2005). *Designing authenticity into language learning materials*. Bristol, England: Intellect.

Morrow, K. (1977). Authentic texts and ESP. In S. Holden (Ed.), *English for specific purposes* (pp. 13–17). London: Modern English Publications.

Mulling, R., & Smith, R. (1999). *Electrical wiring commercial* (10th ed.). Albany, NY: Delmar.

Murphy, J., & Kandil, M. (2004). Word-level stress patterns in the academic word list. *System, 32,* 61–75.

Nafisi, A. (2003). *Reading Lolita in Tehran: A memoir in books*. New York: Random House.

Nagelberg, M. M. (1948). *Drama in our time*. New York: Harcourt Brace.

Nation, I. S. P. (2001). *Learning vocabulary in another language*. Cambridge: Cambridge University Press.

Nattinger, J. R., & DeCarrico, J. S. (1992). *Lexical phrases and language teaching*. Oxford: Oxford University Press.

Norton, B., & Toohey, K. (2002). Identity and language learning. In R. B. Kaplan (Ed.), *The Oxford handbook of applied linguistics* (pp. 115–123). Oxford: Oxford University Press.

Nunan, D. (1989). *Designing tasks for the communicative classroom*. Cambridge: Cambridge University Press.

Nunan, D. (1996). Issues in second language acquisition research: Examining substance and procedure. In W. Ritchie & T. K. Bhatia (Eds.), *Handbook of second language acquisition* (pp. 349–374). San Diego, CA: Academic Press.

Nunan, D. (2004). *Task-based language teaching*. Cambridge: Cambridge University Press.

Oreto, R., & Carlson, M. (2006). Adapting social work theory to ITA training. *ITAIS Newsletter, 11*(2). Retrieved January 20, 2006, from http://www.tesol.org//s_tesol/article.asp?vid=180&DID=7307&sid=1&cid=747&iid=7303&nid=3205

Owen, D., Silet, C. L. P., & Brown, E. (1998). Teaching television to empower students. *The English Journal, 87*(1), 28–33.

Owen, H. (2003). The value of using CALL with tertiary students studying ESL: Attitudes and implications. In B. Morrison, C. Green, & G. Motteram (Eds.),

Directions in CALL (pp. 33–49). Hong Kong: English Language Centre, The Hong Kong Polytechnic University.

Owen, H. (2005). Sociocultural theory: An interpretative framework for computer assisted language learning? In J. B. Son & S. O'Neill (Eds.), *Enhancing learning and teaching: Pedagogy, technology and language* (pp. 195–214). Tenerife, Queensland, Australia: Post Pressed.

Owen, H., & Allardice, R. (2008). Managing the implementation of blended e-learning initiatives with the unconverted in a climate of institutionally driven change. *The International Journal of Learning, 14*(9), 179–192.

Owen, H., & Madsen, L. (2008). Literacy issues in the Gulf: Best practices. In *Best practice of English language teaching* (pp. 98–105). Dubai, United Arab Emirates.

Oxford, R. L. (1990). *Language learning strategies: What every teacher should know.* Boston: Heinle & Heinle.

Paulsen, G. (1996). *Hatchet.* New York: Aladdin Paperbacks.

Peng, J. (2005, August 31). Katrina caught some Hispanics by surprise. *The Hattiesburg American*, p. 7A.

Pennycook, A. (2007). Language, localization, and the real: Hip-hop and the global spread of authenticity. *Journal of Language, Identity, and Education, 6*(2), 101–115.

Petro, A. N. (2006). Addressing the cultural and linguistic needs of students. In D. Kaufman & B. Brownworth (Eds.), *Professional development of international teaching assistants* (pp. 151–163). Alexandria, VA: TESOL.

Pica, T. (2005). Classroom learning, teaching, and research: A task-based perspective. *The Modern Language Journal, 89*(3), 339–352.

Pollock, P. (November 11, 2005). *Creating integrated assignments with television and video resources.* Workshop presented at the New York TESOL Conference.

Pommerance, B. (1979). *The elephant man: A play.* New York, NY: Grove Press.

Powell, W., & Ponder, R. (2001). Sourcebooks in a sustained-content curriculum. *TESOL Journal, 10*(2/3), 18–22.

Prescott, J. (2003). *The power of Readers' Theater.* Retrieved September 16, 2007, from http://teacher.scholastic.com/products/instructor/readerstheater.htm

Radalet, A. (2005, September 4). Hispanics–Katrina's hidden victims. *The Hattiesburg American*, p. 4A.

Raimes, A. (1983). *Techniques in teaching writing.* New York: Oxford University Press.

Ratliff, G. (1999). *Introduction to Readers Theatre: A guide to classroom performance.* Colorado Springs, CO: Meriwether.

Rawson, K., Dunlosky, J. & Thiede, K. (2000). The rereading effect: Meta-comprehension accuracy improves across reading trials. *Memory & Cognition, 28*(6), 1004–1010.

Rhoads, R. A., & Howard, J. P. F. (Eds.). (1998). *Academic service learning: A pedagogy of action and reflection.* San Francisco, CA: Jossey-Bass.

Richards, J. C. (2002). *Methodology in language teaching: An anthology of current practice.* Cambridge: Cambridge University Press.

Richardson, W. (2006). *Blogs, wikis, podcasts, and other powerful web tools for classrooms.* Thousand Oaks, CA: Corwin Press.

Rilling, S. (1996). Lexical phrases as organization markers in academic lectures: A corpus-and computer-based approach to research and teaching. *ORTESOL Journal, 17*, 19–40.

Rizzo, M., & Brown, J. (2006). *Building character through community service.* Lanham, MD: Rowman and Littlefield Education.

Roberts, C., & Sarangi, S. (2003). Uptake of discourse research in interpersonal settings: Reporting from medical consultancy. *Applied Linguistics, 24*(3), 338–359.

Rodgers, D. (1998). *Business communications: International case studies in English.* Cambridge: Cambridge University Press.

Ross, B. (Ed.). (1993). *Haiku moment: An anthology of contemporary North American haiku.* Boston: Tuttle.

Rowley-Jolivet, E., & Carter-Thomas, S. (2005). The rhetoric of conference presentation introductions: Context, argument and interaction. *International Journal of Applied Linguistics, 15*(1), 45–70.

Ruchkin, D., Berndt, R., Johnson, R., Jr., Grafman, J., Ritter, W., & Canoune, H. (1999). Lexical contributions to retention of verbal information in working memory: Event-related brain potential evidence. *Journal of Memory and Language, 41*, 345–364.

Rumi, J. M. (2005). *Masnavi-i ma'navi, the spiritual couplets of Maulana Jalalu'd-din Muhammad Rumi* (E. H. Whinfield, Trans.). Tehran: Yassavoli Publications.

Schmidt, R. (2001). Attention. In P. Robinson (Ed.), *Cognition and second language instruction* (pp. 3–32). Cambridge: Cambridge University Press.

Schultz, J. (2000). Computers and collaborative writing in the foreign language curriculum. In M. Warschauer & R. Kern (Eds.), *Networked-based language teaching: Concepts and Practice* (pp. 121–150). New York: Cambridge University Press.

Schumann, J. H. (1997). *The neurobiology of affect in language.* Oxford: Blackwell.

Scribner, A. (1999). Lessons from high performing Hispanic schools—an introduction. *Lessons from high performing Hispanic schools* (pp. 1–17). New York: Teachers College Press.

Seargeant, P. (2005). "More English than England itself": The simulation of authenticity in foreign language practice in Japan. *International Journal of Applied Linguistics, 15*(3), 326–345.

SEZ AG. (2004, February). *SEZ annual report 2003.* Retrieved September 1, 2004, from http://www.sez.com/AnnualReport2003_eng.SEZ

SEZ AG. (Producer). (2004). *SEZ image video* [DVD]. Villach, Austria.

Smith, S. (1984). *The theatre arts and the teaching of languages.* New York: Addison-Wesley.

Shine, J. (Ed.). (1997). *Service learning.* Chicago: University of Chicago Press.

Sifakis, N. S. (2003). Applying the adult education framework to ESP curriculum development: An integrative model. *English for Specific Purposes, 22,* 195–211.

Skehan, P. (1996). Second language acquisition research and task-based instruction. In J. Willis & D. Willis (Eds.), *Challenge and change in language teaching* (pp. 17–30). Oxford: Heinemann.

Skehan, P. (1998). *A cognitive approach to language learning.* Oxford: Oxford University Press.

Snyder, J., & Drumsta, M. (1990). *The dynamics of acting.* Chicago: National Textbook Company.

Stephen, W., & Gallagher, S. (1993). Problem-based learning: As authentic as it gets. *Educational Leadership, 51,* 25–28.

Stern, S. (1980). Drama in second language learning from a psycholinguistic perspective. *Language Learning, 30*(1), 11–91.

Sullivan, N., & Pratt, E. (1996). A comparative study of two ESL writing environments: A computer-assisted classroom and a traditional oral classroom. *System, 24*(4), 491–501.

Swales, J. M., & Feak, C. B. (2004). *Academic writing for graduate students* (2nd ed.). Ann Arbor, MI: University of Michigan Press.

Szelenyi, K., & Chang, J. C. (2002). Educating immigrants: The community college's role. *Community College Review, 30*(2), 55–73.

Takatsuki, H. (2003–2008). *High moon cartoon gallery. Japan for sustainability.* Retrieved March 25, 2007, from http://www.japanfs.org/

Technical career ladders. (n.d.). Charlotte, NC: Central Piedmont Community College. Retrieved October 24, 2007, from http://www1.cpcc.edu/esl/career-ladders/technical-career-ladders-for-ells

TESOL. (2006, March). Position statement against discrimination of nonnative speakers of English in the field of TESOL. Alexandria, VA: Author. Available at http://www.tesol.org/s_tesol/bin.asp?CID=32&DID=5889&DOC=FILE.PDF

Think sheets. (n.d.). Retrieved March 4, 2007, from http://literacy.kent.edu/eureka/strategies/writing.html

Thomas, J. W. (2000). *A review of research in project-based learning.* The Autodesk Foundation. http://www.autodesk.com/

Thomas, J. W., & Mergendoller, J. R. (2000). *Managing project-based learning: Principles from the field.* Paper presented at the Annual Meeting of the American Educational Research Association, New Orleans, LA. Retrieved August 15, 2007, from http://www.bie.org/files/researchmanagePBL.pdf

Thorne, S. L. (2003). Artifacts and cultures-of-use in intercultural communication. *Language Learning & Technology, 7*(2), 38–67.

Thurber, J. (1939). *The little girl and the wolf.* Retrieved September 14, 2007, from http://www.andromeda.rutgers.edu/~lcrew/quotes/picnicba/html

Thurber, J. (1940). *The unicorn in the garden.* Retrieved September 14, 2007, from http://english.glendale.cc.ca.us/unicorn1.html

Tinker Sachs, G. (2001). Transforming extensive reading lessons. *New Horizons in Education, 43,* 78–90.

Ur, P. (1996). *A course in language teaching.* Cambridge: Cambridge University Press.

Ur, P. (1998). *Beginning to write.* Cambridge: Cambridge University Press.

Ur, P. (1981). *Discussions that work: Task-centered fluency practice.* Cambridge: Cambridge University Press.

U.S. Central Intelligence Agency. (n.d.). *The world factbook.* Washington, DC. Retrieved February 10, 2008, from https://www.cia.gov/library/publications/the-world-factbook/

Vygotsky, L. (1986). *Thought and language* (A. Kozulin, Trans.). Cambridge, MA: MIT Press.

Wade, R. C. (Ed.). (1997). *Community service-learning: A guide to including service in the public school curriculum.* Albany, NY: State University of New York Press.

Wajnryb, R. (1996). *Death, taxes and jeopardy: Systematic omissions in EFL texts, or "life was never meant to be an adjacency pair."* Paper presented at the 9th Educational Conference, Sydney, Australia.

Walters, D. E., & Walters, G. C. (2002). *Scientists must speak.* London: Routledge.

Warschauer, M. (1997). Computer-mediated collaborative learning: Theory and practice. *Modern Language Journal, 81,* 470–481.

Warschauer, M. (2004). Technology and writing. In C. Davidson & J. Cummins (Eds.), *Handbook of English language teaching* (pp. 907–917). Dordrecht, Netherlands: Kluwer.

Warschauer, M. (2000). The changing global economy and the future of English teaching. *TESOL Quarterly, 34*(3), 511–535.

Weidauer, M. H. (2000). *Tapestry writing 3*. Boston: Heinle & Heinle.

Wessels, C. (1987). *Drama*. Oxford: Oxford University Press.

Wessels, C. (1991). From improvisation to publication on an English through drama course. *ELT Journal, 45*(4), 230–6.

Wicks, M. (2000). *Imaginative projects: A resource book of project work for young students*. Cambridge: Cambridge University Press.

Widdowson, H. G. (1998). Context, community, and authentic language. *TESOL Quarterly, 32*(4), 705–716.

Widdowson, H. G. (2003). *Defining issues in English language teaching*. Oxford: Oxford University Press.

Willis, J. (1996). *A framework for task-based learning*. Harlow, Essex, England: Longman.

Willis, J., & Edwards, C. (2005). *Teachers exploring tasks in English language teaching*. Houndmills, England: Palgrave Macmillan.

Willis, J., & Willis, D. (1996). *Challenge and change in language teaching*. Oxford: Heinemann.

Wilson, B., & Ryder, M. (n.d.). *Dynamic learning communities: An alternative to designed instructional systems*. Retrieved September 5, 2007, from http://carbon .cudenver.edu/~mryder/dlc.html

Woodward, T. (1996). Paradigm shift and the language teaching profession. In J. Willis & D. Willis (Eds.), *Challenge and change in language teaching* (pp. 4–9). Oxford: Heinemann.

YouTube. (n.d.). Wikipedia. Retrieved June 3, 2008, from http://en.wikipedia.org/ wiki/YouTube

Index

Page numbers followed by an *f*, *n*, or *t* indicate figures, notes, or tables.

A

À la carte courses, 47–60
Aaron Shepard's RT Page, 97
Accents, text selection and, 160–161
Access
    technology and, 3, 234
    text selection and, 161
Accuracy, task development and, 163–164
Action
    film and, 185–186
    integration with talk/text, 2
    Readers' Theater and, 91
Activity, purpose and, 3
Adaptability, culture-based activities and, 50
Age considerations, service learning and, 114
American Rhetoric, 179
Analysis
    authenticity and, 1
    competence in, 37
    discourse, 233–234
    evaluation of Internet sources, 139–140
    Readers' Theater and, 92
Annual reports, as material, 102–105, 103*f*
Aoyama Gakuin University, 170
Apple Student Gallery, 178, 179
Assessment. *See also* Feedback
    community-based activities and, 115
    content areas and, 72–73
    culture-based activities and, 30, 31–32, 33*f*,
      53

of interests, 110
    needs, 122*f*
    project-based learning and, 41–42, 43*f*, 229
    self-, 236–237
    Technical Career Ladders program and, 120
    Wiki use and, 205–206
Atlassian, 222
Audience
    localization and, 4
    Readers' Theater and, 90, 92
    technology and, 3
Audio visuals, text selection and, 161
Aural skills. *See* Listening skill development
Australia, 23–24. *See also* Culture-based
    activities
Austria, 99. *See also* Materials, development of
Authenticity
    Goal setting and, 101–102
    history of, 1–2
    judgment of, 64
    materials and. *See* Materials
    perspectives/teaching implications of, 158*f*
    task-based curriculum and. *See* Task-based
      curriculum
    texts and, 64–65. *See also* Texts, selection of
Average Student activity, 82

B

Background knowledge, text selection and,
    160–161, 184
BBC Writers Room, 179
BINGO!, 81
Blogger, 196

Blogs, restaurant review, 191–197
Brainstorming, 149
Brazil, 11
British Columbia Ministry of Education, 179
Brown University, 214
Business Communications: International Case Studies in English (Rodgers), 93

C

Cambridge Schools, 182
Campus Movie Fest, 178, 179
Canada, 201. *See also* Culture-based activities
Carinthia University of Applied Sciences, 99
Carnegie Mellon University, 49
Cartooning, project-based learning and, 132–133
Catalyst, 213–222, 219f, 220f
CBC Fifth Estate, 172, 179
Central Piedmont Community College, 118
Challenge, variation in, 162f
Characters
   Readers' Theater and, 92
   text selection and, 88f, 160–161, 184
Chiff.com, 97
City Guides, 29–35
Class considerations, text selection and, 66, 67–68
Climate change, project-based learning and, 129–142
Climax, Readers' Theater and, 91
CLT. *See* Communicative language teaching
Clubs, reading, 63–70
CNN International, 172–173
Cognition
   authenticity and, 1
   learners and, 1
   meta-, 236–237
   processes of, 2
Collaboration
   authenticity and, 1
   cross-institutional, 206
   project-based learning and, 195
   Readers' Theater and, 89
   Wiki use and, 199–211, 203f
Comic Life, 180
Commercial scripts, 171–172, 177
Common European Framework of Reference for Languages, 99–100, 100f

Communication
   culture-based activities and, 32–33
   Vygotsky model of, 87t
Communicative competence, 156f
Communicative language teaching, 1
Community. *See* Culture-based activities
Community-based activities. *See also* Culture-based activities
   assessment of, 115
   basic components of, 122f
   collaborative projects and, 206–207
   context regarding, 109
   curriculum/tasks/materials for, 110–113
   project-based learning and, 133–135
   reflections regarding, 113–114, 123–124
   sample materials, 124–127
   survey regarding, 114–115
Competence, communicative, 156f
Complexity, task development and, 163–164
Complication, Readers' Theater and, 91
Comprehension skills, Readers' Theater and, 92
Computer skills. *See* Technology
Computer-mediated communication, 200. *See also* Technology
Conflict
   Readers' Theater and, 91
   text selection and, 88f
Consolidation, Wiki use and, 203f, 205
Content
   culture-based activities and, 53
   task-based curriculum and, 13t
Content areas
   additional exercises, 220f
   context regarding, 71–76, 213–215, 232
   curriculum/tasks/materials for, 76–82, 215–219
   importance of authenticity in, 71
   options for term selection, 216f
   reflections regarding, 82–83, 220–221, 236–237
   sample chart for, 80f
   sample homepage for, 218f
   sample vocabulary, 219f
   student characteristics, 72t
   syllabus for, 77t
   technology screen shot, 78f, 79f
Context, authenticity of. *See* Authenticity
Conversation. *See* Dialogue

Cooperation, project-based learning and, 44
Cost effectiveness
    culture-based activities and, 50
    ESP material development and, 99–106
CPCC. *See* Central Piedmont Community
    College
Creating a Readers Theater Script, 96
Critical analysis. *See* Analysis
CUAS. *See* Carinthia University of Applied
    Sciences
Cultural awareness
    collaborative projects and, 208
    competence in, 37
    content areas and, 73, 75
    NNES and, 48
    text selection and, 66–68
Culture-based activities. *See also* Project-based
    learning; Task-based curriculum
    context regarding, 19–20, 29–30, 182,
        200–201
    curriculum/tasks/materials for, 20–24,
        30–34, 49–56, 182–187, 201–206
    handout for, 25–26
    importance of authenticity in, 47–48,
        181–182, 199
    overview of ICC courses, 57–58
    reflections regarding, 24, 56–57, 188,
        206–209
    resources for, 27
    sample brochure for, 27
    sample fact sheet, 205*f*
    sample grammar monitoring activity, 60
    sample Oral Qualifier activity, 59
    sample presentation activity, 58–59
    sample site visit worksheet, 34*f*
    sample student transcript from ICC, 55*f*
    scavenger hunt game, 31*f*
    stages of Wiki-based project, 203*f*
    think sheet, 32*f*
    think sheet rubric, 33*f*
Curriculum
    community-based activities and, 110–113,
        119–123
    content areas and, 76–82, 215–219,
        232–236
    culture-based activities and, 20–24, 30–34,
        49–56, 182–187, 201–206
    learner needs/interests and, 3
    material development and, 101–105

project-based learning and, 130, 131–137,
    193–197, 225–227
Readers' Theater and, 87–94
task-based, 12–15
task-based curriculum and, 145–151,
    170–178
text selection and, 65–69

D

Density, text selection and, 160–161
Design, project-based learning and, 41
Dialogue
    culture-based activities and, 54
    Readers' Theater and, 89, 90, 92
    reading clubs and, 68–69
    text selection and, 88*f*
Dictation, running, 79–80
Difficulty, text selection and, 160–161
Directions, as culture-based activity, 33–34
Disaster preparedness, task-based curriculum
    and, 143–152
Disciplinary differences, cultural considerations
    regarding, 48
Discourse analysis, 233–234
Discourse competence, 156*f*
DMC. *See* Dubai Men's College
Documents, as material, 101, 102–105
Drew's Script-o-rama, 180, 188
Dubai Men's College, 200
DVDs, as material, 102–105
Dynamic information, 146*f*

E

EAP. *See* English for academic purposes
Early childhood centers, service learning and,
    111
Eastern Michigan University, 223
Editing, project-based learning and, 41
Education centers, service learning and, 111
EFL. *See* English as a foreign language
Electricians, sample materials for, 124–127
Elements, text selection and, 160–161
E-mailing, project-based learning and,
    195–196
Emergency Management District Brochure
    (State of Mississippi), 148*f*

Emergency preparedness, task-based curriculum and, 143–152
EMP. *See* English for medical purposes
EMU. *See* Eastern Michigan University
Engagement
    authenticity and, 1
    technology and, 3
England, 23. *See also* Culture-based activities
English, Western-centric standards for, 3–4
English as a foreign language, 11, 37, 63, 182, 200
English as a second language, 30, 47, 110, 129, 181, 200, 213, 223
English for academic purposes, 169, 213
English for medical purposes, 236
English for specific purposes, 71, 93, 99–106, 117–127, 232
English for Tour Guides, 19–27
English Language Fellow program, 66
English Learner Movie Guides, 189
English Trailers, 180, 189
Environment, project-based learning and, 129–142
ESL. *See* English as a second language
ESP. *See* English for specific purposes
Ethnicity, text selection and, 66, 67
Evaluation. *See* Assessment
Experience, classroom instruction and, 2
Exposition, Readers' Theater and, 91

F

Facilitators, reading clubs and, 68
Fact sheets, Wiki use and, 204, 205*f*
Facts About X, 80
Falling action, Readers' Theater and, 91
Feedback. *See also* Assessment
    content areas and, 220
    culture-based activities and, 54
    skills instruction for, 207–208
    Wiki use and, 204
Fifth Estate, 172, 179
Film
    as material, 166–168, 181–189
    script reading and, 169–180
    student-made, 176–177, 177*f*
    video defined, 181*n*
Fluency, task development and, 163–164
Food pantries, service learning and, 111

Framework development, 122*f*
Freesound Project, 180
Fulbright program, 66
Future Changes, 222

G

Gender considerations, text selection and, 66, 68
Genre
    Readers' Theater and, 87–93
    text selection and, 64–65, 160–161
Globalization, English as a *lingua franca* and, 105
Goal setting
    authenticity and, 1, 101–102
    content areas and, 75
    task-based curriculum and, 12
    technology and, 3
Grammar in Context (Elbaum), 32
Grammar skills
    culture-based activities and, 53, 60
    text selection and, 160–161
Grant procurement, 65–66
Grocery stores, as culture-based activity, 34
Group work
    culture-based activities and, 20–24, 54
    project-based learning and, 39, 44
    Readers' Theater and, 85–97
    reading clubs and, 63–70
    task-based curriculum and, 14–15, 16*f*
    Wiki use and, 203*f*, 204
Guided walks, as culture-based activity, 20–24

H

Habit formation, project-based learning and, 44
Handouts
    Information for Foreigners, 17
    Magazine, 40*f*
    as material, 102–105
    material development and, 104*f*
Hatchet (Paulsen), 68
Homeless shelters, service learning and, 111
Homophones, 74
Hospitals, service learning and, 111
Hot topics, project-based learning and, 129–142

I

ICC. *See* Intercultural Communication Center
ICT. *See* Technology
Idiomatic language, text selection and, 160–161
IEP. *See* Intensive English programs
IMovie Tutorial, 180
IMRD. *See* Introduction-methods-results-discussion
Independence, student, 35
Indonesia, 11
Information, static vs. dynamic, 146*f*
Information and communication technologies. *See* Technology
Information for Foreigners, 11–18
Institutional support, importance of, 124
Instruction
    authenticity of. *See* Authenticity
    format/medium variation and, 207
    implications of authenticity on, 158*f*
    potential of, 5
    target culture and, 4
    tips for, 210–211
    Webcasts and, 234–236
Instructional design. *See* Curriculum
Integration of skills, project-based learning and, 192
Intensive English programs. *See* Service learning
Interactions, authenticity and, 3
Intercultural Communication Center, 49
Interests
    assessment of, 110
    curriculum and, 3
    film and, 181–182
    text selection and, 88*f*, 159, 183
Internal transition devices, 233
International teaching assistant training, 47–60, 213–222
Internet. *See* Technology
Internet Movie Database, 171, 188
Internet Resources for Conducting Readers Theatre, 96
Interviews
    project-based learning and, 133–134, 141, 142
    Wiki use and, 203*f*, 205
Introduction-methods-results-discussion, 231–233

Investigation, project-based learning and, 130
ITAs. *See* International teaching assistant training

J

Japan, 19, 22, 157, 170, 182. *See also* Culture-based activities; Materials; Script reading
Jargon, content areas and, 73–74
Journaling, 113, 115, 127

K

Kanda University of International Studies, 182
Kaohsiung Medical University, 232
KMU. *See* Kaohsiung Medical University

L

Language
    cultural considerations regarding, 48
    purpose and, 3
    text selection and, 66, 67
Large groups. *See* Group work
Length, text selection and, 160–161
Lexical phrases, Webcasts and, 231–238
Linguistic competence, 156*f*
Listening skill development
    project-based learning and, 40–41, 192, 228
    task development and, 163
"Little Girl and the Wolf, The" (Thurber), 89
Localization, importance of, 3–4
Locations, as culture-based activity, 33–34
London Walks Ltd., 27

M

Magazine, 37–45
Marketing materials, as material, 102–105
Masnavi-i Ma'navi, The (Rumi), 65
Masters of Disaster series (Red Cross), 147, 151
Materials. *See also* Technology; Texts
    authenticity and, 157, 234. *See also* Authenticity
    challenge/support of, 162*f*
    community-based activities and, 110–113, 119–123

Materials *(continued)*
content areas and, 76–82, 215–219, 232–236
context regarding, 157
culture-based activities and, 20–24, 30–34, 49–56, 182–187, 201–206
development of, 99–106, 103*f*, 104*f*
importance of authenticity in, 155–157
material development and, 101–105
project-based learning and, 131–137, 193–197, 225–227
Readers' Theater and, 87–94
reflections regarding, 165–166
revision of, 122*f*
sample using *Secrets & Lies*, 166–168
selection of, 159–162, 183–184
task development and, 162–166
task-based curriculum and, 12–15, 145–151, 170–178
text selection and, 65–69
textbooks and, 157–159
Math, 71–83
Measure It!, 82
Media, as material, 155. *See also* Materials
Mentoring, encouragement of, 208–209
Metacognition, 236–237
Microsoft, 202, 204
Motivation
content areas and, 236
culture-based activities and, 51
material development and, 105, 106
project-based learning and, 193
task-based curriculum and, 12
of teachers, 124
Movies, script reading and, 173
Museums, service learning and, 111

N

National Trust, The, 27
Natural disasters, task-based curriculum and, 143–152
Near homophones, 74
Needs
assessment of, 122*f*
curriculum and, 3
text selection and, 160
News announcing, script reading and, 172–173

Nonnative English speakers (NNES)
cultural support for, 48
TESOL position statement regarding, 4
North Seattle Community College (NSCC), 71, 72*t*
Northwest Sustainability Conference. *See* Sustainability
Note-taking skills, 227
Nursing homes, service learning and, 111
NWT Literacy Council, 96

O

Observation, project-based learning and, 39
Okinawa University, 19
Oman, 71, 77–78. *See also* Math
Open mindedness, 122*f*
Oral language development
project-based learning and, 40, 192, 228
script reading and, 169–170
task-based curriculum and, 15–16
Webcasts and, 231–238
Oral Qualifier, 53, 59
Orientation, stages of Wiki-based project, 203*f*
Outreach, Technical Career Ladders program and, 120
Ownership, project-based learning and, 208

P

Pairs. *See* Group work
Partnering. *See* Group work
Peanut Butter Wiki, 201
Peer review, 223–229. *See also* Group work
Performance
successive cycles of, 134–135, 135*f*
task-based curriculum and, 170, 172*t*
Photo editing, project-based learning and, 195–196
Photo strips, script reading and, 174, 175*f*
Plays, Readers' Theater and, 90–93
Poetry, Readers' Theater and, 87–88
Portfolios, 42, 223–229
Post-listening tasks, task development and, 163
Postproduction phase, 177*f*
Posttask phase, 145, 150–151, 170, 172*t*
Pragmalinguistic competence, 156*f*

Pre-listening tasks, task development and, 163

Preproduction phase, 177*f*

Presentation

assessment of, 229

culture-based activities and, 53, 58–59

project-based learning and, 41, 134–137, 135*f*, 137*f*, 225–227

Pretask phase, 145, 149, 170, 172*t*

Printing, project-based learning and, 41

Privacy, technology and, 195, 224*f*, 225*f*

Problem solving, authenticity and, 1

Processing skills, project-based learning and, 44

Production phase, 177*f*

Products

project-based learning and, 44

task-based curriculum and, 17–18

Progress assessment, 42

Project assessment, 42

Project-based learning. *See also* Culture-based activities; Task-based curriculum

assessment sample, 43*f*

comment function, 227*f*

conference guidelines, 42*f*

context regarding, 38, 192–193, 223–225

curriculum/tasks/materials for, 38–42, 131–137, 193–197, 225–227

evaluation of Internet sources, 139–140

handout for, 40*f*

interviewing an expert and, 141, 142

overview of, 130–132

poster presentation, 137*f*

reflections regarding, 42–44, 137–138, 227–228

student instructions for definition tasks, 138–139

Pronunciation skills, text selection and, 183–184

Proofreading, project-based learning and, 41

Public information, task-based curriculum and, 143–152

Purpose

language and, 3

technology and, 3

Q

Questioning

content areas and, 80*f*

film and, 186

by instructors, 218

project-based learning and, 130

Readers' Theater and, 92

by students, 218

task-based curriculum and, 149

R

Readers' Theater, 85–97

Reading clubs, 63–70

Reading development

project-based learning and, 41, 192

task-based curriculum and, 16

text selection and. *See* Texts, selection of

ReadWriteThink, 97

Real-world learning. *See* Authenticity

Recording, script reading and, 176

Recordkeeping, culture-based activities and, 55

Recruitment, Technical Career Ladders program and, 120

Reflective teaching practices, importance of, 124

Regional proximity, text selection and, 66

Registration, Technical Career Ladders program and, 120

Rehabilitation centers, service learning and, 111

Rehearsal, Readers' Theater and, 90, 92

Religious considerations, text selection and, 66, 67

Reports, as material, 102–105

Research

content areas and, 80*f*

project-based learning and, 133, 228

Restaurant review blogs, 191–197

Rikkyo University, 169

Rising action, Readers' Theater and, 91

"Road Not Taken, The" (Frost), 88

Role play, task-based curriculum and, 150

Roles

negotiation of, 207

text selection and, 88*f*

Rotten Tomatoes, 188

Running dictation, 79–80

S

Scavenger hunt game, 31*f*
Scene writing, script reading and, 174–175
Scheduling, culture-based activities and, 50
Script reading, 169–180
Script Shack, The, 180
Script-o-rama, 180, 188
Scriptsmart, 179
Seattle Area Restaurant Reviews, 197
Secrets & Lies, 165, 166–168
Selection criteria, text selection and, 164–165
Self-study
   content areas and, 220
   project-based learning and, 44
Senior centers, service learning and, 111
Service learning, 109–115
Service Learning (Schine), 110
SEZ Group, 102–105
Shabanu (Staples), 69
Shelters, service learning and, 111
Short stories, Readers' Theater and, 89–90
Simulation, task-based curriculum and, 150
Skill-based projects, Technical Career Ladders
     program and, 121–122
Slogans, as culture-based activity, 33–34
Small groups. *See* Group work
Social class. *See* Class considerations
Social networks
   language use and, 4
   learners and, 1
Sociopragmatic competence, 156*f*
Soup kitchens, service learning and, 111
Speaking skills. *See* Oral language development
Speech rates, text selection and, 160–161
Speeches, script reading and, 173
Speedy Math, 81–82
SQU. *See* Sultan Qaboos University
Staged Reading Rehearsals, 97
Stand-alone texts, text selection and, 161
Standards, Western-centric, 3–4
Static information, 146*f*
"Stopping by Woods on a Snowy Evening"
   (Frost), 88
Storyboards, script reading and, 173–174
Strategic competence, 156*f*
Strategy training
   authenticity and, 3
   competence in, 37
   content areas and, 73, 75–76

Subtitles, film and, 186
Success, text selection and, 162–163
Successive cycles of performance, 134–135,
   135*f*
Sultan Qaboos University, 71, 72*t*
Support
   content areas and, 219
   institutional, 124
   Technical Career Ladders program and,
     120–121
   technology and, 208
   text selection and, 184
   variation in, 162*f*
Sustainability, project-based learning and,
   129–142
Syllabus creation, 122*f*, 164
Syntax, text selection and, 160–161
Synthesis skill, project-based learning and, 44

T

Taiwan, 232. *See also* Webcasts
Tajikistan, 65. *See also* Texts, selection of
Talk, integration with action/text, 2
Tapestry in Writing 3 (Weidauer), 93
Task-based curriculum. *See also* Culture-based
     activities; Project-based learning
   context regarding, 11–12, 144–145, 170
   curriculum/tasks/materials for, 12–15,
     145–151, 170–178
   importance of authenticity in, 11
   phases of, 172*t*
   reflections regarding, 15–18, 178–179
   sample tasks for, 16*f*
   static vs. dynamic information, 146*f*
   theme/content for, 13*t*
Tasks
   community-based activities and, 110–113,
     119–123
   content areas and, 76–82, 215–219,
     232–236
   culture-based activities and, 20–24, 30–34,
     49–56, 182–187, 201–206
   development of, 162–165
   material development and, 101–105
   project-based learning and, 131–137,
     193–197, 225–227
   Readers' Theater and, 87–94
   sample back story comic, 175*f*

task-based curriculum and, 12–15, 145–
151, 170–178
text selection and, 65–69
Teachers, potential of, 5
Technical Career Ladders program (TCL),
117–127
Technology
competence in, 37
content areas and, 77–78
evaluation of Internet sources, 139–140
limitations of utilizing, 196–197
as material, 155, 169. *See also* Materials
potential of, 3
project-based learning and, 41, 133
Technical Career Ladders program and,
117–127
Webcasts and, 231–238
Wiki use and, 199–211, 213–222
YouTube and, 178, 223–229, 224*f*, 225*f*
Teen centers, service learning and, 111
Television
as material, 169
script reading and, 173
Television walk, as culture-based activity, 24
TESOL
Electronic Village, 96
NNES and, 4
TESOL Quarterly, 225
Test of English as a Foreign Language, 47
Texts
integration with talk/action, 2
Readers' Theater and, 85–97
selection of, 63–70, 88*f*, 159–162
textbooks and, 157–159, 182–183
Thainguyen University of Education, 37
Think Sheet, 32*f*
Tic Tac Toe, 81
Time management
culture-based activities and, 52–56
text selection and, 88*f*
Timelessness, text selection and, 162
TOEFL. *See* Test of English as a Foreign
Language
Tokyo International University of America
(TIUA), 129
Town agencies, service learning and, 111
Traditional considerations, text selection and,
66, 67
Training, technology and, 208

Transcripts. *See also* Script reading
film and, 187
sample, 55*f*
Transition words, 233
Trivial Review, 81
Turning point, Readers' Theater and, 91
$20,000 Pyramid, 81–82

U

UAE. *See* United Arab Emirates
"Unicorn in the Garden, The" (Thurber), 89
Uniformity, task-based curriculum and, 17
United Arab Emirates, 200. *See also* Culture-
based activities
United States, 49, 71, 76–77, 109, 118,
129, 144, 182, 214. *See also* Content
areas; Culture-based activities; Project-
based learning; Task-based curriculum;
Technical Career Ladders program
University of Hawaii, 180
University of Toronto, 201
University of Wisconsin, 109
U.S. Department of State, 65–66
Using Wiki in Education, 222
UT. *See* University of Toronto

V

Variety, text selection and, 160
Video. *See* Film
Vietnam, 37. *See also* Project-based learning
Visuals
film and, 186
text selection and, 160–161
Vocabulary acquisition
content areas and, 216–217
journal for, 127
project-based learning and, 131–132,
138–139, 144
Readers' Theater and, 92
reading and, 63
task-based curriculum and, 16–17
text selection and, 88*f*, 160–161, 183–184
Vygotsky model of communication, 87*t*

W

Warm-ups, Readers' Theater and, 95
Webcasts, 231–238
Western-centric standards for English, 3–4
Wiki use, 199–211, 203*f*, 213–222, 216*f*,
    218*f*, 219*f*, 220*f*
Wikipatterns, 222
Willamette University, 130
Windows XP, 180
Word-processing, project-based learning and,
    195–196
Writing development
    culture-based activities and, 31–32, 32*f*

project-based learning and, 41, 136, 192,
    228
Readers' Theater and, 89
reading and, 63
script reading and, 174–175
task-based curriculum and, 16
Wiki use and, 199–211

Y

YouTube, 178, 223–229, 224*f*, 227*f*

Also Available From TESOL

TESOL Classroom Practice Series
M. Dantas-Whitney, S. Rilling, and L. Savova, Series Editors

Classroom Management
Thomas S. C. Farrell, Editor

Language Games: Innovative Activities for Teaching English
Maureen Snow Andrade, Editor

Insights on Teaching Speaking in TESOL
Tim Stewart, Editor

❈ ❈ ❈ ❈ ❈

Language Teacher Research Series
Thomas S. C. Farrell, Series Editor

Language Teacher Research in Asia
Thomas S. C. Farrell, Editor

Language Teacher Research in Africa
Leketi Makalela, Editor

Language Teacher Research in Europe
Simon Borg, Editor

Language Teacher Research in the Americas
Hedy McGarrell, Editor

Language Teacher Research in the Middle East
Christine Coombe and Lisa Barlow, Editors

Language Teacher Research in Australia and New Zealand
Jill Burton and Anne Burns, Editors

❈ ❈ ❈ ❈ ❈

Perspectives on Community College ESL Series
Craig Machado, Series Editor

Volume 1: Pedagogy, Programs, Curricula, and Assessment
Marilynn Spaventa, Editor

Volume 2: Students, Mission, and Advocacy
Amy Blumenthal, Editor

Volume 3: Faculty, Administration, and the Working Environment
Jose A.Carmona, Editor

❋ ❋ ❋ ❋ ❋

Collaborative Partnerships Between ESL and Classroom Teachers Series
Debra Suarez, Series Editor

Helping English Language Learners Succeed in Pre-K–12 Elementary Schools
Jan Lacina, Linda New Levine, and Patience Sowa

Helping English Language Learners Succeed in Middle and High Schools
F. Pawan and G. Sietman, Editors

❋ ❋ ❋ ❋ ❋

TESOL Language Curriculum Development Series
Kathleen Graves, Series Editor

Planning and Teaching Creatively Within a Required Curriculum for Adult Learners
Burns and H. de Silva Joyce, Editors

Revitalizing an Established Program for Adult Learners
A. Rice, Editor

Developing a New Curriculum for Adult Learners
Michael Carroll, Editor

Developing a New Course for Adults
L. Kamhi-Stein and A. Snow, Editors

❋ ❋ ❋ ❋ ❋

CALL Environments: Research, Practice, and Critical Issues, 2nd ed.
Joy Egbert and E. Hanson-Smith, Editors

Learning Languages through Technology
Elizabeth Hanson-Smith and Sarah Rilling, Editors

Global English Teaching and Teacher Education: Praxis and Possibility
Seran Dogancay-Aktuna and Joel Hardman, Editors

ESOL Tests and Testing
Stephen Stoynoff and Carol A. Chapelle

Standards for Teachers of ESL Adult Learners

Local phone: (240)646-7037
Fax: (301)206-9789
E-Mail: tesolpubs@brightkey.net
Toll-free: 1-888-891-0041
Mail Orders to TESOL, P.O. Box 79283, Baltimore, MD 21279-0283
ORDER ONLINE at www.tesol.org and click on "Bookstore"